Credits

Author
Iwan 'e1' Rahabok

Reviewers
Sunny Dua
Lior Kamrat
Craig Risinger
Chris Killian Sexsmith

Commissioning Editor
Ashwin Nair

Acquisition Editor
Vinay Argekar

Content Development Editor
Ajinkya Paranjape

Technical Editors
Humera Shaikh
Aman Preet Singh

Copy Editors
Roshni Banerjee
Adithi Shetty

Project Coordinator
Harshal Ved

Proofreaders
Simran Bhogal
Samuel Redman Birch
Jonathan Todd

Indexer
Mariammal Chettiyar

Graphics
Sheetal Aute

Production Coordinator
Komal Ramchandani

Cover Work
Komal Ramchandani

VMware vRealize Operations Performance and Capacity Management

A hands-on guide to mastering performance and capacity management in a virtual data center

Iwan 'e1' Rahabok

PUBLISHING

BIRMINGHAM - MUMBAI

VMware vRealize Operations Performance and Capacity Management

First published: December 2014

Production reference: 1221214

Published by Packt Publishing Ltd.
Livery Place
35 Livery Street
Birmingham B3 2PB, UK.

ISBN 978-1-78355-168-2

www.packtpub.com

Foreword

My team launched vCenter Operations in early 2011. Since then, it has surpassed VMware's expectations in terms of adoption, both internally and externally. Externally, customers have created their own custom dashboards and super metrics. VMware partners have also created management packs, extending vRealize Operations coverage beyond VMware. Internally, the product has become the central piece in VMware's management strategy. It has become the de facto companion to vSphere and a key component of VMware's SDDC strategy.

I travel extensively to meet customers and partners. They like vRealize Operations and they want to do more with it. One frequent request from customers is for us to document the metrics better, explaining them from a customer's viewpoint and providing practical guidance. This is where this book comes in. Iwan, whom I met during our R&D conference in San Francisco, has volunteered to address it. He has been working closely with my team and has become a virtual extension of the Management Business Unit. As a VMware CTO Ambassador, he is also one of the internal curators for the product.

vRealize Operations 6.0 is our groundbreaking release, with a brand new architecture, and it adds a lot of major functionalities. This book has been timed to coincide with the product launch. Having said that, considering the large existing installation base, the book provides good coverage for the vRealize Operations 5.8 release. You will still benefit significantly from the book even if you decide to wait for an update to the 6.0 release. My team will be taking sample pages from the book as a lot of the material is relevant for both releases.

Operating a Software-Defined Data Center becomes much more difficult if you do not get the architecture right. Iwan has explained it concisely in the first two chapters of this book. These are my favorite chapters as I see them often during my interaction with customers.

The book highlights one key differentiator of vRealize Operations. When we build the product, we do not want to simply regurgitate the information from vSphere. We want to build intelligence and simplify our operations. We started afresh and invented a set of derived metrics, formalizing VMware's recommendations on how you should operate a vSphere environment. This book explains these derived metrics and shows you how you can apply them in your environment.

This little book is a perfect complement to the product. I highly recommend you read it.

Ramin Sayar
SVP and GM
Management BU, VMware

Ramin Sayar was associated with VMware till the last few days of publishing of this book.

Foreword

I have the privilege of leading the technical services organization in VMware, Asia Pacific and Japan. In the past 7 years, my team of architects, engineers, and technical account managers have partnered with our key accounts in thousands of engagements across the region. I have met with many CIOs and Heads of Infrastructure, and what is clear to me is that they value the expertise we bring to the table and it is important that we extend this expertise to all customers and not just our large customers. This is why when Iwan approached my management team with the idea of writing a book on the management of the Software-Defined Data Center, he had our full support.

Data center management is a large and complex discipline in IT. This is further amplified with virtualization. The nature of virtualization means IT departments are nowadays running applications with a lot less hardware. As a result, performance and capacity management have risen to be critical components in the realm of management. They are a fundamental part of Infrastructure-as-a-Service, and if you get them wrong, there is a strong likelihood that you will struggle in your journey to become an internal service provider.

The challenge, in real life, is certainly cost. You need to deliver high performance while keeping excess capacity low. This is where architecture plays a major role. In this book, Iwan shares architecture best practices that help you balance these competing requirements. He explains, in depth, the concept of contention and how it should drive your performance SLA for the business. Keeping the contention value below the agreed SLA goes a long way in proving that the shared infrastructure delivers the required resources.

Chapter 3, *Mastering the Key Counters in SDDC*, to *Chapter 7*, *Storage Counters*, cover all the key metrics in both vCenter and vRealize Operations. This is the first time I've seen the counters in our flagship products documented from a customer's point of view. This is refreshing and practical, and knowing Iwan, this doesn't surprise me. In the 6 years that I have known Iwan, he will always look at situations from a customer's perspective. He founded the ASEAN user group, and today this group is probably one of the largest VMware community groups on Facebook.

Chapter 8, Dashboard Examples and Ideas, is my favorite chapter. This is where field expertise from the many implementations of my team in operationalizing vRealize Operations is harnessed, shared, and explained. Practical examples and applied best practices are clearly documented and explained. Within the VMware Technical Services organization, we look at vRealize Operations as a key technology to manage the Software-Defined Data Center.

I hope you enjoy the book as much as I do.

Peter Zeglis
VP, Technical Services
VMware, Asia Pacific and Japan

About the Author

Iwan 'e1' Rahabok was the first VMware SE for strategic accounts in ASEAN.
Joining VMware in 2008 from Sun Microsystems, he has seen how enterprises adopt
virtualization firsthand, reaping the benefits while overcoming the challenges. It is
a journey that is still going on and the book reflects a subset of that undertaking.
Globally, he was one of the first to achieve the VCAP-DCD certification and has
since helped others to achieve the same with the help of his participation in the
community. He started the user community in ASEAN, and today the group is one
of the largest VMware communities on Facebook. He is a member of VMware CTO
Ambassadors, representing ASEAN region at the global level and the product team
and CTO office to the ASEAN customers. He is a vExpert 2013 and vExpert 2014 and
has been helping others to achieve this global recognition for their contribution to the
VMware community. He graduated from Bond University, Australia, with a degree
in IT in 1994.

Acknowledgments

This book covers materials that were previously not documented and topics that needed experts' opinion. I knew that behind every author there are many people involved who help to make the book possible. What I did not expect was the generosity shown by so many folks to ensure that I completed this book! Besides the four reviewers, I would like to specially thank the following individuals:

- The VMware vRealize Operations product team:
  - David LaVigna, Director, Product Management
  - Sam McBride, Senior Staff Engineer
  - Tom Findling, Staff Engineer
  - Dave Overbeek, Group Manager, Technical Marketing and Enablement
  - Hicham Mourad, Staff Technical Marketing Manager
  - James Ang, Senior Manager, R&D

- The VMware vSphere product team:
  - Ravi Soundararajan, Principal Engineer
  - Anne Holler, Principal Engineer
  - Guolin Yang, Staff Engineer
  - Emre Celebi, Staff Engineer
  - Seongbeom Kim, Staff Engineer
  - Fei Guo, Staff Engineer
  - Haoqiang Zheng, Staff Engineer

- VMware Asia Pacific management:
  - Sanjay Mirchandani, SVP and GM
  - Mike Sumner, Senior Director, Systems Engineering

- VMware ASEAN management:
    - Ron Goh, VP and GM
    - Santoso Suwignyo, Senior Director, Technical Services
    - Colin Png, Senior Director, Marketing
    - Leslie Ong, Director, Singapore
- The VMware Global Support Services team:
    - Ramprasad, Senior Staff Technical Support Engineer
- The VMware CTO Ambassador group:
    - Ben Fathi, CTO
    - Paul Strong, CTO, Global Field
    - Kevin Lees, Principal Architect, Global Center of Excellence
    - Shannon Schofield, Program Manager, Office of the CTO
- Others:
    - Tessa Davis, Systems Engineer, ASEAN, VMware
    - Prasenjit Sarkar, Solutions Architect, Global CoE, VMware
    - David Nelson, Director, Academy Program
    - John Arrasjid, Senior Consulting Technologist, Office of the CTO, EMC

About the Reviewers

Sunny Dua works as a solution architect for VMware's professional services organization, which is focused on India and SAARC countries. He is a two-time vExpert (2013 and 2014) and an active member of the VMware community. With his industry experience of more than 11 years, he has worked on large-scale virtualization and cloud deployments in various roles at VMware, Hewlett Packard, and Capgemini. In his current role, he is focused on providing IT transformation roadmaps to large-enterprise customers on their journey toward the adoption of cloud computing. He also helps enterprise shops by providing them with directions on virtualizing business-critical applications on the VMware virtualization platform.

Operations management in the virtual infrastructure is one of his core competencies, and he has been sharing his experience on the transformation of IT operations through his personal blog, `http://www.vxpresss.blogspot.in/`. He is a guest blogger on VMware management and consulting blogs as well. The industry and vCommunity have recognized his work as his blog ranks in the top 30 in the virtualization and cloud industry. He is also a co-author for *vSphere Design Pocketbook*, published by *CreateSpace Independent Publishing Platform*, written by highly respected members of the VMware virtualization community.

Sunny's Twitter handle is `@sunny_dua`, and he can also be found on LinkedIn at in.linkedin.com/in/duasunny/.

Lior Kamrat is a senior professional services consultant at VMware, where he specializes in vSphere performance, cloud operations management, business-critical applications, and designing enterprise-scale vRealize Operations and SDDC projects.

He also speaks regularly at the VMware User Groups conferences and enjoys spreading knowledge about performance and capacity management in the virtual world.

Previously a virtualization architect and a VMware customer, today Lior spends his time on cloud operations management and writes on the official VMware Cloud Management blog as well as on his personal blog at http://imallvirtual.com/. His Twitter handle is @LiorKamrat.

He holds several certifications, including VCP, VCAP-DCA, and VCAP-DCD, and was also recognized as a VMware vExpert for several years.

Craig Risinger is a consulting architect and VCDX #006 who has been with VMware since 2004. His previous experience includes running help desks and small-shop all-around IT system administration. With VMware, he helped design virtualization infrastructures and operations for everything from small shops to defense contractors to Fortune 50 financial enterprises. His particular interests include performance management, storage design, and delivering clear and precise technical writing and training. He has had the pleasure of helping to review several books written by his colleagues, including those by Duncan Epping and Frank Denneman, John Arrasjid, Prasenjit Sarkar, and Mostafa Khalil.

Chris Killian Sexsmith spent years as a consultant before joining VMware as a systems engineer. He is now a staff solutions architect and ambassador to the CTO. Chris lives in Vancouver, British Columbia, and enjoys hockey and beer like a good Canadian. He is currently working on two publications for 2015, so look out for his work soon!

> I want to thank my team, the Screwballs, for both their friendship and support in everything we do.

www.PacktPub.com

Support files, eBooks, discount offers, and more

For support files and downloads related to your book, please visit www.PacktPub.com.

Did you know that Packt offers eBook versions of every book published, with PDF and ePub files available? You can upgrade to the eBook version at www.PacktPub.com and as a print book customer, you are entitled to a discount on the eBook copy. Get in touch with us at service@packtpub.com for more details.

At www.PacktPub.com, you can also read a collection of free technical articles, sign up for a range of free newsletters and receive exclusive discounts and offers on Packt books and eBooks.

https://www2.packtpub.com/books/subscription/packtlib

Do you need instant solutions to your IT questions? PacktLib is Packt's online digital book library. Here, you can search, access, and read Packt's entire library of books.

Why subscribe?

- Fully searchable across every book published by Packt
- Copy and paste, print, and bookmark content
- On demand and accessible via a web browser

Free access for Packt account holders

If you have an account with Packt at www.PacktPub.com, you can use this to access PacktLib today and view nine entirely free books. Simply use your login credentials for immediate access.

Instant updates on new Packt books

Get notified! Find out when new books are published by following @PacktEnterprise on Twitter or the *Packt Enterprise* Facebook page.

The book is dedicated to my wife Felicia. It's been a joy walking with her as the life partner for the past two decades. I want to thank her for the two little babies (well, they are teens now!) Marie and Marielle.

Table of Contents

Preface

I joined VMware in May 2008 as the first presales engineer (Account SE is the industry term) in ASEAN for VMware strategic accounts. That was more than 6 years ago—a long time in the rapidly-evolving world of virtualization. I have been fortunate to meet many different customers in the ASEAN region. In a sense, the book documents the lessons that my customers and I have learned in their *journey* to the fully virtualized data center. It is *very rare* for customers to master the virtual world, both architecturally and operationally, part of the reason for this is that Software-Defined Data Center (SDDC) is not yet matured. The biggest reason, however, is the lack of an *in-depth* understanding of what exactly virtualization means to IT.

There are, in fact, many misunderstandings of even the *fundamentals*. For example, almost all IT professionals will say they understand a Virtual Machine (VM). However, do they really understand the ramifications? A lot of CIOs still manage their virtual data centers the same way they manage their physical data centers. This creates a lot of complexity as the two platforms are radically different.

This book started many years ago with a presentation that I delivered to customers. Some of the presentations were eventually posted on my LinkedIn profile and at `https://communities.vmware.com/` as customers ask for it. There have been requests to convert these presentations into a book, so they can share it with their peers. After a long time, I am both humbled and honored to present to you this book.

What this book covers

Content-wise, the book is split into two main parts. The first part provides the foundation and theory. The second part provides the solutions and sample use cases.

Chapter 1, Virtual Data Center – It's Not a Physical Data Center, Virtualized, aims to clear up the misunderstandings that customers have about SDDC. It explains why a VM is *radically* different from a physical server, and hence a virtual data center is fundamentally different from a physical data center. It then covers the aspects of management that are affected.

Chapter 2, Capacity Management in SDDC, takes the topic of the previous chapter further by discussing how capacity management should be done in a virtual data center. Together with *Chapter 1, Virtual Data Center – It's Not a Physical Data Center, Virtualized*, it is useful if you need to explain these topics to your peers, customers, or management.

Chapter 3, Mastering the Key Counters in SDDC, sets the technical foundations of performance and capacity management by giving you a tour of the four infrastructure elements (CPU, RAM, network, and storage). It also maps these four elements into all the vSphere objects, so you know what is available at each level.

Chapter 4, CPU Counters, covers CPU counters in detail. It is the first of four chapters that cover the core infrastructure element (CPU, RAM, network, and storage). If you do not *fully* understand the various counters in vSphere and vRealize Operations, how they impact one another, and what values you consider healthy, then these four chapters are good for you. They dive deep into the counters, comparing the counters in vCenter and vRealize Operations. Knowing the counters is *critical*, as choosing the wrong counters, or interpreting the values wrongly, will lead to a wrong conclusion.

Chapter 5, Memory Counters, continues the deep dive by covering memory counters. It explains why VM memory is one of the most complex area to monitor and troubleshoot

Chapter 6, Network Counters, continues the deep dive by covering network counters.

Chapter 7, Storage Counters, completes the coverage by covering storage counters. It explains the multiple layers of storage that occur as a result of virtualization.

Chapter 8, Dashboard Examples and Ideas, covers the practical aspects of this book, as they show how *sample* solutions are implemented. This chapter provides both performance management and capacity management.

What this book is not

The book focuses on the *management* of the SDDC. It does not cover the architecture. So no vCloud Suite design best practices are present in this book. It also does not cover all aspects of operation. For example, it does cover processes, organizational structure, financial management, and audit. Specific to management, the book only focuses on the most fundamental areas, namely:

- Performance
- Capacity

This book does not cover other areas of management, such as configuration management, compliance management, and availability management. For performance management, it focuses on the infrastructure only. It does not cover application management. So there is no discussion of monitoring databases, web, and application servers here.

This book is also a solutions book. It is not a product book. It uses vRealize Operations to apply the solutions. You can probably use other products to apply the use cases. Because it is not a product book, it does not cover all modules of vRealize Operations Suite. For examples, vCenter Infrastructure Navigator, Hyperic, and VMware Configuration Manager are not covered.

For the sake of the environment, I set a hard limit of 250 pages for this book. Plus, I wanted to provide a book that you can finish in one sitting and that is comfortable to hold with one hand. As a result, the book is light on the Capacity Management portion. vRealize Operations 6 introduces a brand new capacity management engine, so I expect that there will be a lot of write-up on it. I have not operationalized this revamped capacity management functionality for my customers. As a result, I am not qualified to write a book on it. Once I gain the implementation experience and see it being used by customers, I will update my blog (`http://virtual-red-dot.info`).

What you need for this book

Because it is not a product book, I assume that you have the products installed and configured. VMware vSphere and vRealize Operations are the products used in this book. There are many blog articles and YouTube videos on installation, configuration, and product overview. In the *References* section of the last chapter, I have provided a link to them as they get updated more frequently than a physical book. Some of the bloggers also have many other materials, which will complete your learning. At a personal level and as a father of two young kids, I'm not keen on killing trees unless it's really necessary.

Who this book is for

This book is for VMware professionals. This can be a VMware administrator, architect, consultant, engineer, or technical support. You may be working for VMware customers, partners, or VMware itself. You may be an individual contributor or a technical leader.

This book is an intermediate-level book. It assumes you have hands-on experience of vSphere 5.5 and vRealize Operations 6.0, and you are capable of performing some level of performance troubleshooting. You also have good overall knowledge of vCloud Suite, Virtual SAN, Horizon View, and NSX. You should also have some level of knowledge of operating systems, storage, network, disaster recovery, and data center.

This book is also for IT professionals who deal with VMware professionals. As such, there is a wide range of roles, as virtualization and VMware covers many aspects of IT. Depending on your role, certain chapters will be more useful to you. The following is the list of roles and the chapters that are relevant to them:

- CIO, Head of Infrastructure, and other senior IT leader
    - *Chapter 1, Virtual Data Center – It's Not a Physical Data Center, Virtualized*
    - *Chapter 2, Capacity Management in SDDC* (the two-tier concept)

- Capacity management team
    - *Chapter 2, Capacity Management in SDDC*
    - *Chapter 8, Dashboard Examples and Ideas* (capacity management portion)

- Network team
    - *Chapter 1, Virtual Data Center – It's Not a Physical Data Center, Virtualized*
    - *Chapter 2, Capacity Management in SDDC* (network portion)
    - *Chapter 3, Mastering the Key Counters in SDDC* (network section)
    - *Chapter 6, Network Counters*
    - *Chapter 8, Dashboard Examples and Ideas* (network portion)

- Storage team
    - *Chapter 1, Virtual Data Center – It's Not a Physical Data Center, Virtualized*
    - *Chapter 2, Capacity Management in SDDC* (storage portion)

- Chapter 3, *Mastering the Key Counters in SDDC* (storage section)
- Chapter 7, *Storage Counters*
- Chapter 8, *Dashboard Examples and Ideas* (storage portion)

- Application architect or developer
  - Chapter 3, *Mastering the Key Counters in SDDC*
  - Chapters 4 to 7

- Enterprise architect
  - Chapter 1, *Virtual Data Center – It's Not a Physical Data Center, Virtualized*
  - Chapter 2, *Capacity Management in SDDC*
  - Chapter 3, *Mastering the Key Counters in SDDC* (first half)

- Help desk and operations
  - Chapter 8, *Dashboard Examples and Ideas*

Conventions

In this book, you will find a number of text styles that distinguish between different kinds of information. Here are some examples of these styles and an explanation of their meaning.

Code words in text, database table names, folder names, filenames, file extensions, pathnames, dummy URLs, user input, and Twitter handles are shown as follows: "This includes the drive where the OS resides (the c:\ drive in Windows)."

New terms and **important words** are shown in bold. Words that you see on the screen, for example, in menus or dialog boxes, appear in the text like this: "Notice that I did not select the **Host to VM** and **VM to datastore** relationship options, and it got way too complicated when I did."

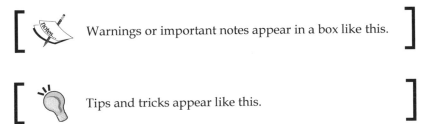

Warnings or important notes appear in a box like this.

Tips and tricks appear like this.

Reader feedback

Feedback from our readers is always welcome. Let us know what you think about this book—what you liked or disliked. Reader feedback is important for us as it helps us develop titles that you will really get the most out of.

To send us general feedback, simply e-mail feedback@packtpub.com, and mention the book's title in the subject of your message.

If there is a topic that you have expertise in and you are interested in either writing or contributing to a book, see our author guide at www.packtpub.com/authors.

Customer support

Now that you are the proud owner of a Packt book, we have a number of things to help you to get the most from your purchase.

Downloading the color images of this book

We also provide you a PDF file that has color images of the screenshots/diagrams used in this book. The color images will help you better understand the changes in the output. You can download this file from: https://www.packtpub.com/sites/default/files/downloads/1682EN_Graphics.pdf.

Errata

Although we have taken every care to ensure the accuracy of our content, mistakes do happen. If you find a mistake in one of our books—maybe a mistake in the text or the code—we would be grateful if you could report this to us. By doing so, you can save other readers from frustration and help us improve subsequent versions of this book. If you find any errata, please report them by visiting http://www.packtpub.com/submit-errata, selecting your book, clicking on the **Errata Submission Form** link, and entering the details of your errata. Once your errata are verified, your submission will be accepted and the errata will be uploaded to our website or added to any list of existing errata under the Errata section of that title.

To view the previously submitted errata, go to https://www.packtpub.com/books/content/support and enter the name of the book in the search field. The required information will appear under the **Errata** section.

Piracy

Piracy of copyrighted material on the Internet is an ongoing problem across all media. At Packt, we take the protection of our copyright and licenses very seriously. If you come across any illegal copies of our works in any form on the Internet, please provide us with the location address or website name immediately so that we can pursue a remedy.

Please contact us at `copyright@packtpub.com` with a link to the suspected pirated material.

We appreciate your help in protecting our authors and our ability to bring you valuable content.

Questions

If you have a problem with any aspect of this book, you can contact us at `questions@packtpub.com`, and we will do our best to address the problem.

1
Virtual Data Center – It's Not a Physical Data Center, Virtualized

In this chapter, we will dive into why seemingly simple technology, a hypervisor and its management console, have a large ramification for the IT industry. In fact, it is turning a lot of things upside down and breaking down silos that have existed for decades in large IT organizations. We will cover the following topics:

- Why virtualization is not what we think it is
- A comparison between a physical server and a **Virtual Machine (VM)**
- What exactly is a Software-Defined Data Center?
- A comparison between a physical data center and a virtual data center
- The impact on how we manage a data center once it is virtualized

Our journey into the virtual world

The change caused by virtualization is much larger than the changes brought forward by previous technologies. In the past two or more decades, we transitioned from mainframes to the client/server-based model to the web-based model. These are commonly agreed upon as the main evolution in IT architecture. However, all of these are just technological changes. It changes the architecture, yes, but it does not change the operation in a fundamental way. Both the client-server and web shifts did not talk about the "journey". There was no journey to the client-server based model. However, with virtualization, we talk about the virtualization journey. It is a journey because the changes are massive and involve a lot of people.

Gartner correctly predicted the impact of virtualization in 2007 (`http://www. gartner.com/newsroom/id/505040`). More than 7 years later we are still in the midst of the journey. Proving how pervasive the change is, here is the following summary on the article from Gartner:

"Virtualization will be the most impactful trend in infrastructure and operations through 2010, changing:

- How you plan
- How, what and when you buy
- How and how quickly you deploy
- How you manage
- How you charge
- Technology, process, culture"

Notice how Gartner talks about change in culture. So, virtualization has a cultural impact too. In fact, I think if your virtualization journey is not fast enough, look at your organization's structure and culture. Have you broken the silos? Do you empower your people to take risk and do things that have never been done before? Are you willing to flatten the organization chart?

So why exactly is virtualization causing such a fundamental shift? To understand this, we need to go back to the very basics, which is what exactly virtualization is. It's pretty common that **Chief Information Officers (CIOs)** have a misconception about what this is.

Take a look at the following comments. Have you seen them in your organization?

- "VM is just Physical Machine virtualized. Even VMware said the Guest OS is not aware it's virtualized and it does not run differently."

- "It is still about monitoring CPU, RAM, Disk, Network. No difference."

- "It is a technology change. Our management process does not have to change."

- "All of these VMs must still feed into our main Enterprise IT Management system. This is how we have run our business for decades and it works."

If only life was that simple, we would all be 100 percent virtualized and have no headaches! Virtualization has been around for years, and yet most organizations have not mastered it.

Not all "virtualizations" are equal

There are plenty of misconceptions about the topic of virtualization, especially among nontechnical IT folk. The CIOs who have not felt the strategic impact of virtualization (be it a good or a bad experience) tend to carry this misconceptions. Although virtualization looks similar on the cover to a physical world, it is completely re-architected under the hood.

So let's take a look at the first misconceptions: what exactly is virtualization? Because it is an industry trend, virtualization is often generalized to include other technologies that are not virtualized. This is a typical strategy by IT vendors who have similar technology. A popular technology often branded under virtualization is **Partitioning**; once it is parked under the umbrella of virtualization, both should be managed in the same way. Since both are actually different, customers who try to manage both with a single piece of management software struggle to do well.

Partitioning and virtualization are two very different architectures in computer engineering, resulting in major differences in functionalities. They are shown in the following figure:

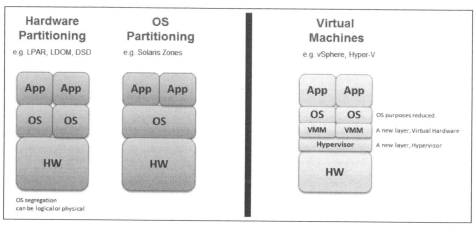

Virtualization versus Partitioning

With partitioning, there is no hypervisor that virtualizes the underlying hardware. There is no software layer separating the **Virtual Machine (VM)** and the physical motherboard. There is, in fact, no VM. This is why some technical manuals in the partitioning technology do not even use the term VM. The manuals use the term domain or partition instead.

There are two variants in the partitioning technology, the hardware level and the OS level, which are covered in the following bullet points:

- In the hardware-level partitioning, each partition runs directly on the hardware. It is not virtualized. This is why it is more scalable and has less of a performance hit. Because it is not virtualized, it has to have an awareness of the underlying hardware. As a result, it is not fully portable. You cannot move the partition from one hardware model to another. The hardware has to be built for a purpose to support that specific version of the partition. The partitioned OS still needs all the hardware drivers and will not work on other hardware if the compatibility matrix does not match. As a result, even the version of the OS matters, as it is just like the physical server.

- In the OS partitioning, there is a parent OS that runs directly on the server motherboard. This OS then creates an OS partition, where other "OS" can run. I use the double quotes as it is not exactly the full OS that runs inside that partition. The OS has to be modified and qualified to be able to run as a **Zone** or **Container**. Because of this, application compatibility is affected. This is very different to a VM, where there is no application compatibility issue as the hypervisor is transparent to the Guest OS.

We covered the difference from an engineering point of view. However, does it translate into different data center architecture and operations? Take availability, for example. With virtualization, all VMs become protected by **HA (High Availability)**—100 percent protection and that too done without VM awareness. Nothing needs to be done at the VM layer, no shared or quorum disk and no heartbeat network. With partitioning, the protection has to be configured manually, one by one for each LPAR or LDOM. The underlying platform does not provide that. With virtualization, you can even go beyond five 9s and move to 100 percent with **Fault Tolerance**. This is not possible in the partitioning approach as there is no hypervisor that replays the CPU instructions. Also, because it is virtualized and transparent to the VM, you can turn on and off the Fault Tolerance capability on demand. Fault tolerance is all defined in the software.

Another area of difference between partitioning and virtualization is **Disaster Recovery (DR)**. With the partitioning technology, the DR site requires another instance to protect the production instance. It is a different instance, with its own OS image, hostname, and IP address. Yes, we can do a SAN boot, but that means another LUN is required to manage, zone, replicate, and so on. DR is not scalable to thousands of servers. To make it scalable, it has to be simpler. Compared to partitioning, virtualization takes a very different approach. The entire VM fits inside a folder; it becomes like a document and we migrate the entire folder as if the folder is are one object. This is what **vSphere Replication** in Site Recovery Manager does. It does a replication per VM; no need to worry about SAN boot. The entire DR exercise, which can cover thousands of virtual servers, is completely automated and with audit logs automatically generated. Many large enterprises have automated their DR with virtualization. There is probably no company that has automated DR for their entire LPAR or LDOM.

I'm not saying partitioning is an inferior technology. Every technology has its advantages and disadvantages, and addresses different use cases. Before I joined VMware, I was a Sun Microsystems SE for five years, so I'm aware of the benefit of UNIX partitioning. I'm just trying to dispel the myth that partitioning equals virtualization.

As both technologies evolve, the gaps get wider. As a result, managing a partition is different than managing a VM. Be careful when opting for a management solution that claims to manage both. You will probably end up with the most common denominator.

Virtual Machine – it is not what you think!

VM is not just a physical server virtualized. Yes, there is a P2V process. However, once it is virtualized, it takes on a new shape. That shape has many new and changed properties, and some old properties are no longer applicable or available. My apologies if the following is not the best analogy:

"We P2V the soul, not the body."

On the surface, a VM looks like a physical server. So let's actually look at the VM property. The following screenshot shows a VM setting in vSphere 5.5. It looks familiar as it has a CPU, Memory, Hard disk, Network adapter, and so on. However, look at it closely. Do you see any property that you don't usually see in a physical server?

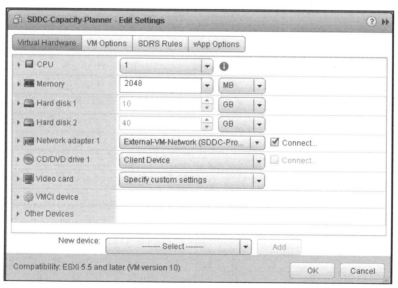

VM property in vSphere 5.5

Let me highlight some of the properties that do not exist in a physical server. I'll focus on those properties that have an impact on management, as management is the topic of this book.

At the top of the dialog box, there are four tabs:

- **Virtual Hardware**
- **VM Options**
- **SDRS Rules**
- **vApp Options**

The **Virtual Hardware** tab is the only tab that has similar properties to a physical server. The other three tabs do not have their equivalent server. For example, **SDRS Rules** pertains to Storage DRS. That means the VM storage can be automatically moved by **vCenter**. Its location in the data center is not static. This includes the drive where the OS resides (the `C:\` drive in Windows). This directly impacts your server management tool. It has to have awareness of Storage DRS, and can no longer assume that a VM is always located in the same datastore or LUN. Compare this with the physical server. Its OS typically resides on a local disk, which is part of the physical server. You don't want your physical server's OS drive being moved around in a data center, do you?

In the **Virtual Hardware** tab, notice the **New device** option at the bottom of the screen. Yes, you can add devices, some of them on the fly while Windows or Linux is running. All the VM's devices are defined in the software. This is a major difference to the physical server, where the physical hardware defines it and you cannot change it. With virtualization, you can have the **ESXi** host with two sockets but the VM has five sockets. Your server management tool needs to be aware of this and recognize that the new **Configuration Management Database (CMDB)** is now vCenter.

The next screenshot shows a bit more detail. I've expanded the CPU device. Again, what do you see that *does not exist* in a physical server?

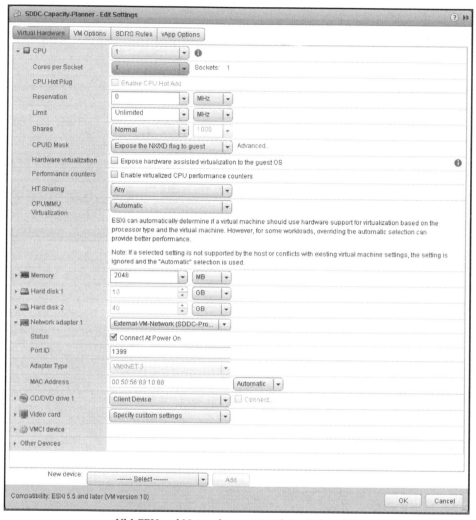

VM CPU and Network property tab in vSphere 5.5

Let me highlight some of the options. Look at **Reservation**, **Limit**, and **Shares**. None of them exist in a physical server, as a physical server is standalone by default. It does not share any resource on the motherboard (CPU and RAM) with another server. With these three levers, you can perform **Quality of Service (QoS)** in a virtual data center. Another point: QoS is actually built into the platform. This has an impact on management, as the platform is able to do some of the management by itself. There is no need to get another console to do what the platform provides you out of the box.

Other properties in the previous screenshot, such as **Hardware virtualization**, **Performance counters**, **HT Sharing**, and **CPU/MMU Virtualization** also do not exist in the physical server. It is beyond the scope of this book to explain every feature, and there are many blogs and technical papers freely available on the Internet that explain them. Some of my favorites are `http://blogs.vmware.com/performance/` and `http://www.vmware.com/vmtn/resources/`.

The next screenshot shows the **VM Options** tab. Again, what properties do you see that *do not exist* in a physical server?

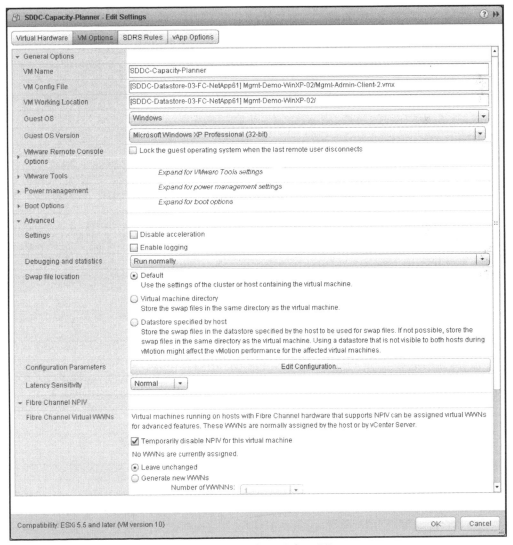

VM Options tab in vSphere 5.5

I'd like to highlight a few of the properties present in the **VM Options** tab. The **VMware Tools** property is a key and highly recommended component. It provides you with drivers and improves manageability. The **VMware Tools** property is not present in a physical server. A physical server has drivers but none of them are from VMware. A VM, however, is different. Its motherboard (virtual motherboard, naturally) is defined and supplied by VMware. Hence, the drivers are supplied by VMware. **VMware Tools** is the mechanism to supply those drivers. **VMware Tools** comes in different versions. So now you need to be aware of **VMware Tools** and it becomes something you need to manage.

I've just covered a few VM properties from the **VM setting** dialog box. There are literally hundreds of properties in VM that do not exist in the physical world. Even the same properties are implemented differently. For example, although vSphere supports **N_Port ID Virtualization (NPIV)**, the Guest OS does not see the **World Wide Name (WWN)**. This means the data center management tools have to be aware of the specific implementation by vSphere. And these properties change with every vSphere release. Notice the sentence right at the bottom. It says **Compatibility: ESXi 5.5 and later (VM version 10)**. This is your VM motherboard. It has dependency on the ESXi version and yes, this becomes another new thing to manage too.

Every vSphere release typically adds new properties too, making a VM more manageable than a physical machine, and differentiating a VM further than a physical server.

Hopefully, I've driven home the point that a VM is very different from a physical server. I'll now list the differences from the *management* point of view. The following table shows the differences that impact how you manage your infrastructure. Let's begin with the core properties:

Property	Physical server	Virtual machine
BIOS	A unique BIOS for every brand and model. Even the same model (for example, HP DL 380 Generation 7) can have multiple versions of BIOS. BIOS needs updates and management, often with physical access to a data center. This requires downtime.	This is standardized in a VM. There is only one type, which is the VMware motherboard. This is independent from the ESXi motherboard. VM BIOS needs far less updates and management. The inventory management system no longer needs the BIOS management module.

Property	Physical server	Virtual machine
Virtual HW	Not applicable	This is a new layer below BIOS. It needs an update on every vSphere release. A data center management system needs to be aware of this as it requires a deep knowledge of vSphere. For example, to upgrade the Virtual Hardware, the VM has to be in the power-off stage.
Drivers	Many drivers are loaded and bundled with the OS. Need to manage all of these drivers. This is a big area in the physical world, as they vary from model to model and brand to brand. The management tool has rich functionalities, such as checking compatibility, rolling out drivers, rolling back if there is an issue, and so on.	Almost no drivers are loaded with the OS; some drivers are replaced by VMware Tools. VMware Tools is the new driver, replacing all other drivers. Even with NPIV, the VM does not need the FC HBA driver. VMware Tools needs to be managed, with vCenter being the most common management tool.
Hardware upgrade	It is done offline and is complex. OS reinstallation and updates are required, hence it is a complex project in the physical world. Sometimes, a hardware upgrade is not even possible without upgrading the application. Virtualization decouples the application from hardware dependency.	It is done online and is simple. A VM can be upgraded from a 5-year-old hardware to a new one, moving from the local SCSI disk to 10 Gb FCoE, from dual core to a 15-core CPU. So yes, MS-DOS can run on 10 Gb FCoE accessing SSD storage via the PCIe lane. You just need to perform vMotion to the new hardware. As a result, the operation is drastically simplified.

In the preceding table, we compared the core properties of a physical server with a VM. Let's now compare the surrounding properties. The difference is also striking when we compare the area related to the physical server or VM:

Property	Physical server	Virtual machine
Storage	For servers connected to SAN, they can see the SAN and FC fabric. They need HBA drivers and have FC PCI cards, and have multipathing software installed. Normally needs an advanced filesystem or volume manager to RAID local disk.	No VM is connected to FC fabric or the SAN. VM only sees the local disk. Even with NPIV, the VM does not send FC frames. Multipathing is provided by vSphere, transparent to VM. There is no need for RAID local disk. It is one virtual disk, not two. Availability is provided at the hardware layer.
Backup	Backup agent and backup LAN needed in the majority of cases.	Not needed in the majority of cases, as backup is done via vSphere VADP API. Agent is only required for application-level backup.
Network	NIC teaming is common. Typically needs two cables per server. Guest OS is VLAN aware. It is configured inside the OS. Moving VLAN requires reconfiguration.	NIC teaming provided by ESXi. VM is not aware and only sees one vNIC. VLAN is provided by vSphere, transparent to VM. VM can be moved from one VLAN to another live.
Antivirus (AV)	The AV agent is installed on Guest. AV consumes OS resources and can be seen by the attacker. AV signature updates cause high storage throughput.	An AV agent runs on the ESXi host as a VM (one per ESXi). AV does not consume the Guest OS resources and it cannot be seen by the attacker from inside the Guest OS. AV signature updates do not require high IOPS inside the Guest OS. The total IOPS is also lower at the ESXi host level as it is not done per VM.

Lastly, let's take a look at the impact on management and monitoring. As can be seen next, even the way we manage the servers changes once they are converted into VMs:

Property	Physical server	Virtual machine
Monitoring	An agent is commonly deployed. It is typical for a server to have multiple agents. In-Guest counters are accurate. A physical server has an average of 5 percent CPU utilization due to the multicore chip. As a result, there is no need to monitor it closely.	An agent is typically not deployed. Certain areas such as application and Guest OS monitoring are still best served by an agent. The key in-Guest counters are not accurate. A VM has an average of 50 percent CPU utilization as it is right sized. This is 10 times higher when compared with a physical server. As a result, there is a need to monitor closely, especially when physical resources are oversubscribed. Capacity management becomes a discipline in itself.
Availability	HA is provided by clusterware such as MSCS and Veritas Cluster. Cloning a physical server is a complex task and requires the boot drive to be on the SAN or LAN, which is not typical. Snapshot is rarely done, due to cost and complexity.	HA is a built-in core component of vSphere. Most clustered physical servers end up as just a single VM as vSphere HA is good enough. Cloning can be done easily. It can even be done live. The drawback is that the clone becomes a new area of management. Snapshot can be done easily. In fact, this is done every time as part of backup process. Snapshot also becomes a new area of management.
Asset	The physical server is an asset and it has book value. It needs proper asset management as components vary among servers. Here, the stock-take process is required.	VM is not an asset as it has no accounting value. A VM is like a document. It is technically a folder with files in it. Stock-take is no longer required as the VM cannot exist outside vSphere.

Software-Defined Data Center

We covered how a VM differs drastically compared to a physical server. Now let's take a look at the big picture, which is at the data center level. A data center consists of three functions—compute, network, and storage. I use the term *compute* as we are entering the converged infrastructure era, where the *server* performs storage too and they are physically in one box. There is no more separation and we cannot say *this is the boundary where the server stops and the storage starts.*

VMware is moving to virtualize the network and storage functions as well, resulting in a data center that is fully virtualized and defined in the software. The software *is* the data center. We no longer prepare the architecture in the physical layer. The physical layer is just there to provide resources. These resources are not aware of one another. The stickiness is reduced and they become a commodity. In many cases, the hardware can even be replaced without incurring downtime to the VM.

The next diagram shows *one* possibility of a data center that is defined in the software. I have drawn the diagram to state a point, so don't take this as the best practice for SDDC architecture. Also, the technology is still evolving, so expect changes in the next several years. In the diagram, there are two physical data centers. Large enterprises will have more physical data centers. The physical data centers are completely independent. Personally, I believe this is a good thing. Ivan Pepelnjak, someone I respect highly on data center networking architecture, states that:

> *Interconnected things tend to fail at the same time*

 This specific sentence can be found at `http://blog.ipspace.net/2012/10/if-something-can-fail-it-will.html`. I also found the following article to be very useful: `http://blog.ipspace.net/2013/02/hot-and-cold-vm-mobility.html`.

Each of these physical functions (compute, network, and storage) is supported, or shall I say instantiated, in the physical world, by the respective hardware vendors. For a server, you might have vendors (for example, Nutanix, HP, Lenovo, Dell, and so on) that you trust and know. I have drawn two vendors to show the message that they do not define the architecture. They are there to support the function of that layer (for example, **Compute Function**). So, you can have 10 vSphere clusters: 3 clusters could be Vendor A, and 7 clusters could be Vendor B.

The same approach is then implemented in **Physical Data Center 2**, but without the mindset that the data centers have to be of the same vendor. Take **Storage Function**, as an example. You might have Vendor A on data center 1, and Vendor B on data center 2. You are no longer bound by the hardware compatibility; storage array replication normally requires the same model and protocol. You can do this as the physical data centers are completely independent of each other. They are neither connected nor stretched. The replication is done at the hypervisor layer. vSphere 5.5 has built-in host-based replication via TCP/IP. It can replicate individual VMs, and provides finer granularity than LUN-based replication. Replication can be done independently from a storage protocol (FC, iSCSI, or NFS) and VMDK type (thick or thin). You might decide to keep the same storage vendor but that's your choice, not something forced upon you.

On top of these physical data centers, you can define and deploy your virtual data centers. A virtual data center is no longer contained in a single building bound by a physical boundary. Although, bandwidth and latency are still limiting factors, the main thing here is you can architect your physical data centers as one or more logical data centers. You should be able to automatically, with just one click in SRM 5.5, move thousands of servers from data center A to data center B; alternatively, you can perform DR from four branch sites to a common HQ data center.

You are not bound to have one virtual data center per site, although it is easier to map it one-on-one with the current release of vSphere. For example, it is easier if you just have one vCenter per physical data center.

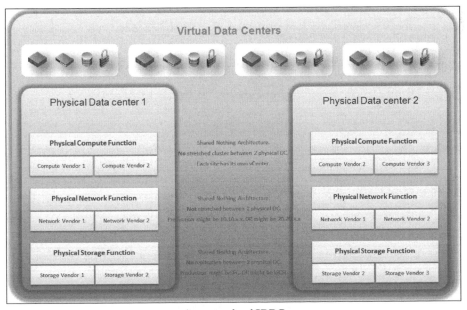

An example of SDDC

The next screenshot shows what a vCenter looks like in vSphere 5.5, the foundation of vCloud Suite. VMware continues integrating and enhancing vCloud Suite, and I would not be surprised to see its capability widening in future releases.

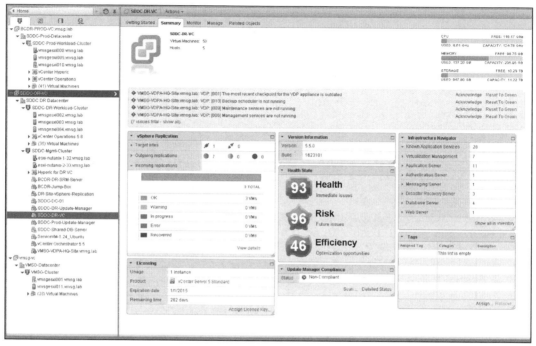

vCenter 5.5

I will zoom in to a part of the screenshot as it's rather small. The left part of the screenshot, shown next, shows that there are three vCenter Servers, and I've expanded each of them to show their data centers, clusters, hosts, and VMs:

From here, we can tell that we no longer need another inventory management software, as we can see all objects and their configurations and how they relate to one another. It is clear from here how many data centers, clusters, ESXi hosts, and VMs we have.

We also get more than static configuration information. Can you see what live or dynamic information is presented here? These are not the types of information you get from CMDB or the inventory management system.

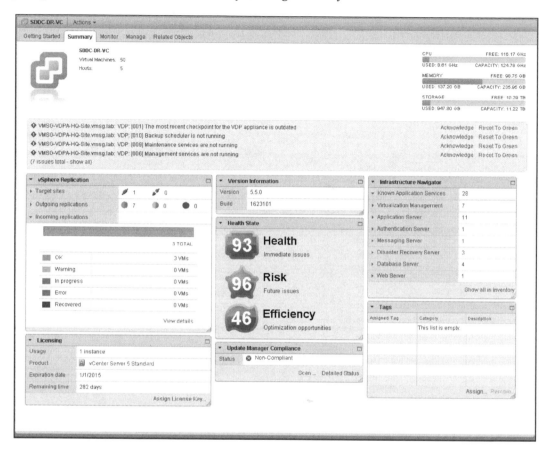

You will notice from the preceding screenshot that I get warnings and alerts, so this is a live environment. I also get information on the capacity and health. At the corner of the screen, you can see the data center CPU, memory, storage capacity, and usage. In the **vSphere Replication** box, you can see the VM replication status. For example, you can see that it has 7 outgoing replications and 3 incoming replications. In the middle of the screen, you can see **Health State**, which, by the way, comes from vRealize Operations. In the **Infrastructure Navigator** box, you get to see what applications are running, such as **Application Server** and **Database Server**. This information also comes from vRealize Operations. So, many of the management functions are provided out of the box. These functions are an *integral* part of vCloud Suite.

The compute function

As a virtualization engineer, I see a cluster as the *smallest* logical building block in vSphere. I treat it as one computer. You should also perform your capacity management at the cluster level and not at the host level. This is because a VM moves around within a cluster with DRS and Storage DRS. In the virtual data center, you think in terms of a cluster and not a server.

Let's take a look at the cluster called *SDDC-Mgmt-Cluster*, shown in the next screenshot. We can tell that it has 3 hosts, 24 processors (that's cores, not socket or threads), and 140 GB of RAM (about 4 GB is used by the three instances of VMkernel). We can also tell that it has EVC Mode enabled, and it is based on the Intel Nehalem generation. This means I can add an ESXi host running a newer Intel processor (for example, Westmere) live inside the cluster, and perform vMotion across the CPU generation. On the top-right corner, we can see the capacity used, just like we can see at the vCenter level. In a sense, we can drill down from the vCenter level to the cluster level.

We can also see that HA and DRS are turned on. DRS is set to fully automated, which is what I would recommend as you do not want to manually manage the ESXi host one by one. There is a whole book on vSphere Cluster, as there are many settings on this features. My favorite is by Duncan Epping and Frank Denneman, which is available at http://www.yellow-bricks.com/my-bookstore/.

The ramification of this is that the data center management software needs to understand vSphere well. It has to keep up with the enhancements in vSphere and vCloud Suite. A case in point: vSphere 5.5 in the Update 1 release added Virtual SAN, a software-defined storage integrated into vSphere.

Notice **Health State**. Again, this information comes from vRealize Operations. If you click on it, it will take you to a more detailed page, showing charts. If you drill down further, it will take you to vRealize Operations.

The **Infrastructure Navigator** box is useful so you know what applications are running in your cluster. For example, if you have a dedicated cluster for Microsoft SQL Server (as you want to optimize the license) and you see SQL in this cluster (which is not supposed to run the database), you know you need to move the VM. This is important because sometimes as an infrastructure team, you do not have access to go inside the VM. You do not know what's running on top of Windows or Linux.

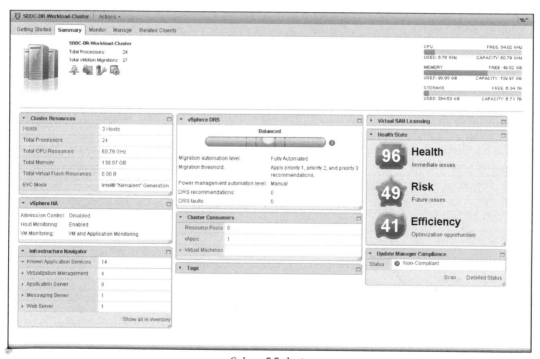

vSphere 5.5 cluster

The network function

We covered compute. Let's move on to network. The next screenshot shows a distributed virtual switch. As you can see, the distributed switch is an object at the data center level. So it extends across clusters. In some environments, this can result in a very large switch with more than 1,000 ports. In the physical world, this would be a huge switch indeed!

A VM is connected to either a standard switch or a distributed switch. It is not connected to the physical NIC in your ESXi host. The ESXi host physical NICs become the switch's uplinks instead, and generally you have 2 x 10 GE ports. This means that the traditional top-of-rack switch has been entirely virtualized. It runs completely as software, and the following screenshot is where you create, define, and manage it. This means the management software needs to understand the distributed vSwitch and its features. As you will see later, vRealize Operations understands virtual switches and treats networking as a first-class object.

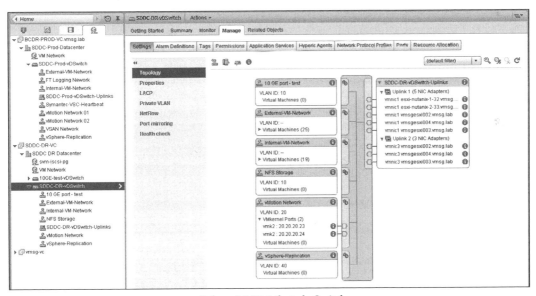

vSphere 5.5 Distributed vSwitch

The previous screenshot shows that the switch has six port groups and two uplinks. Let's drill down into one of the port groups, as shown in the next screenshot. Port group is a capability that is optional in physical switches, but mandatory in a virtual switch. It lets you group a number of switch ports and give it a common property. You can also set policies. As shown in the **Policies** box, there are many properties that you can set. Port group is essential in managing all the ports connected to the switch.

In the top-right corner, you see the **CAPACITY** information. So you know how many ports you configured and how many ports are used. This is where virtual networking is different to virtual compute and virtual storage. For compute and storage, you need to have the underlying physical resources to back it up. You cannot create a VM with a 32-core vCPU if the underlying ESXi has less than 32 physical threads. Virtual network is different. Network is an interconnection; it is not a "node"-like compute and storage. It is not backed by physical ports. You can increase the number of ports to basically any number you want. The entire switch lives on memory! You power off the ESXi and there is no more switch.

In the **Infrastructure Navigator** box, you will again see the list of applications. vRealize Operations is deeply embedded into vSphere, making you feel like it's a single application as it is a single pane of glass. In the past several releases of VMware products; they are becoming one integrated suite and this trend is set to continue.

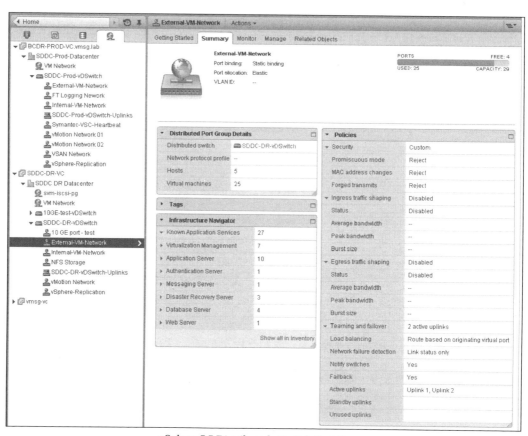

vSphere 5.5 Distributed vSwitch Port Group

The storage function

Let's now move to storage. The next screenshot shows a vSphere 5.5 datastore cluster. The idea behind a datastore cluster is similar to that of a compute cluster. Let's use an example as it's easier to understand. Say you have a cluster of 8 ESXi hosts, with each host sporting 2 sockets, 24 cores, and 48 threads. In this cluster, you run 160 VMs, giving you a 20:1 consolidation ratio. This is reasonable from a performance management view as the entire cluster has 192 physical cores and 384 physical threads. Based on the general guidelines that Intel Hyper-Threading gives around a 50 percent performance boost, you can use 288 cores as the max thread count. This gives you around 1.8 cores per VM, which is reasonable as most VMs are 2 vCPU and have around 50 percent utilization. These 160 VMs are stored in 8 datastores, or around 20 VMs per datastore.

With the compute node, you need not worry about where a VM is running in that cluster. When you provision a new VM, you do not specify which host will run it. You let DRS decide. As the workload goes up and down, you do not want to manage the placement on an individual ESXi host for 160 VMs. You let DRS do the load balancing, and it will use vMotion on the VM automatically. You treat the entire cluster as if it is a single giant box.

With the storage node, you can do the same thing. When you provision a new VM, you do not specify a datastore for it. If you do want to specify it manually, you need to check which datastore has the most amount of space and the least amount of IOPS. The first piece of information is quite easy to check, but the second one is not. This is the first value of the datastore cluster. It picks a cluster based on both capacity and performance. The second value is based on the ongoing operation. As time passes, VM grows at different rates in terms of both capacity and IOPS. Storage DRS monitors this and makes recommendations for you. The major difference here is the amount of data to be migrated. In vMotion, we normally migrate somewhere between 1 GB to 10 GB of RAM, as the kernel only copies the used RAM (and not the configured RAM). In storage vMotion, we potentially copy 100 GB of data. This takes a lot longer and hence has a greater performance impact. As such, Storage DRS should be performed a lot less frequently, perhaps once a month.

Datastore cluster helps in capacity management, as you basically treat all the datastores as one. You can easily check key information about the datastore cluster, such as the number of VMs, total storage, capacity used, and largest free space you have.

As usual, vRealize Operations provides information about what applications are running in the datastore cluster. This is handy information in a large environment, where you have specific datastores for specific applications.

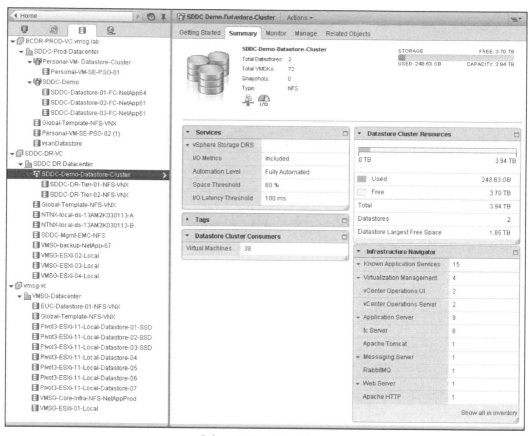

vSphere 5.5 Datastore Cluster

All together now

We covered all the three elements—compute, storage, and network. How are they related? The next screenshot shows the relationship of the key objects managed by vCenter.

It's handy information in a small environment. If you have a large environment, maps such as the one shown in the next screenshot really become much more complex! In this map, I only have 3 ESXi hosts and 7 datastores, and I have to hide some relationships already. Notice that I did not select the **Host to VM** and **VM to datastore** relationship options, because it got way too complicated when I did.

The point of sharing the screenshot is to share that you indeed have your data center in software with the following characteristics:

- You have your VM as the consumer. You can show both powered-on and powered-off VMs.

- You have your compute (ESXi), network (port group), and storage (datastore) as the provider. You can show the relationship between your compute to your network and storage.

- You have the information about the network, storage, and compute your VM is connected to.

Think about it. How *difficult* will it be to have this type of relationship mapped in the physical data center? I've personally heard comments from customers that they do not know exactly how many servers they have, which network they are connected to, and what applications run on that box. The powered-off server is even harder to find! Even if you can implement a data center management system, which can give you the map, one or two years later you cannot be sure that the map is up-to-date. The management system has to be embedded into the platform. In fact, it's the only point of entry to the virtual platform. It cannot be a separate, detached system.

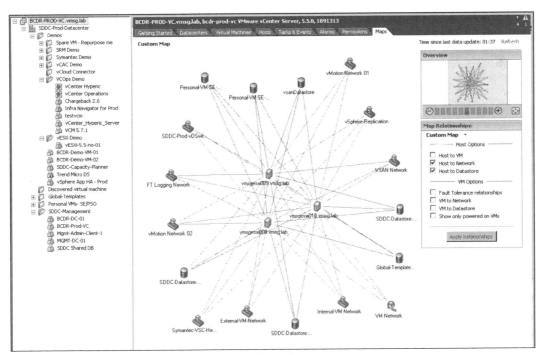

vSphere Maps

The last point I'd like to bring up is that SDDC is a world in itself. It's not simply your data center virtualized. Look at the following table. It lists some of the objects in vSphere. I have not included NSX, Virtual SAN, or vRealize Suite objects here. These objects do not have their physical equivalent. If they do, they have different properties, generate different events, and are measured by different counters. Plus, all these objects have some relationship with one another. You need to look at vCloud Suite in its entirety to understand it well.

Object & Relation	Events	Counters	Properties
• ESXi Host	• vMotion	• CPU Ready	• Share
• Cluster	• DRS	• CPU Latency	• Limit
• Data Center	• DPM	• Co-Stop	• Reservation
• Resource Pool	• Storage vMotion	• Ballooning	• Fault Tolerant
• Folder	• Maintenance mode	• KAVG	• HA
• vCenter	• VM Provisioning	• Memory compression	• Master
• vSwitch	• Storage IOC kicks in	• TPS	• VM
• Distributed vSwitch		• vSphere Replication	• Boot order
• vApp	• Network IOC kicks in	• >100 counters has no physical equivalent...	• Licensing
• vmnic	• Hot Add		• vSphere Replication
• Port Group	• Hot Remove		• Each object in vCloud Suite has many properties
• Datastore	• Network LBT		
• Datastore group	• Each object in vCloud Suite triggers many events		
• Agent VM			
• Devices			
• ... many others			

vSphere Objects and their relationships

The downside of this SDDC is that the upgrade of this "giant machine" is a new project for IT. It has to be planned and implemented carefully because it is as good as upgrading the data center while servers, storage, and network are all still running. Using a physical world analogy, it's like renovating your home while living in it.

A virtual data center versus a physical data center

We covered SDDC to a certain depth. We can now summarize the key differences between a physical data center and a virtual one. To highlight the differences, I'm assuming in this comparison the physical data center is *0 percent virtualized* and the virtual data center is *100 percent virtualized*. For the virtual data center, I'm assuming you have also adjusted your *operation*, because operating a virtual data center with a physical operation mindset results in a lot of frustration and suboptimal virtualization. This means your processes and organization chart have been adapted to a virtual data center.

Data center

The following table summarizes the data centers as physical and virtual data centers:

Physical data center	Virtual data center
This is bounded by one physical site. Data center migration is a major and expensive project.	This is not bound to any physical site. Multiple virtual data centers can exist in one physical data center, and a single virtual data center can span multiple physical data centers. The entire DC can be replicated and migrated.

Server

The following table summarizes servers in physical and virtual data centers:

Physical data center	Virtual data center
1,000 physical servers (just an example, so we can provide a comparison).	It may have 2,000 VMs. The number of VMs is higher for multiple reasons: VM sprawl; the physical server tends to run multiple applications or instances whereas VM runs only one; DR is much easier and hence, more VMs are protected.
Growth is relatively static and predictable, and normally it is just one way (adding more servers).	The number of VMs can go up and down due to dynamic provisioning.
Downtime for hardware maintenance or a technology refresh is a common job in a large environment due to component failure.	Planned downtime is eliminated with vMotion and storage vMotion.

Physical data center	Virtual data center
5 to 10 percent average CPU utilization, especially in the CPU with a high core count.	50 to 80 percent utilization for both VM and ESXi.
Racks of physical boxes, often with a top-of-rack access switch and UPS. The data center is a large consumer of power.	Rack space requirements shrink drastically as servers are consolidated and the infrastructure is converged. There is a drastic reduction in space and power.
Low complexity. Lots of repetitive work and coordination work, but not a lot of expertise required.	High complexity. Less quantity, but deep expertise required. A lot less number of people, but each one is an expert.
Availability and performance monitored by management tools, which normally uses an agent. It is typical for a server to have many agents.	Availability and performance monitoring happens via vCenter, and it's agentless for the infrastructure. All other management tools get their data from vCenter, not individual ESXi or VM. Application-level monitoring is typically done using agents.
The word cluster means two servers joined with a heartbeat and shared storage, which is typically SAN.	The word cluster has a very different meaning. It's a group of ESXi hosts sharing the workload. Normally, 8 to 12 hosts, not 2.
High Availability (HA) is provided by clusterware, such as MSCS and Veritas. Every cluster pair needs a shared storage, which is typically SAN. Typically one service needs two physical servers with a physical network heartbeat; hence, most servers are not clustered as the cost and complexity is high.	HA is provided by vSphere HA, including services monitoring via Application HA. All VMs are protected, not just a small percentage. The need for traditional clustering software drops significantly, and a new kind of clustering tool develops. The cluster for VMware integrates with vSphere and uses the vSphere API.
Fault Tolerance is rarely used due to cost and complexity. You need specialized hardware, such as Stratus ftServer.	Fault tolerance is an on-demand feature as it is software-based. For example, you can temporarily turn it on during batch jobs run.
Anti-Virus is installed on every server. Management is harder in a large environment.	Anti-Virus is at the hypervisor level. It is agentless and hence, is no longer visible by malware.

Storage

The following table summarizes storage in physical and virtual data centers:

Physical data center	Virtual data center
1,000 physical servers (just an example, so we can provide a comparison), where IOPS and capacity do not impact each another. A relatively static environment from a storage point of view because normally, only 10 percent of these machines are on SAN/NAS due to cost.	It has a maximum of 2,000 interdependent VMs, which impact one another. A very dynamic environment where management becomes critical because almost all VMs are on a shared storage, including distributed storage.
Every server on SAN has its own dedicated LUN. Some data centers, such as databases, may have multiple LUNs.	Most VMs do not use RDM. They use VMDK and share the VMFS or NFS datastore. The VMDK files may reside in different datastores.
Storage migration is a major downtime, even within the same array. A lot of manual work is required.	Storage migration is live with storage vMotion. Intra-array is faster due to VAAI API.
Backup, especially in the x64 architecture, is done with backup agents. As SAN is relatively more expensive and SAN boot is complex at scale, backup is done via the backup LAN and with the agent installed. This creates its own problem as the backup agents have to be deployed, patched, upgraded, and managed. The backup process also creates high disk I/O, impacting the application performance. Because the data center is network intensive and carries sensitive data, an entire network is born for backup purposes.	The backup service is provided by the hypervisor. It is LAN-free and agentless. Most backup software use the VMware VADP API to do VM backup. No, it does not apply to databases or other applications, but it is good enough for 90 percent of the VM population. Because backup is performed outside the VM, there is no performance impact on the application or Guest OS. There is also no security risk, as the Guest OS Admin cannot see the backup network.
Storage's QoS is taken care of by an array, although the array has no control over the demand of IOPS coming from servers.	Storage's QoS is taken care of by vSphere, which has full control over every VM.

Network

The following table summarizes the network in physical and virtual data centers:

Physical data center	Virtual data center
The access network is typically 1 GE, as it is sufficient for most servers. Typically, it is a top-of-rack entry-level switch.	The top-of-rack switch is generally replaced with the end-of-row distribution switch, as the access switch is completely virtualized. ESXi typically uses 10 GE.
VLAN is normally used for segregation. This results in VLAN complexity.	VLAN is not required (the same VLAN can be blocked) for segregation by NSX.
Impacted by the spanning tree.	No Spanning Tree.
A switch must learn the MAC address as it comes with the server.	No need to learn the MAC address as it's given by vSphere.
Network QoS is provided by core switches.	Network QoS by vSphere and NSX.
DMZ Zone is physically separate. Separation is done at the IP layer. IDS/IPS deployment is normally limited in DMZ due to cost and complexity.	DMZ Zone is logically separate. Separation is not limited to IP and done at the hypervisor layer. IDS/IPS is deployed in all zones as it is also hypervisor-based.
No DR Test network is required. As a result, the same hostname cannot exist on DR Site, making a true DR Test *impossible* without shutting down production servers.	DR Test Network is required. The same hostname can exist on any site as a result. This means DR Test can be done anytime as it does not impact production.
Firewall is not part of the server. It is typically centrally located. It is not aware of the servers as it's completely independent from it.	Firewall becomes a built-in property of the VM. The rules follow the VM. When a VM is vMotion-ed to another host, the rule *follows* it and is enforced by the hypervisor.
Firewall scales vertically and independently from the workload (demand from servers). This makes sizing difficult. IT ends up buying the biggest firewall they can afford, hence increasing the cost.	Firewall scales horizontally. It grows with demand, since it is deployed as part of the hypervisor (using NSX). Upfront cost is lower as there is no need to buy a pair of high-end firewall upfront.
Traffic has to be deliberately directed to the firewall. Without it, the traffic "escapes" the firewall.	All traffic passes the firewall as it's embedded into the VM and hypervisor. It cannot "escape" the firewall.

Physical data center	Virtual data center
Firewall rules are typically based on the IP address. Changing the IP address equals changing the rules. This results in a database of long and complicated rules. After a while, the firewall admin dare not delete any rules as the database becomes huge and unmanageable.	Rules are not tied to the IP address or hostname. This makes rules much easier. For example, we can say that all VMs in the Contractor Desktop pool cannot talk to each other. This is just one rule. When a VM gets added to this pool, the rule is applied to it.
Load Balancer is typically centrally located. Just like the firewall, sizing becomes difficult and the cost goes higher.	Load Balancer is distributed. It scales with the demand.

Disaster Recovery

The following table summarizes **Disaster Recovery (DR)** in physical and virtual data centers:

Physical data center	Virtual data center
Architecturally, DR is done on a per-application basis. Every application has its own bespoke solution.	DR is provided as a *service* by the platform. It is one solution for all applications. This enables data center-wide DR.
The standby server on the DR site is required. This increases the cost. Because the server has to be compatible with the associated production server, this increases complexity in a large environment.	No need for a standby server. The ESXi cluster on the DR site typically runs the non-production workload, which can be suspended (hibernate) during DR. The DR site can be of a different server brand and CPU.
DR is a manual process, relying on a run book written manually. It also requires all hands on deck. An unavailability of key IT resources when disaster strikes can impact the organization's ability to recover.	The entire DR steps are automated. Once management decides to trigger DR, all that needs to be done is to execute the right recovery process in VMware Site Recovery Manager. No manual intervention.
A complete DR dry run is rarely done, as it is time consuming and requires production to be down.	A DR dry run can be done frequently, as it does not impact the production system. It can even be done on the day before the actual planned DR.

Physical data center	Virtual data center
The report produced after a DR exercise is manually typed. It is not possible to prove that what is documented in the Microsoft Word or Excel document is what actually happened in the data center.	The report is automatically generated, with no human intervention. It timestamps every step, and provides a status whether it was successful or not. The report can be used as audit proof.

Application

The following table summarizes the application in physical and virtual data centers:

Physical data center	Virtual data center
Licensing is bound by the physical server. It is a relatively simple thing to manage.	Licensing is bound by an entire cluster or per VM. It can be more expensive or cheaper, hence it is complex from a management point of view.
All applications are supported.	Most applications are supported. The ones that are not supported are primarily due to the outdated perception by the ISV vendor. When more apps are developed in the virtual environment, this perception will go away.

Infrastructure team

The following table summarizes the infrastructure team in physical and virtual data centers:

Physical data center	Virtual data center
There's a clear silo between the compute, storage, and network teams. In organizations where the IT team is big, the DR team, Windows team, and Linux team could also be separate teams. There is also a separation between the engineering, integration (projects), and operations (business as usual) teams. The team, in turn, needs layers of management. This results in rigidity in IT.	With virtualization, IT is taking the game to the next level. It's a lot more powerful than the previous architecture. When you take the game to the next level, the enemy is also stronger. In this case, the expertise required is deeper and the experience requirement is more extensive. Earlier, you may have needed 10 people to manage 1,000 physical servers. With virtualization, you might only need three people to manage 2,000 VMs on 100 ESXi hosts. However, these 3 people have deeper expertise and more experience than the 10 people combined.

Management disciplines impacted by virtualization

We covered all the changes introduced by virtualization. Virtualization changes the architecture of IT, turning operation as usual from best practice to dated practice. The following table now summarizes from the pillar of management, so that we can see the impact from a specific discipline:

Area impacted	Why is it impacted?
Performance management	This gets *harder* as the performance of ESXi/VM/Datastore can impact one another. The entire environment is no longer static. VM activities such as vMotion, Storage vMotion, provisioning, power on, and so on also add to the workload. So, there is VM workload and infrastructure workload. Performance issues can originate from any component.
	Troubleshooting something that is dynamic is difficult. Unlike a physical data center, the first thing we need to check is the *overall* health because of the interdependency. Only when we are satisfied that the problem is not wide-spread that we zoom in to a specific object (for example, VM, ESXi, and datastore).
	Performance degradations can also be caused by configuration changes. These configuration changes occur more frequently than a physical data center as many of them can be done live.
	QoS becomes *mandatory* due to shared resources.
	A new requirement is application visibility. We can no longer troubleshoot in isolation without knowing which applications run inside that VM.
Availability management	vCloud Suite relies heavily on shared storage. The availability of this storage becomes critical. Enterprise should consider storage as an integral part of the platform, and not a subsystem managed by a *different* team.
	Clustering software is mostly replaced with vSphere.
	Backup is mostly agentless and LAN-free.
	DR becomes a service provided by the platform.
Capacity management	Capacity management becomes a complex process. You need a tool that understands the dynamic nature of vCloud Suite.

Area impacted	Why is it impacted?
Compliance management	Compliance becomes more complex due to the lack of physical segregation.
	vCloud Suite itself is a big area that needs to be in compliance.
Security	Access to vCloud Suite needs to be properly controlled.
Configuration management (related to Change management)	vCloud Suite became the new source of truth, displacing the CMDB (as it is detached from the environment it manages). The need for another database to manage the virtual environment has to be weighed in as there is already a de facto database, which is vCenter. For example, if vCenter shows a VM is running, but there is no record in CMDB, do you power off and delete the VM? Certainly not. As a result, CMDB becomes less important as vCloud Suite itself provides the data.
	VM configuration changes need to be tracked. Changes happen more often and faster.
	vSphere becomes another area where configuration management needs to be applied.
Patch management	The data center itself becomes the software, which needs to be patched and upgraded. This can be automated to a large extent.
	Because it is software, it needs to have a *non-production copy*.
Financial management	Chargeback (or showback at the minimal) becomes mandatory as the infrastructure is no longer owned by the application team. Shared resources means users do not expect to pay the full price.
Asset management	Drastically *simplified* as the VM is not an asset. Most network and storage appliances become software.
	ESXi is the new asset, but it can't be changed without central management (vCenter) being alerted. The configuration is also standardized.
	Stock-take is no longer applicable for the VM and top-of-rack access switch. Inventory is built-in in vSphere and NSX.
Operations management	Although ITIL principles do not change, the details of a lot of processes change drastically. We covered some of them previously.

Summary

I hope you enjoyed the comparison and found it useful. We covered, to a great extent, the impact caused by virtualization and the changes it introduces. We started by clarifying that virtualization is a different technology compared to partitioning. We then explained that once a physical server is converted into a virtual machine, it takes on a very different form and has radically different properties. The changes range from the core property of the server itself to how we manage it. This, in turn, creates a ripple effect in the bigger picture. The entire data center changes once we virtualize it.

In the next chapter, we will cover capacity management in greater depth, as it is an area that is made more complex once you virtualize your data center.

2
Capacity Management in SDDC

Capacity management changes drastically with virtualization. In this chapter, we will explain why it is one of the areas that is greatly impacted by virtualization. We will cover the following topics:

- Why capacity management is split into two distinct areas
- How you should perform capacity management at the VM level
- How you should perform capacity management at the infrastructure level

We explain how each component (compute, storage, and network) are changed and how you should plan for it.

Shift in capacity management

The changes to capacity management can be largely grouped into two areas:

- *Operationally*, virtualization changes the IT infrastructure team from system builder to service provider. The application team no longer own the physical infrastructure, and it is now a shared infrastructure. This creates a two-tier capacity management:

  - At the VM level, capacity management is done by the application team. They determine the size of their VM, and then buy the capacity from the infrastructure team. They need to adjust the size, as oversizing leads to performance issues.

  - At the physical infrastructure level, the infrastructure team must perform capacity management as a single team. The joint team must take care of computing, networking, storage, and DR. The mindset has to change from that of a system builder to a service provider.

- *Architecturally*, the infrastructure moves from a bespoke system to standardized hardware. The application team no longer need to dictate the specifications of the hardware. For example, they do not specify a server brand, model, and CPU frequency. They can only specify how many virtual CPU they need. Sometimes, especially in a large environment, they can only choose small, medium, or large vCPU, and all of these have been preconfigured.

Once you split capacity management into the two distinct layers, it will become natural and it will transform the infrastructure team into the service provider model. You need to see the application team as a customer who does not need to know about the detailed specification of your infrastructure. You provide them a service. To achieve this, you need to unify the three components (compute, network, and storage) as one integrated capacity planning. It is no longer sufficient to look at them as three separate components managed by three different teams.

Capacity management at the VM level

There are some tips you can give to your customers and policies you can set to keep things simple. For a start, keep the building blocks simple—one VM, one OS, one application, and one instance. So, avoid having one OS running the web, app, and DB server or avoid having one Microsoft SQL server running five instances of databases. The workload can become harder to predict as you cannot isolate them. It is recommended to adjust the size of the peak workload for a production environment. A month-end VM needs to be sized based on the month-end workload. For a non-production environment, you may want to tell the application team to opt for a smaller VM, because the vSphere Cluster where the VM is running is oversubscribed. The large VM may not get the CPU it asks for if it asks for too many.

Be careful with those VMs that have two distinct peaks: one for CPU resources and another one for memory resources. I have seen this with a telecommunications client running **Oracle Hyperion**. For example, the first peak needs 8 vCPUs and 12 GB vRAM, and the second peak needs 2 vCPUs and 48 GB vRAM. In this case, the application team tendency is to size for 8 vCPUs and 48 GB vRAM. This results in an unnecessarily large VM, which can result in poor performance for both peaks. It is likely there are two different workloads running in the VM, which should be split into two VMs.

Size correctly. Educate the application team that oversizing results in slower performance in the virtual world. Although I encourage the standardization of VM size to make life simple, you should be flexible for large or extra-large cases. For example, once you pass 8 vCPUs, you need to consider every additional CPU carefully, ensure the VM really needs it, and ensure the application can indeed take advantage of the extra threads. You also need to verify that the underlying ESXi has sufficient physical cores, as it will affect your consolidation ratio, and hence your capacity management. You may see an ESXi that is largely idle yet the VMs on it are not performing, therefore impacting your confidence about adding VMs.

At the VM level, you need to monitor the following five components:

- Virtual CPU
- Virtual RAM
- Virtual network
- Virtual disk IOPS
- Usable disk capacity left in the Guest OS.

Getting vCPU and vRAM into a healthy range requires finding a balance. Undersizing leads to poor performance and oversizing leads to monetary waste *as well as* poor performance. The actual healthy range depends upon your expected utilization, and it normally varies from tier to tier. It also depends on the nature of the workload (online versus batch). For example, in tier 1 (the highest tier), you will have a lower range for the OLTP type of workload as you do not want to hit 100 percent at peak. The overall utilization will be low as you are catering for a spike. For batch workload, you normally tolerate a higher range for long-running batch jobs, as they tend to consume all the resources given to it. In a non-production environment, you normally tolerate a higher range, as the business expectation is lower (because they are paying a lower price).

Generally speaking, virtual network is not something that you need to worry about from a capacity point of view. You can create a super metric in vRealize Operations that tracks the maximum of all of your vNIC utilization from all VMs. If the maximum is, say, 80 percent, then you know that the rest of the VMs are lower than that. You can then plot a chart that shows this peak utilization in the last three months. We will cover this in more detail in one of the use cases discussed in the final chapter.

You should monitor the usable disk capacity left inside the Guest OS. Although vCenter does not provide this information, vRealize Operations does—provided your VM has VMware Tools installed (which it should have as a part of best practice).

You should use **Reservation** sparingly as it impacts the HA slot size, increases management complexity, and prevents you from oversubscribing. In tier 1, where there is no oversubscription because you are guaranteeing resource to every VM, reservation becomes unnecessary from a capacity management point of view. You may still use it if you want a faster boot, but that's not from a capacity point of view. In tier 3, where cost is the number-one factor, using Reservation will prevent you from oversubscribing. This negates the purpose of tier 3 in the first place.

You should avoid using **Limit** as it leads to unpredictable performance. The Guest OS does not know that it is artificially limited.

Capacity management at the infrastructure level

At the infrastructure level, you look at the *big picture*. Hence, it is important that you know your architecture well. One way to easily remember what you have is to keep it simple. Yes, you can have different host specifications—CPU speed, amount of RAM, and so on in a cluster. But, that would be hard to remember if you have a large farm with many clusters.

You also need to know what you actually have at the *physical* layer. If you don't know how many CPUs or how much RAM the ESXi host has, then it's impossible to figure out how much capacity is left. I will use storage as an example to illustrate why this is important. Do you know how many IOPS your storage has?

The majority of shared storage is shared with both ESXi and non-ESXi servers mounted. Even if the entire storage is dedicated to ESXi, there is still the physical backup server mounting it, and it might be doing array-based replication or a snapshot.

Some storage support dynamic tiering (high IOPS, low latency storage fronting the low IOPS, and high latency spindles). In this configuration, the underlying physical IOPS varies from minute to minute. This gives a challenge for ESXi and vRealize Operations to determine the actual physical limit of the array, so you need to take extra care to ensure you accurately account for the resources available. A change in the array configuration can impact your capacity planning. Changing the tier preference of a given LUN can probably be done live, so it can be done *without* you being informed.

Capacity planning at the compute level

Once you know the actual capacity, you are in a position to figure out the usable portion. The next figure shows the relationship. The raw capacity is what you have physically. The **Infrastructure as a Service (IaaS)** workload is all the workload that is not caused by a VM. For example, the hypervisor itself consumes CPU and RAM. When you bring an ESXi host into the maintenance mode, it will trigger mass vMotion for all the VMs running on it. That vMotion will take up the CPU and RAM of both ESXi hosts and the network between them. So the capacity left for VM, the usable capacity, is **Raw Capacity – IaaS workload – Non vSphere workload**.

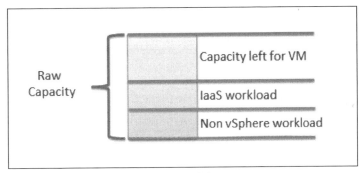

Main consumers of the capacity

So what are these IaaS workloads? Think of SDDC. All the services or functionalities it provides to the consumer (the VM) run as software. Storage services (for example, Virtual SAN, vSphere Replication), network services (for example, L3 switch in NSX, firewall), security services (for example, Trend Micro Antivirus), and availability services (for example, Storage vMotion); the list goes on. It is software, and software consumes physical resources. The next table lists all the IaaS workloads. It is possible that the list will get outdated as more and more capabilities are moved into software. For each of the workloads, I have put a *rough* estimate on the impact. It is an estimate as it depends upon the scale. Using vMotion on a small and idle VM will have minimal impact. Using vMotion on five large memory-intensive VMs will have high impact; the same goes for vSphere Replication. Replicating an idle VM with RPO of 24 hours will generate minimal traffic. Replicating many write-intensive VMs with RPO of 15 minutes will generate high network traffic.

In the list of IaaS workloads here, I'm not including Horizon view. **Virtual Desktop Infrastructure (VDI)** workloads behave differently to server workloads and so they need their own separate breakdown of workload, which have not been included in the table. A VDI (desktop) and VSI (server) farm should be separated physically for performance reasons and so that you may upgrade your vCenter Servers independently. If that is not possible in your environment, then you need to include Horizon view-specific IaaS workloads (recompose, refresh, rebalance, and so on) in your calculations. If you ignore these and only include the desktop workloads, you may not be able to perform recompose during office hours.

IaaS workload	Compute Impact	Network Impact	Storage Impact
vMotion and DRS	Medium	High	Low
Storage vMotion and Storage DRS	Low	Low (vStorage APIs for Array Integration-VAAI) High (non-VAAI)	High
VM operation: snapshot, cloning, hibernate, shutdown, and boot up	Medium	Low	High
Fault Tolerant VM	Medium	Medium	Low
HA and cluster maintenance (can result in all VMs evacuated on affected host)	Medium	High	N/A
Hypervisor-based storage services: vSphere Replication	Low	Medium	Medium
Virtual Storage (for example, VSAN, Nutanix, and so on)	Medium	High	High
Backup (for example, VDP Advanced, VADP API, and so on) with de-dupe Backup vendor can provide the info here For VDP-Advanced, you can see the actual data in vSphere	High	High	High
Hypervisor-based network services: AV, IDS, IPS, FW, L3 switch (NSX), and others	Medium	Medium	Low
Edge of Network services (for example, NSX Edge, F5, and so on)	Low	High	Low
DR Test or Actual (with SRM)	High	High	High

Good capacity management begins with a good design. A good design creates standards that simplify capacity management. If the design is flawed and complex, capacity management may become impossible.

Personally, I'm in favor of dedicated clusters for each service tier in a large environment. We can compare the task of managing the needs of virtual machines to how an airline business manages the needs of passengers on a plane—the plane has dedicated areas for first class, business class, and economy class. It makes capacity management easier as each class has a dedicated amount of space to be divided among the passengers and the passengers are grouped by service level, so it is easier to tell if the service levels for each class are being met overall. Similarly, I prefer to have three smaller clusters rather than one very large, mixed cluster serving all three tiers. Of course, there are situations where it is not possible to have small clusters; it all depends on requirements and budget. Additionally, there are benefits of having one large cluster, such as lower cost and more resources to handle peak periods. In situations where you choose to mix VMs of different tiers, you should consider using **Shares** instead of **Reservations**.

For the compute node, the following table provides an example of cluster design for virtual machine tiers. Your design will likely differ from the following table, as your requirements may differ. The main thing is that you need to have a design, which clearly defines the standard.

Tier	# Host	ESXi Specification	Failure Tolerance	Max #VM	Remarks
Tier 1	Always 6	Always identical	2 hosts	100	Only for critical apps. No resource overcommits.
Tier 2	4-8	Sometimes	1 host	200	A VM can be vMotion-ed to tier 1 during critical run.
Tier 3	4-12	Most likely not	1 host	300	Twice the resource overcommit.
SW	2-12	Sometimes	1-2 hosts	200	Running expensive software. Oracle and SQL are the norms as part of DB as a service.

In the preceding example, capacity planning becomes simple in tier 1, as there is a good chance that we hit the availability limit before we hit the capacity limit. Defining how many VMs will be in a cluster in advance will allow you to set an alert if that number is breached.

Capacity planning at the storage layer

For the storage node, capacity management depends on the chosen architecture. Storage is undergoing an evolution with the arrival of the converged storage, which introduces an alternative to the traditional, external array.

In the traditional, external storage model, there is a physical array (for example, EMC VNX, HDS HUS, and NetApp). As most environments are not yet 100 percent virtualized, the physical array is shared by non-ESXi servers (for example, UNIX). There is often a physical backup server (for example, Symantec NetBackup) that utilizes the VMware VADP API.

The array might have LUNs replicated to a DR site. This replication certainly takes up bandwidth, FC ports, the array CPU, and bandwidth on your inter-data center line.

If the array is not supporting VAAI (or that feature is not yet implemented at the VMkernel level), then the traffic will traverse the path up and down. This can mean a lot of traffic going from the spindle to ESXi and back.

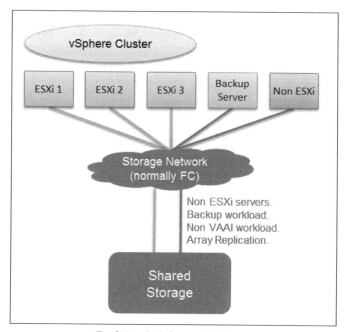

Traditional vSphere architecture

In the second example, there is no longer a separate physical array. It has been virtualized and absorbed into the server. It has truly become a subsystem. Some example products in this category are Nutanix and Virtual SAN. So the object labeled **Storage 1** in the next diagram is just a bunch of local disks (magnetic or solid state) in the physical server. Each ESXi host runs a similar group of local drives, typically with flash, SSD, and SATA. The local drives are virtualized. There is no FC protocol; it's all IP-based storage.

To avoid single point of failure, the virtual storage appliance is able to mirror or copy in real time and there is a need to cater bandwidth for this. I would recommend you use 10 Gb infrastructure for your ESXi if you are adopting this distributed storage architecture, especially in environments with five or more hosts in a cluster. The physical switches connecting your ESXi servers should be seen as an integral part of the solution, not a "service" provided by the network team. Architectural choices such as ensuring redundancy for **Network Interface Cards** (**NIC**) and switches are important.

The following diagram also uses vSphere Replication. Unlike array-replication, this is consuming the resource of ESXi and the network.

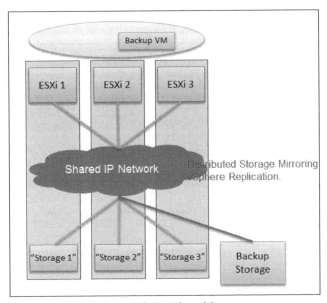

vSphere with Distributed Storage

Once you have confirmed your storage architecture, you will be in the position to calculate your usable capacity and IOPS. Let's now dive deeper into the first architecture, as this is still the most common architecture.

The next diagram shows a typical mid-range array. I'm only showing **Controller 1** as our focus here is capacity, not availability. The top box shows the controller. It has CPU, RAM, and cache. In a tiered storage, there will be multiple tiers and the datastore (or NFS / RDM) can write into any of the tiers seamlessly and transparently. You do not need to have per-VM control over it. The control is likely at the LUN level. I've covered what that means in terms of performance (IOPS and latency). What I'd like to show in this diagram is the trade-off in design between the ability to share resources and the ability to guarantee performance. In this diagram, our array has three volumes. Each volume consists of 16 spindles. In this specific example, each volume is independent of one another. If **Volume 1** is overloaded with IOPS but **Volume 2** is idle, it cannot offload the IOPS to **Volume 2**. Hence, the storage array is not exactly one array. From a capacity and performance point of view, it has *hard* partitions that cannot be crossed. Does it then mean that you create one giant volume so you can share everything? Probably not; the reason is that there is no concept of shares or priority within a single volume. From the diagram, **Datastore 1** and **Datastore 2** live on **Volume 1**. If a non-production VM on **Datastore 1** is performing a high IO task (say someone runs IOmeter), it can impact a production VM on **Datastore 2**.

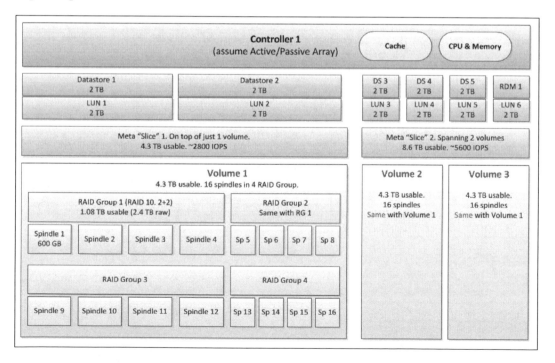

Storage I/O Control (SIOC) will not help you in this case. The scope of SIOC is *within* a datastore. It does not ensure fairness across datastores. I recommend you review Cormac Hogan's blog at http://cormachogan.com/2013/07/11/sioc-and -datastores-spread-across-all-spindles-in-the-array. Duncan Epping has also written some good articles on the topic and a good starting point is the site http://www.yellow-bricks.com/2010/10/19/storage-io-control-best -practices. If you have many datastores, SIOC has the highest chance of hitting fairness across datastores when the number of VMs per datastore is consistent.

As a VMware admin performing capacity management, you need to know the physical hardware where your VMware environment is running on at all layers. Often as VMware professionals, we stop at the compute layer and treat storage as just a LUN provider. There is a whole world underneath the LUNs presented to you.

Now that you know your physical capacity, the next thing to do is estimate your IaaS workload. If you buy an array with 100,000 IOPS, it does not mean you have 100,000 IOPS for your VM. In the next example, you have a much smaller number of usable IOPs. The most important factors you need to be aware of are:

- Frontend IOPS
- Backend IOPS

There are many calculations on IOPS as there are many variables impacting it. The numbers in this table are just examples. The point I hope to get across is that it is important to sit down with the storage architect and estimate the number for your specific environment.

Components	IOPS	Remarks
Raw capacity	100,000	Backend IOPS.
Frontend IOPS	50,000	RAID 10. RAID 5 or RAID 6 will be lower.
Non ESXi workload	5,000	Not recommended to mix as we cannot do QoS or Storage I/O Control.
Backup workload	5,000	You can get the data from the physical array since the backup server is typically a physical server connected to the array. Included in vSphere if VDP Advanced is used.
Array replication	5,000	If used.
vSphere replication	5,000	If used.
Distributed storage mirroring	0	Not applicable in this example as it uses shared array.
Net available	30,000	Only 30 percent left for VM workload!

Capacity planning at the network layer

Similar to calculating capacity for storage, understanding capacity requirements for your network requires knowledge of the IaaS workloads that will compete with your VM workload. The following table provides an example using IP Storage. Your actual design may differ compared to it. If you are using Fiber Channel storage, then you can use the available bandwidth for other purposes.

Purpose	Bandwidth	Remarks
VM	4 Gb	For approximately 20 VMs. vShield Edge VM needs a lot of bandwidth as all the traffic passes through it.
Heartbeat	1 Mb	Minimal as it's purely for heartbeat. Used by Symantec Veritas Cluster.
FT network	2 Gb	Currently, 1 vCPU FT needs around 1 Gb. If FT delivers vSMP in future releases, it should go higher as more vCPUs need to be synchronized.
IP Storage (serving VM)	6 Gb	NFS or iSCSI. Doesn't need 10 Gb as the storage array is likely shared by 10-50 hosts. The array may only have 40 Gb in total for all these hosts (assuming it uses 4 x 10 GE cables). In this example, 7 hosts are enough to saturate it already if each host has 6 Gb.
vMotion & Storage vMotion	6 Gb	vSphere is capable of shared-nothing live migration. This increases the demand as VMDK is much larger than vRAM. Includes multi-NIC vMotion for faster vMotion when there are multiple VMs to be migrated.
Management	1 Gb	Copying a powered-off VM to another host without a shared datastore takes this bandwidth.
vSphere Replication	1 Gb	Should be sufficient as the WAN link is likely the bottleneck.
Total	Approximately 20 Gb	

Summary

In this chapter, we discussed how you should approach capacity management in the virtual data center. We shared that there is a fundamental shift, resulting in a two-tier model. The application team performs capacity management at the VM layer, and the infrastructure team performs at the infrastructure layer.

In *Chapter 1, Virtual Data Center – It's Not a Physical Data Center, Virtualized*, we have explained in depth why virtualization has large ramifications in both architecture and operations. We also covered the impact to how we manage. In this chapter we focused on capacity management. We are now ready to dive deeper into the technical discussion. *Chapter 3, Mastering the Key Counters in SDDC*, will start it by discussing the counters and how they are used.

3
Mastering the Key Counters in SDDC

Starting with this chapter, we will dive deep into the world of vCenter and vCenter Operations counters. The topics we will cover are:

- The need to classify the counters based on the two roles
- Counters related to compute (focusing on CPU and RAM)
- Counters related to storage
- Counters related to network
- All metric groups in vCenter and vRealize Operations
- An example of how vCenter Operations does not simply regurgitate what's in vCenter (it can take a different view from vCenter)

First things first – the purpose

vSphere 5.5 comes with many counters, many more than what a physical server provides. There are new counters that do not have a physical equivalent, such as memory ballooning, CPU latency, and vSphere replication. In addition, some counters have the same name as their physical world counterpart but behave differently in vSphere. Memory usage is a common one, resulting in confusion among system administrators. For those counters that are similar to their physical world counterparts, vSphere may use different units, such as milliseconds.

As a result, experienced IT administrators find it hard to master vSphere counters by building on their existing knowledge. Instead of trying to relate each counter to its physical equivalent, I find it useful to group them according to their *purpose*. Virtualization *formalizes* the relationship between the infrastructure team and application team. The infrastructure team changes from the system builder to service provider. The application team no longer owns the physical infrastructure.

The application team becomes a consumer of a shared service — the virtual platform. Depending on the **Service Level Agreement (SLA)**, the application team can be served as if they have dedicated access to the infrastructure, or they can take a performance hit in exchange for a lower price. For SLAs where performance matters, the VM running in the cluster should not be impacted by any other VMs. The performance must be as good as if it is the only VM running in the ESXi.

Because there are two different counter users, there are two different purposes. The application team (developers and the VM owner) only cares about their own VM. The infrastructure team has to care about both the VM and infrastructure, especially when they need to show that the shared infrastructure is not a bottleneck. One set of counters is to monitor the VM; the other set is to monitor the infrastructure. The following diagram shows the two different purposes and what we should check for each. By knowing what matters on each layer, we can better manage the virtual environment.

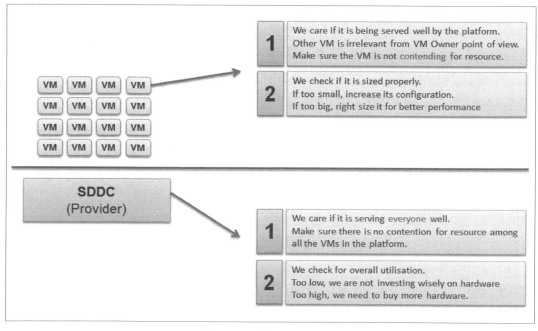

The two-tier IT organization

At the VM layer, we care whether the VM is being served well by the platform. Other VMs are irrelevant from the VM owner's point of view. A VM owner only wants to make sure his or her VM is not contending for a resource. So the key counter here is **contention**. Only when we are satisfied that there is no contention can we proceed to check whether the VM is sized correctly or not. Most people check for utilization first because that is what they are used to monitoring in the physical infrastructure. In a virtual environment, we should check for contention first.

At the infrastructure layer, we care whether it serves everyone well. Make sure that there is no contention for resource among all the VMs in the platform. Only when the infrastructure is clear from contention can we troubleshoot a particular VM. If the infrastructure is having a hard time serving majority of the VMs, there is no point troubleshooting a particular VM.

This two-layer concept is also implemented by vSphere in compute and storage architectures. For example, there are two distinct layers of memory in vSphere. There is the individual VM memory provided by the hypervisor and there is the physical memory at the host level. For an individual VM, we care whether the VM is getting enough memory. At the host level, we care whether the host has enough memory for everyone. Because of the difference in goals, we look for a different set of counters.

In the previous diagram, there are two numbers shown in a large font, indicating that there are two main steps in monitoring. Each step applies to each layer (the VM layer and infrastructure layer), so there are two numbers for each step. Step 1 is used for performance management. It is useful during troubleshooting or when checking whether we are meeting performance SLAs or not. Step 2 is used for capacity management. It is useful as part of long-term capacity planning. The time period for step 2 is typically 3 months, as we are checking for overall utilization and not a one off spike.

With the preceding concept in mind, we are ready to dive into more detail. Let's cover compute, network, and storage.

Compute

The following diagram shows how a VM gets its resource from ESXi. It is a pretty complex diagram, so let me walk you through it.

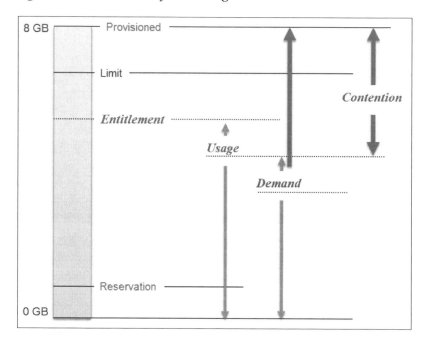

The tall rectangular area represents a VM. Say this VM is given 8 GB of virtual RAM. The bottom line represents 0 GB and the top line represents 8 GB. The VM is configured with 8 GB RAM. We call this **Provisioned**. This is what the Guest OS sees, so if it is running Windows, you will see 8 GB RAM when you log into Windows.

Unlike a physical server, you can configure a **Limit** and a **Reservation**. This is done outside the Guest OS, so Windows or Linux does not know. You should minimize the use of **Limit** and **Reservation** as it makes the operation more complex.

Entitlement means what the VM is entitled to. In this example, the hypervisor entitles the VM to a certain amount of memory. I did not show a solid line and used an italic font style to mark that **Entitlement** is not a fixed value, but a dynamic value determined by the hypervisor. It varies every minute, determined by **Limit**, **Entitlement**, and **Reservation** of the VM itself and any shared allocation with other VMs running on the same host.

Obviously, a VM can only use what it is entitled to at any given point of time, so the **Usage** counter does not go higher than the **Entitlement** counter. The green line shows that **Usage** ranges from 0 to the **Entitlement** value.

In a healthy environment, the ESXi host has enough resources to meet the demands of all the VMs on it with sufficient overhead. In this case, you will see that the **Entitlement**, **Usage**, and **Demand** counters will be similar to one another when the VM is highly utilized. This is shown by the green line where **Demand** stops at **Usage**, and **Usage** stops at **Entitlement**. The numerical value may not be identical because vCenter reports **Usage** in percentage, and it is an average value of the sample period. vCenter reports **Entitlement** in MHz and it takes the latest value in the sample period. It reports **Demand** in MHz and it is an average value of the sample period. This also explains why you may see **Usage** a bit higher than **Entitlement** in highly-utilized vCPU. If the VM has low utilization, you will see the **Entitlement** counter is much higher than **Usage**.

An environment in which the ESXi host is resource constrained is unhealthy. It cannot give every VM the resources they ask for. The VMs demand more than they are entitled to use, so the **Usage** and **Entitlement** counters will be lower than the **Demand** counter. The **Demand** counter can go higher than **Limit** naturally. For example, if a VM is limited to 2 GB of RAM and it wants to use 14 GB, then **Demand** will exceed **Limit**. Obviously, **Demand** cannot exceed **Provisioned**. This is why the red line stops at **Provisioned** because that is as high as it can go.

The difference between what the VM demands and what it gets to use is the **Contention** counter. **Contention** is **Demand** minus **Usage**. So if the **Contention** is 0, the VM can use everything it demands. This is the ultimate goal, as performance will match the physical world. This **Contention** value is useful to demonstrate that the infrastructure provides a good service to the application team. If a VM owner comes to see you and says that your shared infrastructure is unable to serve his or her VM well, both of you can check the **Contention** counter.

The **Contention** counter should become a part of your SLA or **Key Performance Indicator (KPI)**. It is not sufficient to track utilization alone. When there is contention, it is possible that both your VM and ESXi host have low utilization, and yet your customers (VMs running on that host) perform poorly. This typically happens when the VMs are relatively large compared to the ESXi host. Let me give you a simple example to illustrate this. The ESXi host has two sockets and 20 cores. Hyper-threading is not enabled to keep this example simple. You run just 2 VMs, but each VM has 11 vCPUs. As a result, they will not be able to run concurrently. The hypervisor will schedule them sequentially as there are only 20 physical cores to serve 22 vCPUs. Here, both VMs will experience high contention.

Hold on! You might say, "There is no **Contention** counter in vSphere and no memory **Demand** counter either." This is where vRealize Operations comes in. It does not just regurgitate the values in vCenter. It has implicit knowledge of vSphere and a set of derived counters with formulae that leverage that knowledge.

You need to have an understanding of how the vSphere CPU scheduler works. The following diagram shows the various states that a VM can be in:

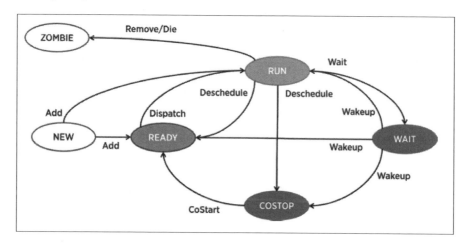

The preceding diagram is taken from *The CPU Scheduler in VMware vSphere® 5.1: Performance Study* (you can find it at `http://www.vmware.com/resources/techresources/10345`). This is a whitepaper that documents the CPU scheduler with a good amount of depth for VMware administrators. I highly recommend you read this paper as it will help you explain to your customers (the application team) how your shared infrastructure juggles all those VMs at the same time. It will also help you pick the right counters when you create your custom dashboards in vRealize Operations.

Network

From the point of performance and capacity management, network has different fundamental characteristics of CPU or RAM:

- The first difference is that the resources available to your VM (which is what we care about at the end of the day) are a lot lower and more dynamic. The ESXi host has a fixed specification (for example, 2 CPUs, 36 cores, 256 GB RAM, 2 x 10 GEs) and we know the upper physical limit. However, the hypervisor consumes a relatively low proportion of resources, almost negligible, for CPU and RAM. Even if you add a software-defined storage such as Virtual SAN, you are looking at around 10 percent total utilization. The same cannot be said about network. Mass vMotion (for example, when the host enters maintenance mode), storage vMotion (for IP storage), VM provisioning or cloning (for IP storage), and Virtual SAN all take up significant bandwidth. In fact, the non-VM network takes up the majority of the ESXi resources.

- The second difference with the VM network is the resource that is given to a VM itself. With CPU and RAM, we can configure a granular size of CPU and RAM. For the CPU, we typically assign one, two, four, six, or eight vCPUs. With network, we cannot specify a configured vNIC speed. It takes the speed of the ESXi vmnic assigned to the VM port group. So each VM will either see 1 GE or 10 GE (assuming you have the right vNIC driver, obviously). For example, you cannot configure 500 Mbps or 250 Mbps in the Guest OS. In the physical world, we tend to assume that each server has 1 GE and the network has sufficient bandwidth. You cannot assume this in a virtual data center as you no longer have 1 GE for every VM at the physical level. It is shared and typically oversubscribed.

- The third difference in resource management for networks is that the hardware itself can provide different functionalities. For compute, you have servers. While they may have different form factors or specifications, they all serve the same purpose—to provide processing power and a set of working memory for applications. For network, you have a variety of network services (firewall and load balancer) in addition to the basic network functionalities (switch and router). You need to monitor all of them to get a complete picture. These functionalities are software defined in NSX. vRealize Operations provides a management pack for both VMware **vCloud Networking and Security (vCNS)** and NSX. I have implemented the vCNS management pack at a banking client and it provides visibility into these network services.

- Finally, there is a fundamental difference between the nature of the network and other resources that need to be monitored. The network is an interconnection; compute and storage are nodes. When you have a CPU or RAM performance issue on one host, it doesn't typically impact another host on a different cluster. The same thing happens with storage. When a physical array has a performance issue, generally speaking it does not impact other arrays in the data center. Network is different. A local performance issue can easily be a data center-wide problem.

Because of all these differences, the way you approach network monitoring should also be different. If you are not the network expert in your data center, the first step is to partner with the experts. The network team will be a good source of advice when you are designing your vRealize Operations custom dashboard and policies.

As of late 2014, most companies have either implemented or are planning to adopt 10 GE. Network monitoring is both simpler and harder in a 10 Gb environment. It is simpler as you have a lot less cables and more bandwidth. It is harder as you cannot differentiate between traffic types as the physical capacity is now shared. In a 1 GE environment, you may not need to enable **Network I/O Control** (although you should, for the reason I will explain later). In 10 GE, you almost have to enable it because the non-VM network can spike and consume a large bandwidth. The following screenshot shows the default configuration for **Network I/O Control**. As you can see, the VM network takes up a small portion:

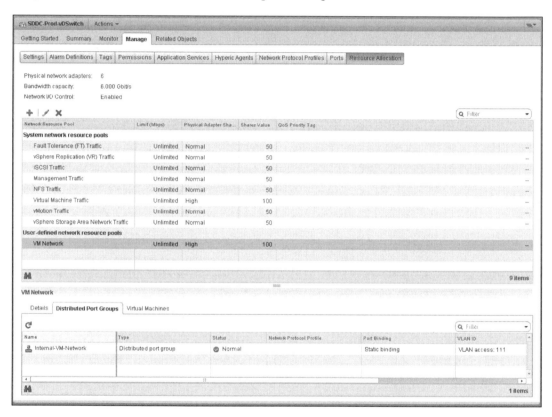

Relying on load-based teaming to balance the load for performance needs may not provide enough sensitivity to meet SLAs, as it kicks in every 30 seconds. For a discussion about **Network I/O Control (NIOC)**, I'd recommend you review Frank's blog at `http://frankdenneman.nl/2013/01/17/a-primer-on-network-io-control` and Duncan's blog at `http://www.yellow-bricks.com/2013/10/29/virtual-san-network-io-control` so that you can configure your settings correctly. Incorrect configuration will make both performance management and capacity management difficult.

Because the physical capacity of the network is shared, you have a dynamic upper limit for each workload. The **VM Network** port group will have more bandwidth when there is no vMotion happening. Further more, each VM has a dynamic upper limit as it shares the **VM Network** port group with other VMs. In the previous screenshot, I have created a network resource pool and mapped the **VM Network** port group to it. Even if you dedicate a physical NIC to the **VM Network** port group, that 1 Gb NIC is still shared among all the VMs. If you have 20 VMs on that host at one time, it means that an average of 50 Mbps is available per VM. You may not always have 20 VMs due to vMotion and DRS, so the upper threshold is dynamic. The limit changes from host to host. Within the same host, the limit changes as time progresses. Unlike **Storage I/O Control**, **Network I/O Control** does not provide any counters that tell you that it has capped the bandwidth.

In some situations, the bandwidth within the ESXi host may not be the smallest pipe between the originating VM and its destination. Within the data center, there could be firewalls, load balancers, routers, and other hops that the packet has to go through. Once it leaves the data center, the WAN and Internet are likely to be a bottleneck. Because of this practical consideration, vRealize Operations does not make the assumption that the physical vmnic is the bandwidth available. It is certainly the physical limit, but it may not always be the actual bandwidth available. vRealize Operations observes the peak utilized bandwidth and sets this as the upper limit. The following chart shows that a vCenter 5.5 VM network usage varies between 18,000 KBps and 25,772 KBps during the past three days. vRealize Operations observes the range and sets the maximum network usage to near the peak (25,772 KBps). This counter is useful in that it tells you that the utilization never exceeds the amount.

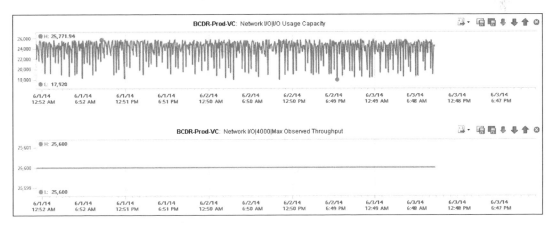

As you can see from the preceding chart, the maximum observed throughput number is also adjusted dynamically. The next chart shows two ESXi hosts in the same cluster. The spike could be due to a mass vMotion in that cluster.

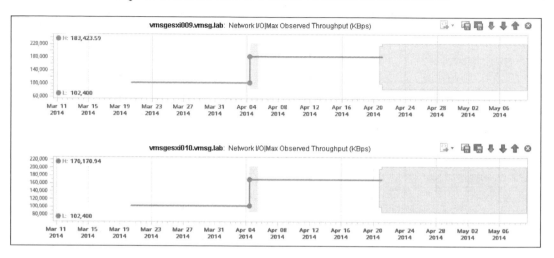

NIOC can help to limit the network throughput for a particular workload or VM. If you are using 10 GE, you do want to enable NIOC so that a burst in one network workload does not impact your VM. For example, mass vMotion can saturate the 10 Gb link if you do not implement NIOC. In vCenter 5.5, there is no counter that tracks when NIOC caps the network throughput. As a result, vRealize Operations will not tell you that NIOC has taken action.

vRealize Operations does not track the vmnic speed, since that's considered a configuration element. Because you normally set the network to autonegotiate, sometimes the speed can drop (for example, from 1 Gbps to 100 Mbps). This is something you need to check manually if you encounter network slowness while your network utilization is below 100 Mbps. In this case, the maximum observed counter can give a clue.

Based on all the preceding factors, the maximum observed counter is a much more practical indicator of the network resource available to a VM than the physical configuration of the ESXi vmnic. You should use this counter as your VM maximum bandwidth. For ESXi, you should also use the physical vmnic as a guideline.

vRealize Operations provides the **Workload** (in percent) counter or **Demand** (in percent) counter that is based on this maximum observed value. For example, if the VM **Usage** counter shows 100 KBps, and **Maximum Observed Throughput** shows 200 KBps, then the **Demand** (in percent) counter will be 50 percent.

Storage

If you look at the ESXi and VM metric groups for storage in the vCenter performance chart, it is not clear how they relate to one another at first glance. You have storage network, storage adapter, storage path, datastore, and disk metric groups that you need to check. How do they impact on one another?

I have created the following diagram to explain the relationship. The beige boxes are what you are likely to be familiar with. You have your ESXi host, and it can have **NFS Datastore**, **VMFS Datastore**, or **RDM** objects. The blue colored boxes represent the metric groups.

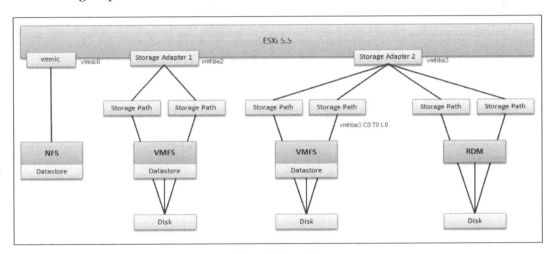

From ESXi to disk

NFS and VMFS datastores differ drastically in terms of counters, as NFS is file-based while VMFS is block-based. For NFS, it uses the vmnic, and so the adapter type (FC, FCoE, or iSCSI) is not applicable. Multipathing is handled by the network, so you don't see it in the storage layer. For VMFS or RDM, you have more detailed visibility of the storage. To start off, each ESXi adapter is visible and you can check the counters for each of them. In terms of relationship, one adapter can have many devices (disk or CDROM). One device is typically accessed via two storage adapters (for availability and load balancing), and it is also accessed via two paths per adapter, with the paths diverging at the storage switch. A single path, which will come from a specific adapter, can naturally connect one adapter to one device. The following diagram shows the four paths:

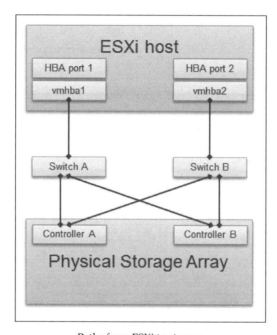

Paths from ESXi to storage

A storage path takes data from ESXi to the LUN (the term used by vSphere is **Disk**), not to the datastore. So if the datastore has multiple extents, there are four paths per extent. This is one reason why I did not use more than one extent, as each extent adds four paths.

If you are not familiar with extent, Cormac Hogan explains it well
on this blog post:

`http://blogs.vmware.com/vsphere/2012/02/vmfs-`
`extents-are-they-bad-or-simply-misunderstood.html`

For **VMFS**, you can see the same counters at both the **Datastore** level and the **Disk**
level. Their value will be identical if you follow the recommended configuration to
create a 1:1 relationship between a datastore and a LUN. This means you present an
entire LUN to a datastore (use all of its capacity).

The following screenshot shows how we manage the ESXi storage. Click on the ESXi
you need to manage, select the **Manage** tab, and then the **Storage** subtab. In this
subtab, we can see the adapters, devices, and the host cache. The screen shows an ESXi
host with the list of its adapters. I have selected **vmhba2**, which is an FC HBA. Notice
that it is connected to 5 devices. Each device has 4 paths, so I have 20 paths in total.

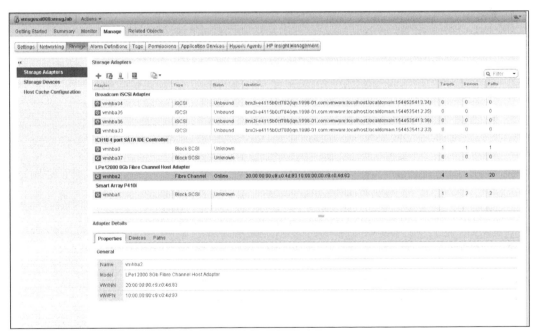

ESXi adapter

Let's move on to the **Storage Devices** tab. The following screenshot shows the list of devices. Because NFS is not a disk, it does not appear here. I have selected one of the devices to show its properties.

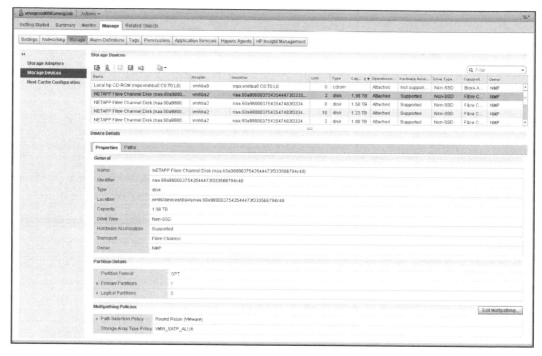

ESXi device

If you click on the **Paths** tab, you will be presented with the information shown in the next screenshot, including whether a path is active. Note that not all paths carry I/O; it depends on your configuration and multipathing software. Because each LUN typically has four paths, path management can be complicated if you have many LUNs.

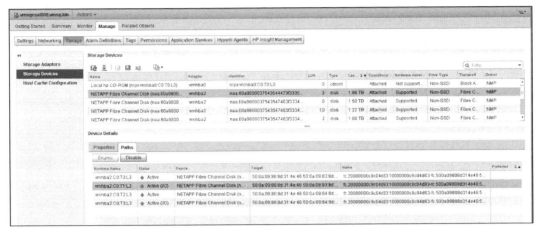

ESXi paths

The story is quite different on the VM layer. A VM does not see the underlying shared storage. It sees local disks only. So regardless of whether the underlying storage is NFS, VMFS, or RDM, it sees all of them as virtual disks. You lose visibility in the physical adapter (for example, you cannot tell how many IOPSs on vmhba2 are coming from a particular VM) and physical paths (for example, how many disk commands travelling on that path are coming from a particular VM). You can, however, see the impact at the **Datastore** level and the physical **Disk** level. The **Datastore** counter is especially useful. For example, if you notice that your IOPS is higher at the **Datastore** level than at the virtual **Disk** level, this means you have a snapshot. The snapshot IO is not visible at the virtual **Disk** level as the snapshot is stored on a different virtual disk.

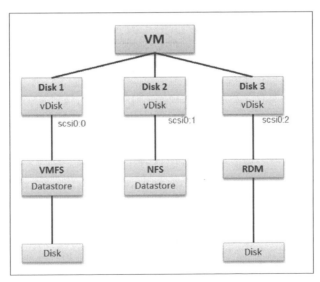

From VM to disk

Metric groups

So far we have covered the concepts of compute, storage, and network monitoring. Now we are ready to dive into the counters. While we will not be covering the counters in **esxtop**, we are going to cover the counters in both vCenter and vRealize Operations. These three tools serve different purposes:

- The esxtop operates at an individual host level, providing the deepest and most granular detail. It can go down to a granularity of 2 seconds. This is useful when you already know which ESXi host and VM you want to troubleshoot.

- vCenter Server complements esxtop by providing a view across hosts and other objects in vSphere. However, its granularity is at an interval of 20 seconds.

- vRealize Operations complements vCenter by extending the coverage beyond vSphere. It can go up to the application level or down to the physical infrastructure. It also allows you to slice and dice the combined data. However, its default granularity is at an interval of 5 minutes.

I have used the term counter and metric interchangeably, as vCenter 5.5 uses both terms. You can see that the next screenshot has the words **Chart Metrics** and **Select counters for this chart**. We call metrics and counters grouped together a **metric group**. You will notice that vRealize Operations has many more metric groups than vCenter. The following table provides a set of common metric groups that vRealize Operations adds to each vSphere object. Not all metric groups are applicable for all objects. For example, the metric group **Summary** does not exist for **Datastore cluster**. I have shown it as blank instead of N for ease of visual comparison. **vDS** is the shortform for **vSphere Distributed Switch**.

Metric group	vRealize Operations generated	Badge	Summary	vSphere configuration limit	Configuration
VM	Y	Y	Y	Y	Y
ESXi	Y	Y	Y	Y	Y
Resource pool	Y	Y	Y		
Cluster	Y	Y	Y	Y	Y
Datastore	Y	Y	Y		
Datastore cluster	Y	Y			
vDS	Y	Y	Y		

Metric group	vRealize Operations generated	Badge	Summary	vSphere configuration limit	Configuration
DC	Y	Y	Y	Y	
vCenter	Y	Y	Y	Y	
World	Y	Y	Y		

Let's quickly review the preceding five metric groups:

- The **vRealize Operations generated** metric group provides information on the analytics. For example, it tracks the number of metrics and how many of them are categorized as a KPI. As a result, you do not normally use it to troubleshoot.

- The **Badge** metric group, on the other hand, provides the actual metrics used to represent the badges. So if you want to see the history value of a badge, this is where you go. The metrics under the **Badge** metric group vary per object, and are not limited to just the minor and major badges.

- The **Summary** metric group covers capacity. Its metrics also vary by object. The **Summary** group provides useful information, such as the number of vMotion operations and the number of running VMs in a host. For a cluster, it tells you the number of running hosts and VMs. I have used some of these metrics when performing troubleshooting on problems that occurred in the past and customers did not know about the exact behavior of the environment at that time. Using some of these metrics, we were able to reconstruct what the environment looked like at that particular moment when the performance problems began.

- The **vSphere configuration limit** metric group covers capacity. You do not normally use this group for performance use cases.

- The **Configuration** metric group provides information such as the number of vCPUs for a VM object and the failover level for a cluster object.

In addition to the preceding points, vRealize Operations 6 provides a set of metric groups for capacity management. You will notice that it has many more metric groups compared to version 5.x. This is because the capacity engine has now been integrated.

VM – metric groups

The following screenshot shows the vCenter metric groups for a VM. They are listed on the left-hand side under the **Chart Metrics** heading. I have selected **Virtual disk** in the screenshot and the details are shown. Notice that the two virtual disks of the VM are shown on the right-hand side.

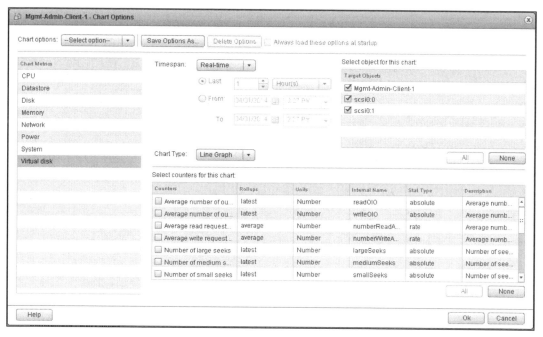

VM metric groups in vCenter

From the list in the preceding screenshot, you may notice that there is no metric group for **Virtual flash** and **vSphere Replication**. They are only available at the ESXi level. This means that you will not be able to know the metric for a given VM. You have to go to the ESXi to see it. At the host level, you can choose **Stacked Graph (per VM)** to see the data per VM.

vRealize Operations provides many more metric groups for VMs, and the next table shows the comparison. These additional metric groups, and their associated metrics, are very valuable in both performance and capacity management. I have excluded the five default vRealize Operations metric groups, as they have been covered earlier. I'm not listing them in alphabetical order, but in the following type: **CPU**, **RAM**, **Network**, **Storage**, and **Others**. I have left the value under the vCenter 5.5 column blank so that you can easily see which metric groups are unique to vRealize Operations.

Scope	vCenter 5.5	vRealize Operations
CPU	CPU	CPU
CPU		CPU – allocation model
CPU		CPU utilization for resources
RAM	Memory	Memory
RAM		Memory (host)
RAM		Memory – allocation model
Network	Network	Network I/O
Network		Network I/O (host)
Storage	Datastore	Datastore I/O
Storage	Disk	Disk
Storage		Disk space – allocation model
Storage		Disk space reclaimable
Storage		Guest file system statistics (visible only with VMware tools installed on the VM)
Storage	Virtual disk	Virtual disk
Others	Power	Power (not shown by default)
Others	System	System

ESXi – metric groups

The next screenshot shows the vCenter metric groups for a host. For some of the counters, you can get the information at the individual component level. For example, CPU core and individual vmnic. For others, the values are only available at the host level. The value of the individual components can be useful during performance troubleshooting. In the following screenshot, I have selected the **CPU** metric group. The individual cores are shown on the right-hand side. Knowing the data at the CPU core level is useful because a typical ESXi host has many cores (for example, 2 sockets, 36 cores, 72 threads (hyper threading enabled)). Plotting a chart at the core level can reveal whether the utilization is balanced or not. If you have many large VMs in the host, you may notice that some cores are highly utilized while others are idle.

Note that **vSphere Replication** and **Virtual flash** are given their own groups. This makes it easier to monitor the environment. In a large environment where you have many VMs protected, you can track the total TX and RX to see the patterns.

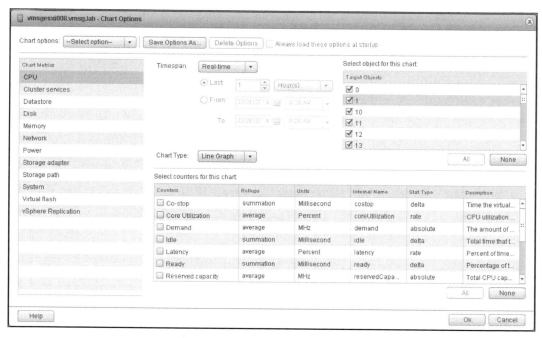

ESXi metric group

As you can guess by now, vRealize Operations provides additional metric groups, and the following table shows the comparison. Just like the comparison for VM, I have excluded standard vRealize Operations metric groups. You will see later that vRealize Operations also provides more at the individual core and vmnic level too.

Scope	vCenter 5.5	vRealize Operations
CPU	CPU	CPU
CPU		CPU utilization for resources
RAM	Memory	Memory
Network	Network	Network I/O
Storage	Datastore	Datastore I/O
Storage	Storage adapter	Storage adapter
Storage	Storage path	
Storage	Disk	Disk
Storage		Disk space

Scope	vCenter 5.5	vRealize Operations
Storage		Disk space reclaimable
Storage		Storage
Storage	Virtual flash	vFlash module
Storage	vSphere Replication	vSphere Replication (only appears if the host has vSphere replication)
Others	Cluster services	
Others	Power	Power (not shown by default)
Others	System	System
Others		Hardware

You may notice that there is a metric group called **Cluster services** in vCenter. This is applicable if the host is part of a DRS cluster. It only has two components—**CPU** and **Memory** fairness. It calculates the fairness of distribution among members of the cluster. It is not necessary to actively track the cluster services, as an unbalanced cluster does not mean you have a performance issue. For example, assume that you have an 8-node cluster. Host 1 is running at 90 percent utilization, while host 2 to host 8 are running at 0 percent utilization. So long as host 1 does not experience contention, balancing the cluster does not give you increased performance. In fact, if your workload is network intensive between VMs (for example, in a three-tier application), the VMs are better off running in the same host as the traffic between VMs never needs to travel on the physical network. The cluster services are shown in the following screenshot. Notice the **Rollup** is **Latest**. This makes sense as you want to know the latest data, not the average.

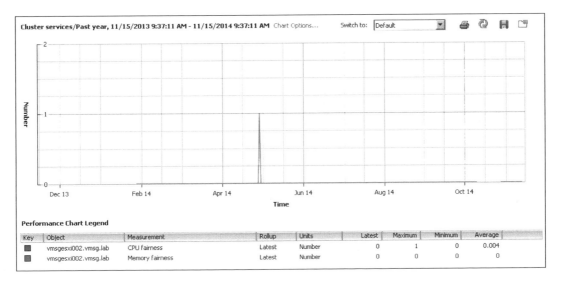

Cluster – metric groups

The next screenshot shows the vCenter metric groups for a cluster. As you can see, it has a lot less information than the host metric groups. For example, information related to storage and network do not appear in the cluster metrics. As a result, monitoring and troubleshooting becomes difficult at the cluster level in vCenter. You need to check individual hosts one by one.

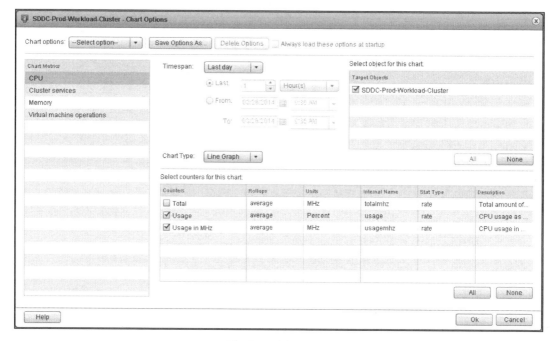

Cluster metric groups

This is where vRealize Operations comes in. It provides more metric groups at the cluster level, and the following table shows the comparison. I've deliberately shown blank columns for easier visual comparison. For example, you can see that it provides network and storage counters that are missing in vCenter. Because of these additional metrics, you can now do performance and capacity management at the cluster level.

Scope	vCenter 5.5	vRealize Operations
CPU	CPU	CPU
RAM	Memory	Memory
Network		Network I/O
Storage		Datastore I/O
Storage		Disk
Storage		Disk space
Storage		Disk space reclaimable
Storage		Storage
Others	Cluster services	
Others	VM operations	

Datastore – metric groups

The screenshots of the vCenter metric groups for the other objects (VM, host, and cluster) shared earlier were shown in the **Advanced** option of the **Performance** tab. vCenter does not have this **Advanced** option for datastore objects. Instead, it presents you with a fixed list of charts, as can be seen in the next screenshot. Therefore we cannot list the vCenter metric groups for datastores as we did for the other objects.

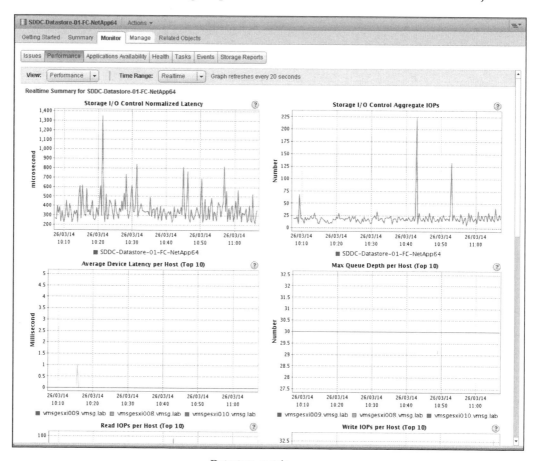

Datastore metric groups

vRealize Operations again complements vCenter by providing a more extensive list of metric groups, as shown in the following table. This enables us to see the key storage counters (IOPS, throughput, latency, and capacity).

Scope	vRealize Operations
Storage	Capacity
Storage	Datastore I/O

Scope	vRealize Operations
Storage	Devices (Logically this is applicable for VMFS or RDM, and not NFS)
Storage	Disk space
Storage	Disk space reclaimable
Storage	Capacity

Datastore cluster – metric groups

As for individual datastores, vCenter does not have the **Advanced** option for the datastore cluster **Performance** tab. It presents you with a fixed list of charts, as can be seen in the next screenshot.

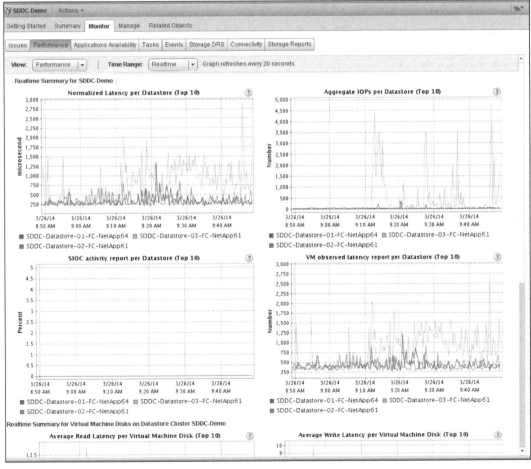

Datastore cluster metric groups

vRealize Operations provides two metric groups, which are shown in the next table. The datastore metric group provides all the key metrics (IOPS, latency, and throughput). It provides the breakdown for read, write and total. The disk space metric group provides capacity information, including the space used for snapshot.

Scope	vRealize Operations
Storage	Datastore
Storage	Disk space

The distributed switch

The following screenshot shows that vCenter does not provide performance counters for the distributed switch. In fact, there is no **Performance** tab. This means you need to monitor the switch at the individual ESXi level. This can make correlation difficult, as there are types of traffic that are inter-ESXi in nature, for example, vMotion, storage vMotion, and distributed storage. Being able to see how much bandwidth they consume on the shared physical NICs can be useful for both performance troubleshooting and capacity planning.

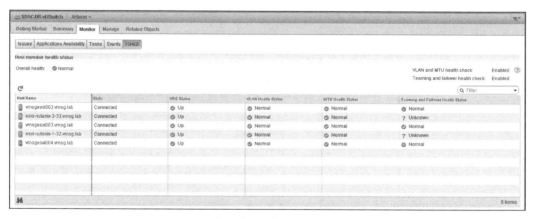

Distributed switch metric group

vRealize Operations provides this visibility across the distributed switch with the metric groups shown in the following table. It also introduces a new object for the distributed port group. With these two objects, you can check the network performance from the network point of view. You can check both the ingress and egress traffic at either the switch level or port group level.

Object	Scope	vRealize Operations
Distributed switch	Network	Network
Distributed switch	Others	Host
Distributed port group	Network	Network

For the standard switch, the counters are provided as part of the ESXi host as it is not an object that resides outside the host. While all standard switches are completely independent of each other, all virtual switches that communicate with each other over the physical network are related from the performance point of view. There is a value in being able to view a summary of the switches across hosts at a higher level. With ESXi moving from 1 GE NIC to 10 GE NIC, the reason to choose a distributed switch becomes stronger.

Data center – metric groups

The next screenshot shows the vCenter metric groups for a data center. As you can see, there is even less information than for a cluster object. We lost all the information on CPU, RAM, network, and storage. It provides only VM operations, such as power on and reboot. Information at the data center level is actually useful, as both distributed switch and datastore may extend up to, yet rarely beyond, a data center (the exception being a stretched network). vMotion in vSphere 5.5 also does not go across vCenter data centers. Viewing data at the data center level means you know for sure you are not getting partial data.

In a small environment, where one data center has only one cluster, the information at the data center level is logically redundant.

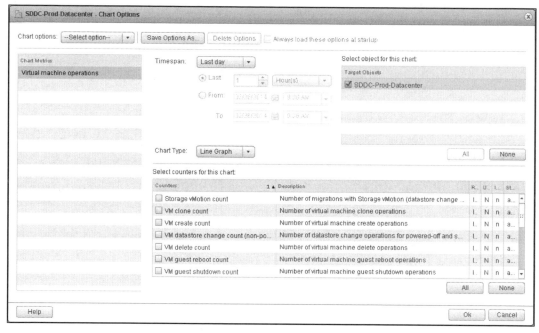

vSphere data center metric group

vRealize Operations, on the other hand, provides a more complete list of metric groups, which is shown in the following table:

Scope	vRealize Operations
CPU	CPU
RAM	Memory
Network	Network I/O
Storage	Storage
Storage	Disk
Storage	Disk space
Storage	Disk space reclaimable
Storage	Datastore I/O

In most deployments, a single vCenter will only manage one vCenter data center. So viewing the information at either level is sufficient as they will provide identical data. There are situations where you may decide to have multiple data center objects in a single vCenter. The following are some examples:

- Your vCenter manages multiple physical data centers. In this case, you create one data center object for each physical data center. In situations where you need long-distance vMotion, you create a single data center spanning two physical data centers.

- You have many remote branches, with limited WAN bandwidth back to headquarter. You prefer to have one vCenter to make management easier and optimize vCenter licenses.

- You have a very large data center spanning multiple floors, with each floor having its own independent network and rows of racks.

- You want to have tighter control, both from a security and an operations point of view. Having a separate data center increases the logical separation.

Let me know if you have other use cases in which you need a separate vCenter data center. In my opinion, vCenter data centers are typically associated with a physical location or boundary, and they have a 1:1 relationship.

vCenter – metric groups

The next screenshot shows that vCenter does not provide performance counters at the vCenter level. There is no **Performance** tab.

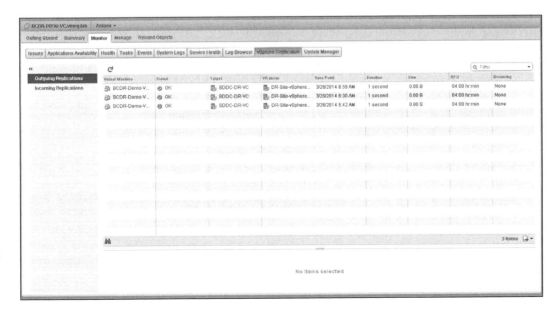

vRealize Operations, on the other hand, provides a list of metric groups, which is shown in the following table. They are useful when you need to see the big picture.

Scope	vRealize Operations
CPU	CPU
RAM	Memory
Network	Network I/O
Storage	Disk
Storage	Disk space
Storage	Disk space reclaimable
Storage	Datastore I/O

In addition to the vCenter level, vRealize Operations goes up even higher, introducing a *World* object. It recognizes that most customers deploy multiple vCenter Servers. The following are the use cases in which you may deploy multiple vCenter Servers:

- There are two vCenter Servers for the **Server VMs (VSI)**, one in each physical data center. They are paired by VMware Site Recovery Manager. The vCenter Servers manage both the production VM and non-production VM.

- There are two vCenter Servers for the **Desktop VMs (VDI)**, one in each physical data center. They are fronted by Horizon View Servers, which create a logical desktop pool spanning both physical data centers in an active/ active configuration.

- Some customers have a very large number of VMs. I work with customers with 45,000 server VMs and more than 50,000 desktop VMs. For these customers, they may want to have a separate pod in which each vCenter Server manages, say, 10,000 VMs.

- For customers who operate in multiple continents or geographical areas, where network latency and stability become an issue, there is a need to deploy a vCenter Server near that continent or area.

- Customers typically have branches that need servers too. Depending on the number of branches, latency, bandwidth, and local IT capability, a vCenter may be required on the remote branch.

- For business workload that is highly confidential, where the business workload has its own physical infrastructure (storage, network, server, rack, UPS, KVM, and so on) and resides on a separate namespace (that is, not part of an Active Directory), a separate vCenter is logically required. The environment is also typically managed by a different administrator.

- One vCenter Server for non-production usage, as the preceding vCenter Servers are all production servers. This allows you to test patches and updates, and upgrade the vCenter Server in the non-production environment first. vCenter has many components (web client server, inventory, database, and so on) and having a test environment lets you test them confidently.

Information at the World level covers all the vCenter Servers, so it provides a bird's-eye view of the entire infrastructure. The increased scalability in vRealize Operations 6 means this can be a global view covering tens of thousands of VMs. vRealize Operations provides the following metric groups at the World level:

Scope	vRealize Operations
CPU	CPU
RAM	Memory
Storage	Disk
Network	Network

Besides the preceding metric groups, the World object has all the vRealize Operations badges and capacity-related metric groups. Together, they can be handy if you want to show the big picture on the big screen for everyone to see.

Counters in vCenter and vRealize Operations

We compared the metric groups between vCenter and vRealize Operations. We know that vRealize Operations provides a lot more detail, especially for larger objects such as vCenter, data center, and cluster. It also provides information about the distributed switch, which is not displayed in vCenter at all. This makes it useful for the big-picture analysis.

We will now look at individual counters. To give us a two-dimensional analysis, I would not approach it from the vSphere objects' point of view. Instead, we will examine the four key types of metrics (CPU, RAM, network, and storage). For each type, I will provide my personal take on what I think is a good guidance for their value. For example, I will give guidance on a good value for CPU contention based on what I have seen in the field. This is not an official VMware recommendation. I will state the official recommendation or popular recommendation if I am aware of it.

You should spend time understanding vCenter counters and esxtop counters. This section of the book is not meant to replace the manual. I would encourage you to read the vSphere documentation on this topic, as it gives you the required foundation while working with vRealize Operations. The following are the links to this topic:

- The link for vSphere 5.5 is `http://pubs.vmware.com/vsphere-55/index.jsp#com.vmware.vsphere.monitoring.doc/GUID-12B1493A-5657-4BB3-8935-44B6B8E8B67C.html`. If this link does not work, visit `https://www.vmware.com/support/pubs/vsphere-esxi-vcenter-server-pubs.html` and then navigate to **ESXi and vCenter Server 5.5 Documentation | vSphere Monitoring and Performance | Monitoring Inventory Objects with Performance Charts**.

- The counters are documented in the vSphere API. You can find it at `http://pubs.vmware.com/vsphere-55/index.jsp#com.vmware.wssdk.apiref.doc/vim.PerformanceManager.html`. If this link has changed and no longer works, open the vSphere online documentation and navigate to **vSphere API/SDK Documentation | vSphere Management SDK | vSphere Web Services SDK Documentation | VMware vSphere API Reference | Managed Object Types | P**. Here, choose **Performance Manager** from the list under the letter **P**.

- The esxtop manual provides good information on the counters. You can find it at `https://www.vmware.com/support/pubs/vsphere-esxi-vcenter-server-pubs.html`.

You should also be familiar with the architecture of ESXi, especially how the scheduler works.

vCenter has a different collection interval (sampling period) depending upon the timeline you are looking at. Most of the time you are looking at the real-time statistic (chart), as other timelines do not have enough counters. You will notice right away that most of the counters become unavailable once you choose a timeline. In the *real-time* chart, each data point has 20 seconds' worth of data. That is as accurate as it gets in vCenter. Because all other performance management tools (including vRealize Operations) get their data from vCenter, they are not getting anything more granular than this. As mentioned previously, esxtop allows you to sample down to a minimum of 2 seconds.

Speaking of esxtop, you should be aware that not all counters are exposed in vCenter. For example, if you turn on 3D graphics, there is a separate SVGA thread created for that VM. This can consume CPU and it will not show up in vCenter. The **Mouse, Keyboard, Screen (MKS)** threads, which give you the console, also do not show up in vCenter.

The next screenshot shows how you lose most of your counters if you choose a timespan other than real time. In the case of CPU, you are basically left with two counters, as **Usage** and **Usage in MHz** cover the same thing. You also lose the ability to monitor per core, as the target objects only list the host now and not the individual cores.

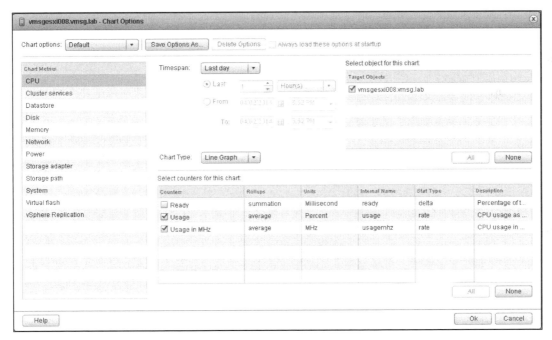

Counters are lost beyond 1 hour

Because the real-time timespan only lasts for 1 hour, the performance troubleshooting has to be done at the *present* moment. If the performance issue cannot be recreated, there is no way to troubleshoot in vCenter. This is where vRealize Operations comes in, as it keeps your data for a much longer period. I was able to perform troubleshooting for a client on a problem that occurred more than a month ago!

vRealize Operations takes data every 5 minutes. This means it is not suitable to troubleshoot performance that does not last for 5 minutes. In fact, if the performance issue only lasts for 5 minutes, you may not get any alert, because the collection may happen exactly in the middle of those 5 minutes. For example, let's assume the CPU is idle from 08:00:00 to 08:02:30, spikes from 08:02:30 to 08:07:30, and then again is idle from 08:07:30 to 08:10:00. If vRealize Operations is collecting at exactly 08:00, 08:05, and 08:10, you will not see the spike as it is spread over two data points. This means, for vRealize Operations to pick up the spike in its *entirety* without any idle data, the spike has to last for 10 minutes or more.

> In some metrics, the unit is actually 20 seconds. vRealize Operations averages a set of 20-second data points into a single 5-minute data point.

The **Rollups** column is important. **Average** means the average of 5 minutes in the case of vRealize Operations. The **summation** value is actually an average for those counters where accumulation makes more sense. An example is **CPU Ready time**. It gets accumulated over the sampling period. Over a period of 20 seconds, a VM may accumulate 200 milliseconds of CPU ready time. This translates into 1 percent, which is why I said it is similar to **average**, as you lose the peak.

Latest, on the other hand, is different. It takes the last value of the sampling period. For example, in the sampling for 20 seconds, it takes the value between 19 and 20 seconds. This value can be lower or higher than the average of the entire 20-second period.

So what is missing here is the peak of the sampling period. In the 5-minute period, vRealize Operations does not collect **low**, **average**, and **high** from vCenter. It takes **average** only.

Let's talk about the **Units** column now. Some common units are milliseconds, MHz, percent, KBps, and KB. Some counters are shown in MHz, which means you need to know your ESXi physical CPU frequency. This can be difficult due to CPU power saving features, which lower the CPU frequency when the demand is low. In large environments, this can be operationally difficult as you have different ESXi hosts from different generations (and hence, are likely to sport a different GHz). This is also the reason why I state that the cluster is the smallest logical building block. If your cluster has ESXi hosts with different frequencies, these MHz-based counters can be difficult to use, as the VMs get vMotion-ed by DRS.

When is a peak not a true peak?

Let's elaborate on peaks. How do you define peak utilization or contention without being overly conservative or aggressive?

There are two dimensions of peaks. You can measure them across time or members of the group. Let's take a cluster with 8 hosts as an example:

- You measure across members of the group. For each sample data, take the utilization from the host with the highest utilization. In our cluster example, let's say at 1:30 pm, host number 7 has the highest utilization among all hosts. It hits 80 percent. We then take it that the cluster peak utilization at 1:30 pm is also 80 percent. You repeat this process for each sample period. You may get different hosts at different times. You will not know which host provides the peak value as that varies from time to time. This method results in over-reporting, as it is the peak of a member. You can technically argue that this is the true peak.

- You measure across time. You take the average utilization of the cluster, roll up the time period to a longer time period, and take the peak of that longer time period. For example, the cluster average utilization peaks at 80 percent at 1:30 pm. You roll up the data for one day. This means the peak utilization for that day is 80 percent. This is the most common approach. The problem of this approach is that it is actually an average. For the cluster to hit 80 percent average utilization, some hosts have to hit over 80 percent. That means you can't rule out the possibility that one host might hit near 100 percent. The same logic applies to a VM. If a VM with 16 vCPUs hits 80 percent utilization, some cores probably hit 100 percent. This method results in under-reporting as it is an average.

The first approach is useful if you want to know detailed information. You retain the 5-minute granularity. With the second approach, you lose the granularity and each sample becomes one day (or one month, depending on your timeline). You do not know what time of the day it hits the peak. The first approach will result in higher average than the second approach, because in most cases, your cluster is not perfectly balanced (identical utilization). In the tier 1 cluster, where you do not oversubscribe, I'd recommend the first approach as it will capture the host with the highest peak. The first approach can be achieved by using super metrics in vRealize Operations. The second approach requires the **View** widget with data transformation.

Does this mean you always use the first approach? The answer is *no*. The first approach can be too aggressive when the number of members is high. If your data center has 500 hosts and you use the first approach, then your overall data center peak utilization will always be high. All it takes is just one host to hit a peak at any given time.

The first approach fits a use case where automatic load balancing should happen. So you expect an overall balanced distribution. A DRS cluster is a good example.

vRealize Operations versus vCenter

I mentioned earlier that vRealize Operations does not simply regurgitate what vCenter has. Some of the vSphere-specific characteristics are not properly understood by traditional management tools. Partial understanding can lead to misunderstanding. vRealize Operations starts by fully understanding the unique behavior of vSphere, then simplifying it by consolidating and standardizing the counters. For example, vRealize Operations creates derived counters such as **Contention** and **Workload**, then applies them to CPU, RAM, disk, and network.

Let's take a look at one example of how partial information can be misleading in a troubleshooting scenario. It is common for customers to invest in an ESXi host with plenty of RAM. I've seen hosts with 256 to 512 GB of RAM. One reason behind this is the way vCenter displays information. In the following screenshot, vCenter is giving me an alert. The host is running on high memory utilization. I'm not showing the other host, but you can see that it has a warning, as it is high too. The screenshots are all from vCenter 5.0 and vCenter Operations 5.7, but the behavior is still the same in vCenter 5.5 Update 2 and vRealize Operations 6.0.

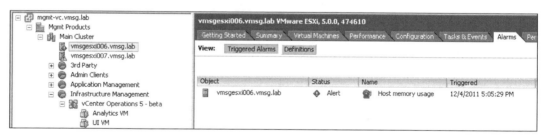

vSphere 5.0 – Memory alarm

I'm using vSphere 5.0 and vCenter Operations 5.x to show the screenshots as I want to provide an example of the point I stated earlier, which is the rapid change of vCloud Suite.

The first step is to check if someone has modified the alarm by reducing the threshold. The next screenshot shows that utilization above 95 percent will trigger an alert, while utilization above 90 percent will trigger a warning. The threshold has to be breached by at least 5 minutes. The alarm is set to a suitably high configuration, so we will assume the alert is genuinely indicating a high utilization on the host.

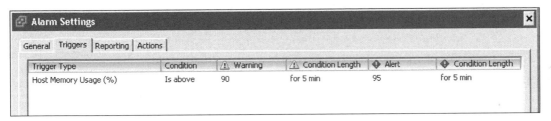

vSphere 5.0 – Alarm settings

Let's verify the memory utilization. I'm checking both the hosts as there are two of them in the cluster. Both are indeed high. The utilization for **vmsgesxi006** has gone down in the time taken to review the **Alarm Settings** tab and move to this view, so both hosts are now in the **Warning** status.

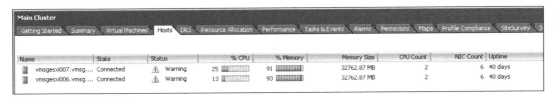

vSphere 5.0 – Hosts tab

Now we will look at the **vmsgesxi006** specification. From the following screenshot, we can see it has 32 GB of physical RAM, and RAM usage is 30747 MB. It is at 93.8 percent utilization.

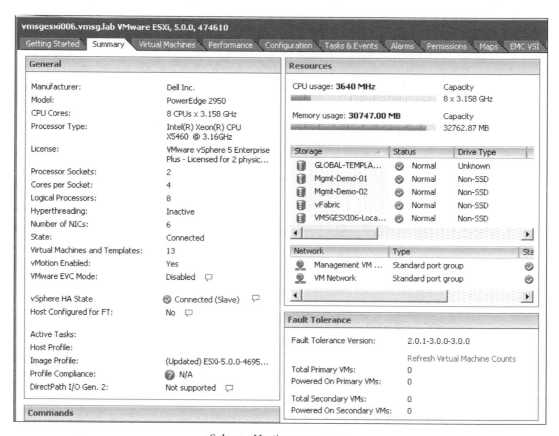

vSphere – Host's summary page

Since all the numbers shown in the preceding screenshot are refreshed within minutes, we need to check with a longer timeline to make sure this is not a one-time spike. So let's check for the last 24 hours. The next screenshot shows that the utilization was indeed consistently high. For the entire 24-hour period, it has consistently been above 92.5 percent, and it hits 95 percent several times. So this ESXi host was indeed in need of more RAM.

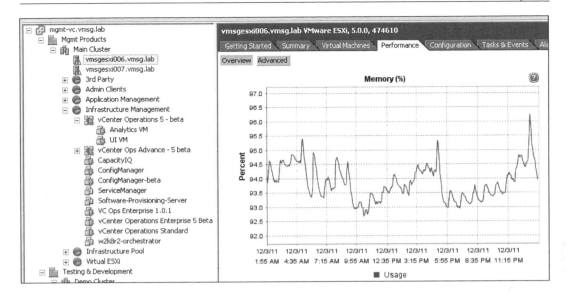

Deciding whether to add more RAM is complex; there are many factors to be considered. There will be downtime on the host, and you need to do it for every host in the cluster since you need to maintain a consistent build cluster-wide. Because the ESXi is highly utilized, I should increase the RAM significantly so that I can support more VMs or larger VMs. Buying bigger DIMMs may mean throwing away the existing DIMMs, as there are rules restricting the mixing of DIMMs. Mixing DIMMs also increases management complexity. The new DIMM may require a BIOS update, which may trigger a change request. Alternatively, the large DIMM may not be compatible with the existing host, in which case I have to buy a new box. So a RAM upgrade may trigger a host upgrade, which is a larger project.

Before jumping in to a procurement cycle to buy more RAM, let's double-check our findings. It is important to ask *what is the host used for?* and *who is using it?*.

In this example scenario, we examined a lab environment, the VMware ASEAN lab. Let's check out the memory utilization again, this time with the context in mind. The preceding graph shows high memory utilization over a 24-hour period, yet no one was using the lab in the early hours of the morning! I am aware of this as I am the lab administrator.

We will now turn to vCenter Operations for an alternative view. The following screenshot from vCenter Operations 5 tells a different story. CPU, RAM, disk, and network are all in the healthy range. Specifically for RAM, it has 97 percent utilization but 32 percent demand. Note that the **Memory** chart is divided into two parts. The upper one is at the ESXi level, while the lower one shows individual VMs in that host.

The upper part is in turn split into two. The green rectangle (**Demand**) sits on top of a grey rectangle (**Usage**). The green rectangle shows a healthy figure at around 10 GB. The grey rectangle is much longer, almost filling the entire area.

The lower part shows the hypervisor and the VMs' memory utilization. Each little green box represents one VM.

On the bottom left, note the **KEY METRICS** section. vCenter Operations 5 shows that **Memory | Contention** is **0** percent. This means none of the VMs running on the host is contending for memory. They are all being served well!

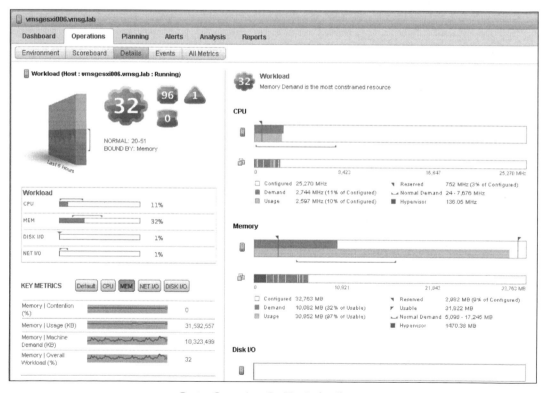

vCenter Operations 5 – Host's details page

I shared earlier that the behavior remains the same in vCenter 5.5. So, let's take a look at how memory utilization is shown in vCenter 5.5. The next screenshot shows the counters provided by vCenter 5.5. This is from a different ESXi host, as I want to provide you with a second example. Notice that the ballooning is 0, so there is no memory pressure for this host. This host has 48 GB of RAM. About 26 GB has been mapped to VM or VMkernel, which is shown by the **Consumed** counter (the highest line in the chart; notice that the value is almost constant). The **Usage** counter shows 52 percent because it takes from **Consumed**. The active memory is a lot lower, as you can see from the line at the bottom. Notice that the line is not a simple straight line, as the value goes up and down. This proves that the **Usage** counter is actually the **Consumed** counter.

vCenter 5.5 Update 1 memory counters

At this point, some readers might wonder whether that's a bug in vCenter. No, it is not. There are situations in which you want to use the consumed memory and not the active memory. In fact, some applications may not run properly if you use active memory. I will cover this when we discuss memory counters in further chapters. Also, technically, it is not a bug as the data it gives is correct. It is just that additional data will give a more complete picture since we are at the ESXi level and not at the VM level. vRealize Operations distinguishes between the active memory and consumed memory and provides both types of data. vCenter uses the **Consumed** counter for utilization for the ESXi host.

 As you will see later in this book, vCenter uses the **Active** counter for utilization for VM. So the **Usage** counter has a different formula in vCenter depending upon the object. This makes sense as they are at different levels.

vRealize Operations uses the **Active** counter for utilization. Just because a physical DIMM on the motherboard is mapped to a virtual DIMM in the VM, it does not mean it is actively used (read or write). You can use that DIMM for other VMs and you will not incur (for practical purposes) performance degradation. It is common for Microsoft Windows to initialize pages upon boot with zeroes, but never use them subsequently.

For further information on this topic, I would recommend reviewing Kit Colbert's presentation on *Memory in vSphere* at VMworld, 2012. The content is still relevant for vSphere 5.x. The title is *Understanding Virtualized Memory Performance Management* and the session ID is INF-VSP1729. You can find it at `http://www.vmworld.com/docs/DOC-6292`. If the link has changed, the link to the full list of VMworld 2012 sessions is `http://www.vmworld.com/community/sessions/2012/`.

Not all performance management tools understand this vCenter-specific characteristic. They would have given you a recommendation to buy more RAM.

Summary

In this chapter, we covered the world of counters in vCenter and vRealize Operations. The counters were analyzed based on their four main groupings (CPU, RAM, disk, and network). We also covered each of the metric groups, which maps to the corresponding objects in vCenter. For the counters, we also shared how they are related, and how they differ.

In the next four chapters, we will dive deeper into each of these four main groupings, dedicating a chapter to each group.

4
CPU Counters

We will continue our venture into the world of counters by focusing on CPU counters in this chapter. We will cover both the contention counters and the utilization counters. The topics that will be covered in this chapter are as follows:

- VM CPU counters
- ESXi CPU counters
- Cluster CPU counters
- CPU counters at high-level objects
- Guidance on the value you should be setting for each service tier

CPU counters at the VM level

The following screenshot shows the VM CPU counters in vCenter 5.5 taken from the C# client. The **Collection Level** column does not apply to vRealize Operations. Changing the collection level does not impact what counters get collected by vRealize Operations. It collects all counters from vCenter using its own filter, which you can customize.

In vCenter, there are 16 counters available at the VM level, and 11 of them are available at a virtual core level too. That means a VM with 2 vCPUs (or 2 virtual cores) will have 38 counters. A vSphere environment with 1,000 VMs with 2 vCPUs as the average VM size will have more than 30,000 counters! In vCenter, you can look at an individual VM to see these counters. Because VMs can impact one another's performance, you need a management tool that can cut across all of these 38 counters across VMs in all vCenter Servers. I find vRealize Operations useful because it allows me to slice and dice all of these counters across VMs. Ronald Buder, a VMware vExpert and an expert in vRealize Operations, describes vRealize Operations as *big data*.

Description	Rollup	Units	Internal Name	Collection Level
☑ Usage	Average	Percent	usage	1
☐ Ready	Summation	Millisecond	ready	1
☐ System	Summation	Millisecond	system	3
☐ Co-stop	Summation	Millisecond	costop	2
☐ Max limited	Summation	Millisecond	maxlimited	2
☐ Idle	Summation	Millisecond	idle	2
☐ Overlap	Summation	Millisecond	overlap	3
☐ Run	Summation	Millisecond	run	2
☐ Entitlement	Latest	MHz	entitlement	2
☐ Latency	Average	Percent	latency	2
☐ Demand-to-entitlement ratio	Latest	Percent	demandEntitlemen…	4
☐ Wait	Summation	Millisecond	wait	3
☐ Demand	Average	MHz	demand	2
☐ Used	Summation	Millisecond	used	3
☐ Swap wait	Summation	Millisecond	swapwait	3
☑ Usage in MHz	Average	MHz	usagemhz	1

VM – CPU counters

The five counters that are not available at the virtual core level are:

- Usage
- Entitlement
- Latency
- Demand-to-entitlement ratio
- Demand

This means you cannot track the CPU latency on a per-core basis. Also, you cannot use **Demand** and **Usage**, and therefore you have to use **Used** (which is in milliseconds) or **Usage** in MHz when looking at metrics at a core level. Counters that provide value in the percentage format are easier to understand than counters that provide value in milliseconds or MHz, as the percentage format takes into account the context of what is available to the VM. Value in MHz can in fact be misleading if the VM is moved to another host running at a different frequency.

vSphere understands virtual socket and virtual core. However, in the vCenter performance chart, it does not distinguish them.

 I recommend you read the post by Mark Achtemichuk at `http://blogs.vmware.com/vsphere/2013/10/does-corespersocket-affect-performance.html` for a deeper understanding of virtual sockets and cores.

A virtual socket can have many virtual cores. There is a difference between 1 socket with 8 cores and 8 sockets with 1 core each from configuration point of view. From a performance point of view, as long as the VM can fit into a single physical socket, there will be little difference. In most cases, it is easier to leave it as the default setting, which is 1 socket, 8 cores. In the performance counters, vCenter 5.5 does not distinguish between virtual socket and virtual cores. A VM with 2 dual-core virtual sockets or 1 quad-core virtual socket will be shown as 1 socket, 4 cores. This is another reason why I prefer to use the default setting and avoid creating a VM with multiple virtual sockets; another reason is the licensing benefit. Some software products are licensed on a per-socket basis with unlimited cores.

Because there are a lot of counters, it is easier to discuss what is missing first. All the available counters are at the vSphere layer. Because the hypervisor does not have visibility inside the Guest OS, you will not see counters inside the VM without extensions in the form of management packs for vRealize Operations. From a CPU point of view, the main missing counter is **CPU run queue**. This is useful when working out if the allocated vCPU is enough or not. Generally, the CPU run queue will be low if the CPU utilization is low, as the queue only develops when the CPU is used. If you can monitor the CPU run queue, you should create a super metric in vRealize Operations that divides the run queue with the number of vCPUs. This gives you a standardized comparison across VMs with different vCPU size. If the value is 3 or higher, and CPU utilization is high, this is a sign of insufficient vCPUs for the VM.

Contention counters

Earlier in the book, we talked about why we must check for contention before utilization. The reason is that you want to make sure your infrastructure is not causing any bottleneck for the VM it is serving.

vCenter does not have a **Contention** counter, but it does have raw counters that signal contention, which are leveraged by vRealize Operations to derive contention. The main ones are **Ready**, **Co-stop**, and **Latency**. The most famous among these three is **Ready**, which is the amount of time a VM waits for a thread to be scheduled. **Co-stop** is the amount of time a multi-vCPU (symmetrical multiprocessing) VM was ready to run but incurred delay while waiting for parallel threads to be scheduled simultaneously. **Latency** is the %LAT_C counter in esxtop. It includes **Ready** and **Co-stop** and is also impacted by the **Hyper-Threading (HT)** busy time and the hardware CPU power state (dynamic voltage frequency scaling). Because of this, vRealize Operations uses **Latency** as its primary source for CPU contention data.

Ready includes **Limit**, but not **Co-stop**. Many VMware administrators simply look at **Ready** and assume that a figure below 5 percent is good. A better practice is to first take CPU latency into account before drawing conclusions.

Co-stop means a VM vCPU is being paused by the hypervisor scheduler to allow its sibling vCPUs to catch up (a feature of relaxed co-scheduling). This naturally happens if the VM has more than 1 vCPU and one of them is waiting for the other. The waiting happens because ESXi does not have enough physical CPUs to serve all the virtual CPUs. This is why you need to adjust the size of the VM. In *Chapter 8, Dashboard Examples and Ideas*, we will cover a use case of adjusting the size of the VM with confidence, using individual virtual core information.

The **Latency** counter is greatly affected by the CPU power management. It can spike if you do not set the CPU power management to maximum. The following screenshot shows the power meter on a HP Proliant server, a popular ESXi host. In **20-Minute History Graph**, notice the power consumption spiked and then went down. I changed the power management from balance to maximum and then back to balance again.

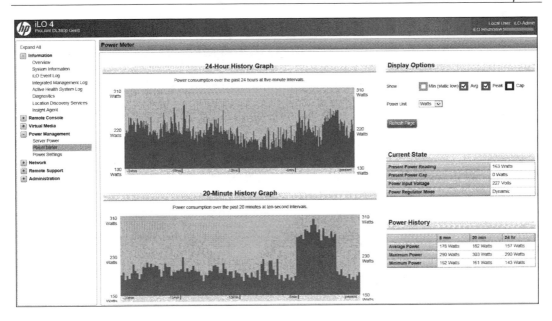

What do you expect we will see at the ESXi level? Specifically, what do you think the CPU latency will be during the spike? Do you think it will go down near 0 percent?

If that is your answer, you are right. The next screenshot shows the latency, which was hovering around 6.4 percent and dropped to 0 percent. It then went up after I changed the power management back to balance.

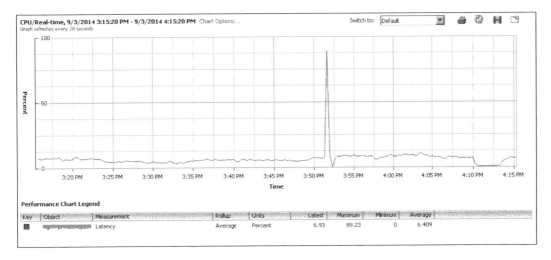

Now, the **Latency** counter impacts the **Contention** counter. You will see that **Contention** hovers around 6.4 percent (in this case), even though the reality is actually closer to 0. Since we are setting SLA based on contention, you need to take this into account.

There are two options to set the CPU maximum performance. You can set it at the hardware level or at the ESXi level. The following screenshot shows the settings in HP Proliant DL 380 G7. The first three choices are managing power at the hardware level. I recommend you manage at the software level by selecting **OS Control mode**, as shown in the screenshot. Changing from hardware level to software level usually requires a reboot of the host.

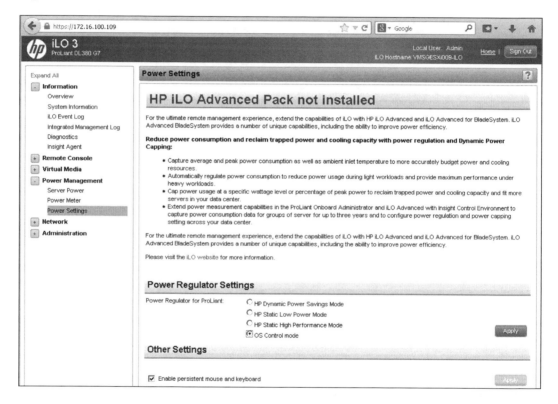

Once **Power Policy Settings** are enabled at the ESXi level, you can control them via vCenter as shown in the following screenshot. None of these changes require a reboot. The default setting is **Balanced**, which I recommend you change to **High performance** if you have workload that is sensitive to CPU latency (for example, VDI or tier 1 applications).

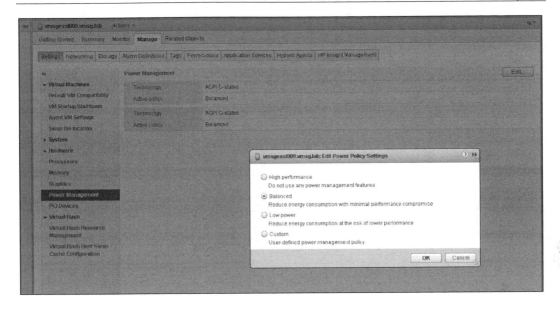

You can track the actual power consumption from vCenter or vRealize Operations. The next screenshot shows the power consumption. This is a HP DL 380 G7 machine with 2 sockets containing Xeon processors and 64 GB RAM. I changed the power policy from **Balanced** to **Low power** at around 5:50 p.m. You can see the power consumption drops from around 150 W to 144 W. The spike in the chart at around 5:10 p.m. is due to vMotion. I vMotion-ed all the VMs from one host to another host. The power consumption remains at around 145 W, which means this is as low as it gets.

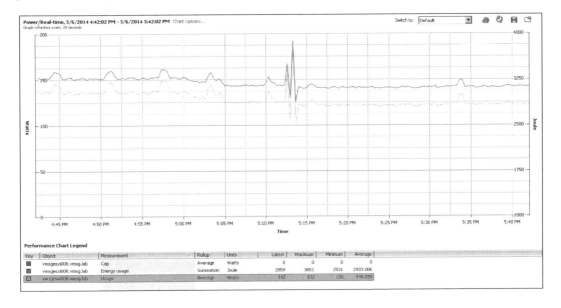

More information about power management can be found at `http://kb.vmware.com/kb/1018206` and `https://www.vmware.com/resources/techresources/10416`. The KB article provides settings for other hardware, and the technical paper goes deeper in explaining the concepts. I also find useful the blog at `http://blogs.vmware.com/performance/2013/05/power-management-and-performance-in-esxi-5-1.html` by Rebecca Grider assuring because the default setting in ESXi is balanced.

If you do not change the CPU power management to maximum performance, you should see **Latency** higher than **Ready**, because **Latency** is affected by change in CPU frequency. In addition, **Latency** also goes up if the VM does not run on its preferred core (which is where it ran previously). **Ready** only goes up if the VM is unable to run at all.

The next screenshot shows that **Latency** is higher than **Ready**, because the ESXi host is set to the default CPU power management. It is a bit difficult to compare **Latency** and **Ready** in vCenter, because they use different units. The **Ready** value is the red line. It fluctuates between 13 milliseconds and 54 milliseconds. As this is a real-time chart, each sample is 20,000 milliseconds per virtual core. The VM has 4 vCPUs, so 54 milliseconds is 0.0675 percent of 80,000 milliseconds. The **Latency** counter however, spikes to 7.23 percent—an amount that is 100 times bigger. The following chart could easily be misinterpreted, as it gives the impression that **Ready** is fluctuating greatly while **Latency** barely moves. It is the opposite that actually happens!

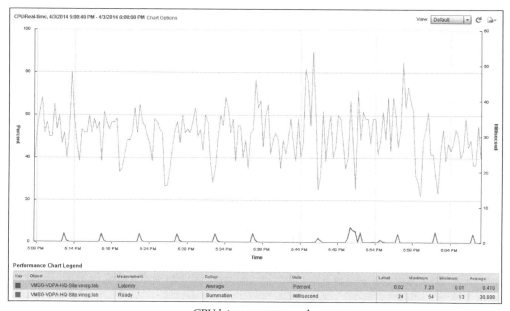

CPU latency versus ready

vRealize Operations simplifies tracking contention by providing a **CPU Contention** counter. The next chart shows that the **CPU Contention** spikes to 10.65 percent when the **Co-stop** value hits 7,391 on March 14 at around 1:45 p.m. It is so much easier to think in percentage than in millisecond. It is hard to remember if the value 7,391 is considered good or bad, as you must multiply 20,000 by the number of virtual cores in the VM. Note that the CPU **Ready** value did not spike even though **Co-stop** spiked, as **Ready** does not include **Co-stop**. Compared to **CPU Ready**, **CPU Contention** also tends to correlate better to **CPU Usage**. The following chart demonstrates that closer correlation. Note that **CPU Usage** and **CPU Contention** have a similar pattern.

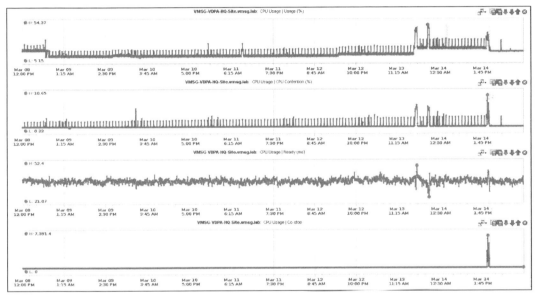

CPU Usage, CPU Contention, CPU Ready, and CPU Co-stop

In the preceding chart, **CPU Ready** shows very little movement. It varies from 21 milliseconds to 52 milliseconds. Since the range is 80,000, this means that the **CPU Ready** counter barely moves—as 50 out of 80,000 is around just 0.06%. Compare this with **CPU Contention**, which spikes to 10 percent! Because of this higher sensitivity, you would only set the SLA on **CPU Contention** to the same level as **CPU Ready** if you configure the maximum CPU power.

In another example, let's use a different time period and a different version of vRealize Operations. The previous chart is from vCenter Operations 5.8.1, and the next one is from vRealize Operations 6. In version 6, units are added for the *y* axis, making it easier to understand the value.

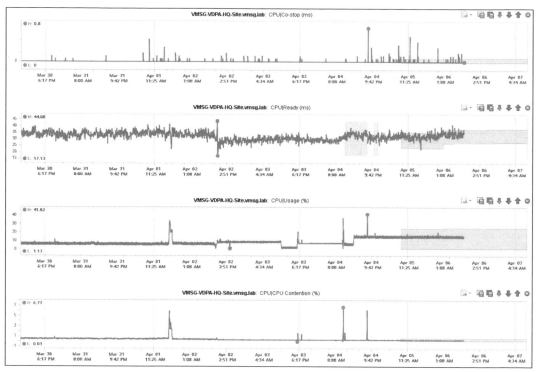

CPU Usage, CPU Contention, CPU Ready, and CPU Co-stop

From the previous chart, we can see that **CPU Contention** spikes when **CPU Usage** spikes, whereas **CPU Co-stop** does not. In this example, we see that **CPU Ready** barely moves, but **CPU Contention** captures the spike. If you set your SLA at 5 percent for **CPU Ready**, you are safe. If you set your SLA to the same 5 percent for **CPU Contention**, you fail to deliver it on three different occasions as there are three spikes in the previous chart that passed 5 percent.

The SLA value you should set depends on your CPU power management. If the CPU power management is set to maximum, the **CPU Contention** counter will show a more realistic number, which is a much lower value. The following two examples show that it can go down to well below 1 percent:

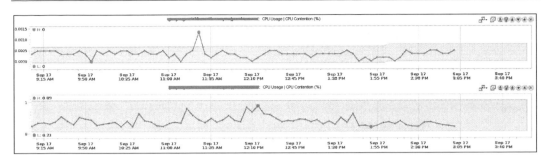

Utilization counters

Once you are satisfied that there is no contention, it is time to check utilization. If it is high and the CPU run queue inside the VM is high, there is a good chance that the VM needs to be given more vCPUs. If it is low, but performance is slow, you need to check if the CPU is waiting for RAM, disk, or network.

For utilization, vCenter provides five counters—that's a lot of counters! You can check the following counters:

- Usage
- Demand
- Run
- Used
- Usage in MHz

The counters have different units. The easiest one is **Usage**, since it is given in percentage. The limitation with **Usage** is that it is not available at a per-core level. The value also tends to be a bit lower than **Demand** as **Demand** is affected by CPU power management. If you have a big VM, you need to look at individual core performance to ensure it is not oversized. A low usage at the VM level does not mean balanced utilization across all cores. If the utilization is not balanced and you see a consistent pattern for months, you should consider reducing the vCPUs to improve performance. Adjusting the size gives better performance than relying on relaxed co-scheduling, as the gap between the leading vCPU and the idle vCPU cannot exceed a certain threshold. Refer to the book *The CPU Scheduler in VMware vSphere® 5.1: Performance Study*, which I mentioned in the previous chapter.

Most of the time, **Usage (%)**, **Usage (MHz)**, **Demand (MHz)**, and **Used (ms)** are identical; they just use different units and scale, as shown in the following chart. Notice that the pattern is identical. They move up and down in tandem; only the scale differs and represents the different units. The chart goes back 7 days and this is a VM with 4 vCPUs, so mathematically, there were plenty of chances for these 4 counters to differ—but they did not.

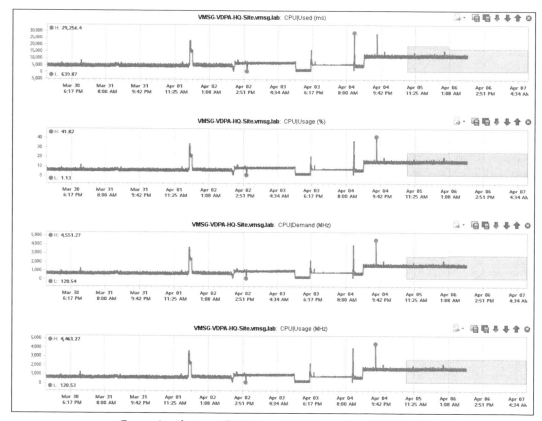

Comparison between CPU Usage, CPU Demand, and CPU Used

If you look carefully at the preceding screenshot, **CPU Demand (MHz)** and **CPU Usage (MHz)** have different values. **Demand** is slightly higher. This is due to power management. When the physical CPU frequency is lowered, **CPU Demand** uses that reduced value as its 100 percent; hence, you get a higher value for **Demand**. According to the manual, the **Demand** counter tracks the amount of vCPUs that the VM would use if there were neither **CPU Contention** nor **CPU Limit**. So if **Demand** is significantly greater than **Usage**, and the two counters do not have an identical pattern, that means there is contention or your CPU power management has kicked in.

Based on the previous chart for the previous example, **CPU Used (ms)** and **CPU Usage (%)** use a different scale. The preceding VM has 4 vCPUs, so the maximum value (equivalent to 100 percent) is 80,000 milliseconds. You might think that since the sampling period is based on 5 minutes, 100 percent means 300 seconds or 300,000 milliseconds. It is not. vRealize Operations takes the real-time chart (which is 20 seconds), and takes the average of these 20-second intervals. It does not sum up.

Going back to the scale, if we divide 29,256 by 80,000, we get 36.6 percent. This is around 13 percent lower than 41.8 percent that we saw in the previous chart. The fact that **CPU Used** takes into account CPU power management impacts its result.

Let's look at another example; this time, we will zoom in to a 1-day interval so we can see more clearly. Also, we have a VM with 2 vCPUs instead of 4. The VM version is vCenter 5.5 Update 1. This is the Linux appliance with an embedded database. It is running embedded SSO that serves two other vCenter Servers. Note the regular pattern; the CPU spikes from 10 percent to 50 percent regularly.

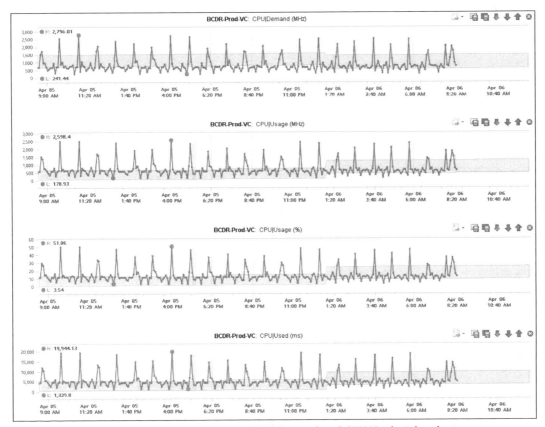

Comparison between CPU usage, CPU Demand, and CPU Used – 1 day chart

From the previous example, we again see a consistent pattern among the four counters. We also see that **Demand (MHz)** shows a slightly higher value than **Usage (MHz)**. **CPU Used (ms)** is again lower than **CPU Usage (%)**. This is a 2 vCPU VM, so the equivalent of 100 percent is 40,000 milliseconds. The peak of **CPU Used (ms)** is 19,944 milliseconds, which is equivalent to 49.9 percent, slightly lower than the peak of **CPU Usage (%)** at 51.06 percent.

Let's take one more example. This time, we go back 30 days. We will be looking at **CPU Used (ms)** and **CPU Usage (%)** this time around. Notice they are identical again, and **CPU Used (ms)** is slightly lower than **CPU Usage (%)**. The peak of **CPU Used (ms)** is around 48 percent, slightly lower than 54 percent.

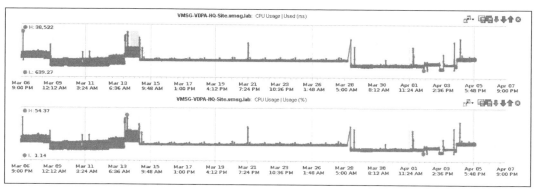

CPU Usage and CPU Used

CPU Run usually takes the same pattern as **CPU Used**. The formula for **CPU Used** is:

Used = Run + System – Overlap

In an environment where the utilization is low and the VMs do not generate a lot of I/O, the value of *System* and *Overlap* will be near zero. You can track the behavior of these two counters in your data center by creating super metrics in vRealize Operations. The super metric tracks the maximum value of each counter. A change in the pattern of the line chart is worth investigating.

Differences in values between CPU **Run** and CPU **Used** can certainly happen. CPU **Used** takes into account hyper-threading, so it can be lower (as shown in the following example). In hyper-threading, two threads share the same physical core, so there is an efficiency loss. Prior to vSphere 5.0, the efficiency loss was valued at 50 percent. This was lowered to 37.5 percent in vSphere 5.0 as the technology improved. In the screenshot, you can see that **Used** is consistently lower than **Run**, as the thick blue line is consistently lower than the thin gray line above it. In this example, the CPU **System** and CPU **Overlap** do not cover the gap. CPU **System** is in fact zero for the entire period.

On the other hand, if you have a CPU that supports turbo mode, the CPU frequency can also be higher than the nominal (rated) frequency. In this case, CPU **Used** could be higher than CPU **Run**.

CPU **Run** does not account for hyper-threading and system time.

The **System** counter tracks the amount of time spent on system processes on each vCPU in the VM. The hypervisor knows whether the VM is accessing ring zero or not and is executing a privileged instruction or not.

The **Overlap** counter tracks the time the VM was interrupted to perform system services on behalf of that VM or other VMs. vCenter does not distinguish between VMs. Having said that, the effect is the same—the VM cannot run as the physical core is used by VMkernel to operate system services.

System and **Overlap** are related at the ESXi level that juggles multiple VMs. If VM number 1 is currently being scheduled on core number 1 and a network packet for VM number 2 is processed by the ESXi VMkernel on the same core, the time spent appears as **Overlap** for VM number 1 and **System** for VM number 2.

The **System** and **Overlap** counters are not captured by default in vRealize Operations.

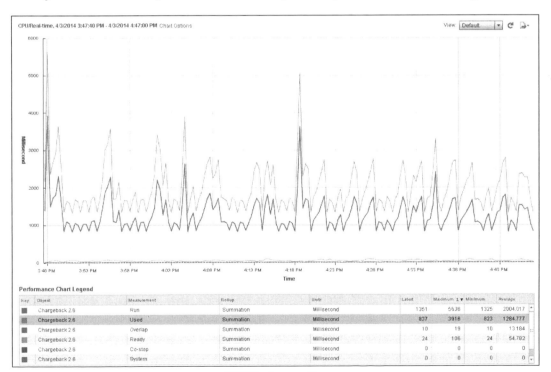

CPU Used versus Run

The **Entitlement** counter tracks the CPU entitlement of the VM. If there is no contention, this value can be relatively flat (as shown in the following chart). The red line at the top is the **Entitlement**. Notice that it is practically a straight line, even though the **Demand** and **Usage** fluctuate. The value is also much higher than both **Demand** and **Usage**, showing a healthy ESXi host.

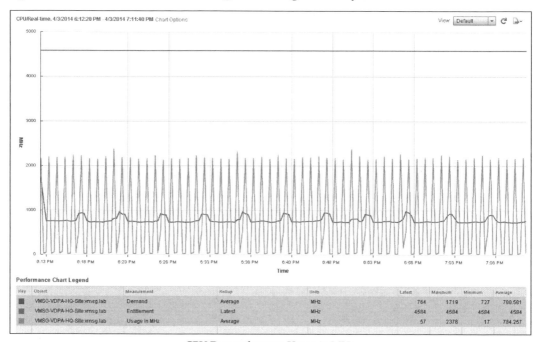

CPU Demand versus Usage in MHz

From the preceding chart, you may think that **Usage** is double that of **Demand**. This is another case of two similar metrics with different units of measurement, which often leads to confusion. The two counters are actually the same, as can be seen in the next chart. Here is the data from the same VM shown in vRealize Operations over the past 30 days, which shows that the values are the same when the units are the same.

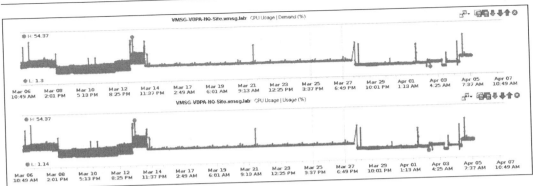

CPU Demand versus CPU Usage

CPU Demand gives a more realistic pattern than **Usage**. The spiky nature of **Usage** does not seem natural, as 20,000 milliseconds is a long time from a CPU point of view (which operates in subnanoseconds). An average taken over a very long period would be relatively flat.

There is another reason why I recommend **CPU Demand** over **CPU Usage**. In an environment where the ESXi is unable to meet the demand of its VMs, you will see **CPU Demand** to be higher than **CPU Usage**. The **CPU Demand** counter shows the utilization that would have happened if there is no contention.

vRealize Operations also provides the **Workload** (percent) counter. It is the **Demand** (%) counter, but rounded to the nearest whole number. The following screenshot shows that the **Workload** chart is simplified, which makes it a little easier to read. I prefer the **Workload** (percent) counter because in an idle VM, it will show a flat line.

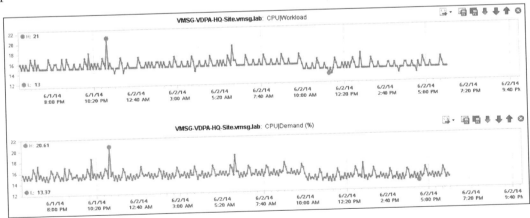

What should the values of **CPU Workload** and **CPU Contention** be in a healthy environment when **Usage** is very high? If the **Usage** is flat at 100 percent, and ESXi is able to meet all the demands, what do you expect the value of **CPU Workload** and **CPU Contention** to be? The following chart shows a VM with 100 percent utilization. The **CPU Workload** counter is slightly higher, as it is based on **Demand** and we expect it to be a bit higher. The **CPU Contention** is low, as the VM is not contending with other VMs for resource.

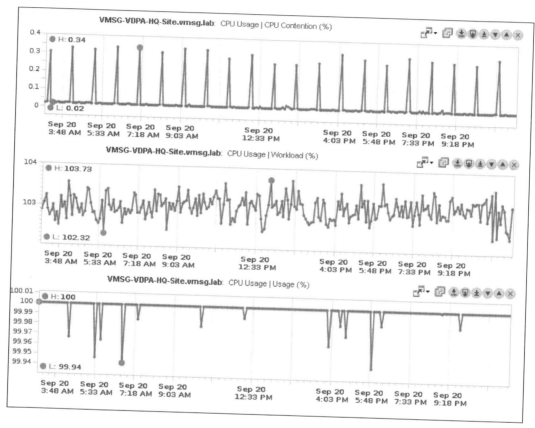

Other counters

Demand-to-entitlement ratio is a useful counter as you do not have to track **Demand** and **Entitlement**. Whenever the value shoots above 100 percent, the VM is experiencing CPU contention. It is not getting what it is asking for.

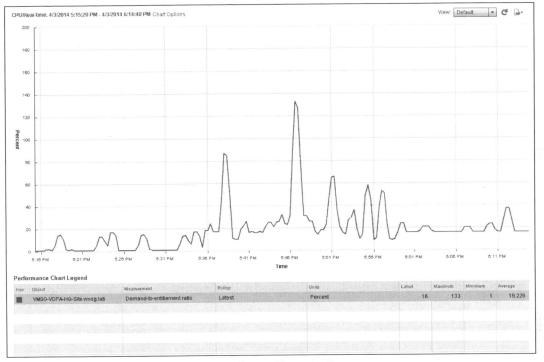

Demand-to-entitlement ratio

CPU **Idle** tracks the time the VM is not doing any work. The majority of VMs in test and development environments are likely to be idle most of the time.

CPU Wait includes **CPU Idle**, **Swap Wait**, and **CPU I/O Wait** states. Because it includes **Idle** time, it can be confusing initially. **CPU Swap Wait** tracks the time an ESXi world (this normally means a VM) is waiting for the VMkernel to swap memory. The value of **CPU Wait**, **CPU Idle**, and **Swap Wait** indicates there is an I/O bound. It means that the VM is being blocked, waiting for an I/O operation. This is shown in vRealize Operations with the **CPU I/O Wait** metric. If your VM does not experience an I/O issue, then **CPU Wait** and **CPU Idle** will be nearly identical. The following screenshot shows such a scenario. This is a VDPA VM with 4 vCPUs. As a backup appliance, it does perform some I/O, but the hypervisor is serving it well.

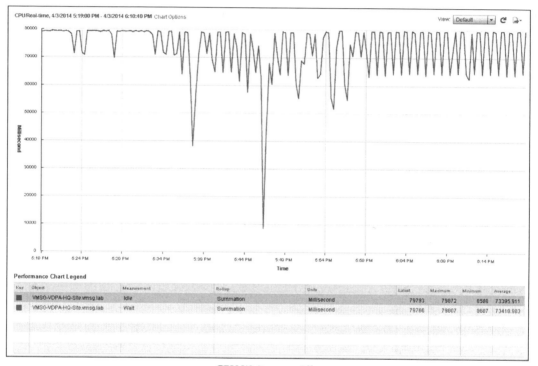

CPU Wait versus Idle

Let's look at another example. This is a 2 vCPU VM, so we expect the total to not exceed 40,000 milliseconds. Again, the values of **Idle** and **Wait** are very similar, indicating I/O is not a bottleneck. This particular VM is a vCenter Appliance 5.5 Update 1.

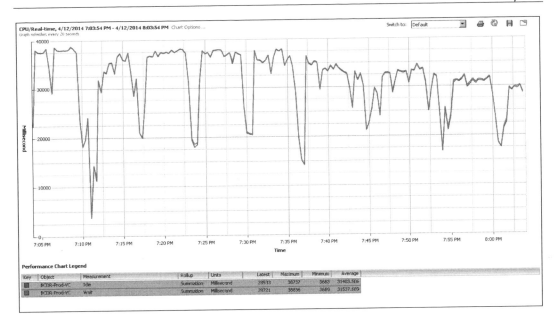

In a healthy environment, the value of **Swap Wait** should be zero. This counter tracks the CPU time spent waiting for memory to be swapped in from disk to DIMM. This counter is actually being used by vRealize Operations to derive the memory **Contention (%)** counter.

Certain counters such as **Max Limited** should always be zero, because you do not want to artificially place a **Limit**. With vRealize Operations, you can create a super metric that tracks the maximum value of **Max Limited** across all VMs in your entire data center. You should end up with a perfectly flat chart as the value for every VM should be zero all the time. You can then create an alert if the value is not zero, which informs you that someone has placed a **Limit** on a VM.

VM CPU key counters

We talked about contention and utilization being the main areas that you check. The following table summarizes the recommendation on what to monitor at a core level or at an overall level (VM level in this case). Notice that vRealize Operations provides the **Ready** counter in percentage at the core level, which is easier to interpret than millisecond.

The following table shows the VM CPU and virtual core level counters:

Purpose	vCenter	vRealize Operations
Contention	Ready (ms) Co-stop (ms) Latency does not exist at the core level	Ready (%) Co-stop (ms) There is no **Contention** counter at the core level
Utilization	Used (ms)	Used (ms) There is no **Demand** counter at the core level

The following table shows the VM CPU and VM level counters:

Purpose	vCenter	vRealize Operations
Contention	Limit (ms) if applicable Latency (%)	Contention (%)
Utilization	Usage (%)	Workload (%)

CPU counters at the ESXi level

The counters at the ESXi level are naturally similar to the ones at the VM level, as the hypervisor is also an OS. The key difference is that there are counters that are not applicable to ESXi hosts, such as **Entitlement**, **Max Limited**, and **System**. The values at the hypervisor level reflect the aggregate value of all VMs in the host plus the hypervisor's own workload. The hypervisor generates its own workload; for example, vMotion, cloning, and other tasks. Kernel modules such as Virtual SAN also take up CPU resources.

Unlike VMs, which have 16 counters for CPU, ESXi comes with 14 counters for CPU. Also, unlike VM, which provides 11 counters at CPU core level, ESXi only provides 5 counters at CPU core level. The remaining 9 counters that are not available at the core level are as follows:

- **Usage in MHz**
- **Total capacity**
- **Wait**
- **Demand**
- **Ready**
- **Reserved capacity**

- **Latency**
- **Swap Wait**
- **Co-stop**

This means you will not be able to track contention at the physical core level by looking at the ESXi host metrics, as all the three counters (**Ready**, **Latency**, and **Co-stop**) are not available. **Reserved Capacity** and **Total Capacity** are obviously not applicable at the physical core level. You cannot use **Demand** and **Usage in MHz**; you have to use CPU **Used (ms)** or **Usage (%)**.

At the physical core level, you have 1 counter to track the **Wait** and four counters to track usage (**Core Utilization**, **Utilization**, **Usage**, and **Used**).

If you recall, at the VM level, you cannot use **Usage (%)** to track individual virtual CPU core, but you can use **Usage in MHz**. The opposite happens for ESXi. At the ESXi level, you cannot use **Usage in MHz** to track individual physical CPU core, but you can use **Usage (%)**.

Description	Rollup	Units	Internal Name	Collection Level
☐ Idle	Summation	Millisecond	idle	2
☐ Usage in MHz	Average	MHz	usagemhz	1
☐ Total capacity	Average	MHz	totalCapacity	2
☐ Core Utilization	Average	Percent	coreUtilization	2
☐ Utilization	Average	Percent	utilization	2
☐ Wait	Summation	Millisecond	wait	3
☐ Usage	Average	Percent	usage	1
☐ Demand	Average	MHz	demand	2
☐ Ready	Summation	Millisecond	ready	1
☐ Used	Summation	Millisecond	used	3
☐ Reserved capacity	Average	MHz	reservedCapacity	2
☐ Latency	Average	Percent	latency	2
☐ Swap wait	Summation	Millisecond	swapwait	3
☐ Co-stop	Summation	Millisecond	costop	2

ESXi – CPU counters

Contention counters

As usual, we will focus on contention first, then utilization. As you would expect, there is no counter for contention in vCenter. Again, similar to the situation for VMs, you need to look at **Ready**, **Latency**, and **Co-stop**. These three counters are shown in the next screenshot. The **Ready** value looks healthy in this example. Notice that it was hovering around 200 milliseconds. As the graph refreshes every 20 seconds, each data point represents 20,000 ms per virtual core.

The graph does not show the number of virtual cores (a VM with 2 vCPUs has 2 virtual cores). Even if there is only 1 VM on the host, and that VM only has 1 vCPU, the 200 milliseconds translates to 1 percent, which is a healthy value. The value drops to near zero when the ESXi host has some activity. The action performed resulting in this graph was executing vMotion for a number of VMs concurrently. When the ESXi has more VMs, it settles for a higher **CPU Ready** level, hovering around 600. This is because I have moved VMs after the mass vMotion operation, and each VM does have **Ready** time. The aggregate is reflected here. It is interesting to see that the **Latency** counter spikes twice, and it spikes to 100 percent! Perhaps work was done on a different physical core, which means **Latency** would go up. Notice that each spike lasted for 20 seconds, so will not show up in vRealize Operations, as each data point is of 5 minutes. During the entire 1-hour period, the **Co-stop** counter barely moved. It only moved once and only reached the value of 16 out of a maximum of 20,000.

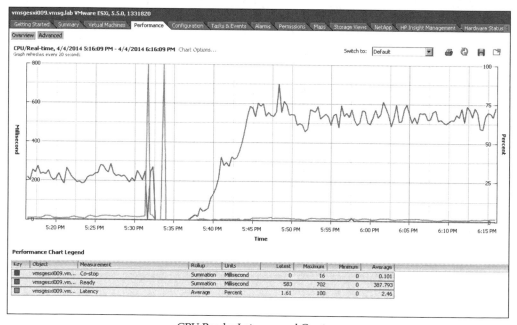

CPU Ready, Latency, and Co-stop

Tracking multiple counters with different units is certainly complex. That is why I prefer to track the **CPU Contention** counter, available in vRealize Operations. **CPU Contention** at ESXi level is the sum of all its VM **CPU Contention (in ms)** divided by 20,000 milliseconds times the number of running VMs' vCPUs. Continuing with the same scenario, the equivalent chart for vRealize Operations is shown next. This is a longer timeline, so we can see the relationship between **Ready** and **Contention** and how those metrics relate to **CPU Demand**. There is a correlation between **CPU Demand** and **CPU Contention**. Similar to what we have observed for VMs, **CPU Contention** is more sensitive than **CPU Ready** on an ESXi host.

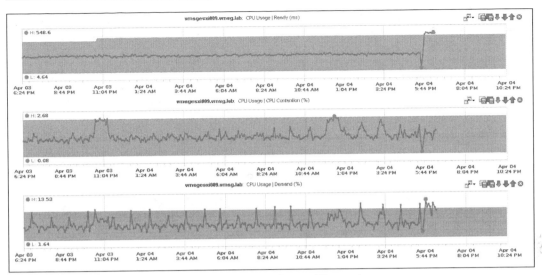

CPU Ready, Contention, and Demand

Here is another example that shows the sensitivity of **CPU Contention**. Notice that it hovers around 10 percent for more than 24 hours. The following chart spans from March 16, 3:00 a.m. to March 18, 12:00 a.m. The **CPU Contention** also correlates with **CPU Demand**, and **CPU Ready** barely moves during the entire period.

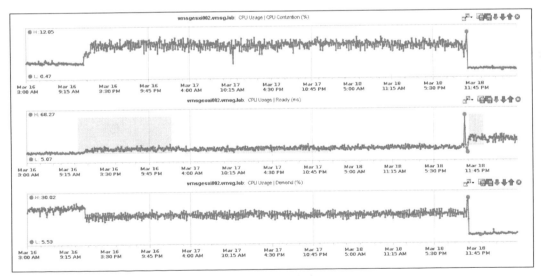

CPU Contention

Can **CPU Ready** go up while **CPU Contention** remains the same? Yes, it can. The following chart is from the same ESXi host, with the view zoomed in to a later time. In this chart, **CPU Ready** goes up a little to 567 milliseconds. **CPU Contention**, however, does not react to it. In fact, the value drops a little. This happens when you have a lot of idle VMs in the ESXi host. Each idle VM has **Ready** time and the aggregate is reflected in the ESXi host. Since they are idle, there is no contention. This is yet another reason why I prefer to use **CPU Contention** over **CPU Ready**.

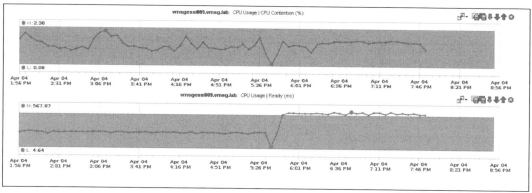

CPU Contention versus Ready

From my experience, **CPU Contention** provides a more reliable value than **CPU Ready**. The following screenshot spans 30 days, which is long enough for a comparison. Notice that **CPU Ready** spikes to a very high number around March 14, yet it does not move at all during a longer period of contention around March 31.

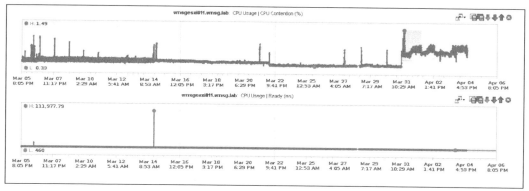

CPU Ready spike – example 1

Here is another example where **CPU Ready** shoots to a high value, whereas **CPU Contention** remains constant. It is interesting to note that both ESXi hosts spike at the same time. They are managed by different vCenter Servers. In addition, the lab has 11 ESXi and the other 9 do not show any spike at all in the same time period.

The 2 ESXi hosts shown in the following screenshot are the only two hosts in a cluster. Notice that both generally have the same value, with the exception of the spike. The spike lasts 10 minutes, as I saw two values when I zoomed in to the chart.

Notice that **CPU Usage (%)** shows no spike. There is also no contention. We do not expect spike in **Contention** in general as the labs consist of small VMs and they are mostly idle.

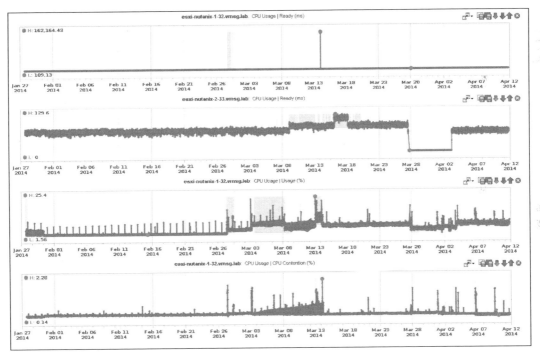

CPU Ready spike – example 2

Utilization counters

For utilization, the counters differ to those of VM. You still have **Usage (%)**, **Usage in MHz**, **Demand (MHz)**, and **Used (ms)**. But instead of **Run**, you have **Utilization (%)** and **Core Utilization (%)**.

Let's compare the values to study them. The following chart shows **Usage** versus **Demand**. Based on the chart we have seen at the VM level, we expect them to be similar but not identical in the real-time chart. This chart shows that we can rely on this assumption:

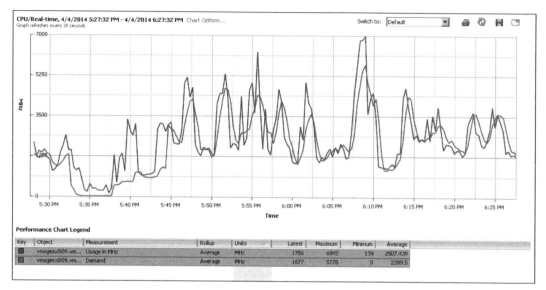

CPU Usage and Demand

We have also come to expect that although **Usage** and **Demand** in vRealize Operations will be on a different scale, their pattern will be identical when there is no contention. The following chart confirms that. As a side note, you can see the dynamic threshold in action in the following chart. vRealize Operations was not expecting a drop in the CPU utilization because it has been stable for days. The yellow area shows the period where the value is not within the range of vRealize Operations predictive analysis. The light gray area is the range that vRealize Operations expected the metrics to fall within. The value drops in this example because all the VMs were moved from this host using vMotion. That is certainly not a normal operation in production.

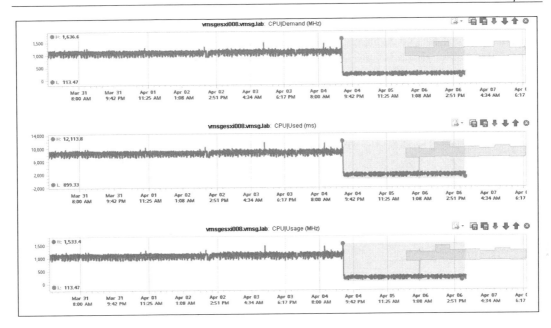

In an environment where there is contention, **CPU Demand** will be higher. The next example shows an ESXi that experienced a spike in demand and was unable to fulfill all the demands. During the period it was able to meet, the **CPU Demand** and **CPU Usage** counters are similar (it's hard to see due to the scale) and the **CPU Contention** counter was low. However, during that sharp spike, both **CPU Demand** and **CPU Contention** rise to reveal the issue. **CPU Usage** only rises to 57 percent. If you were using **CPU Usage** as an alert, you would not get an alert! This is why I do not recommend using **CPU Usage** in the environment.

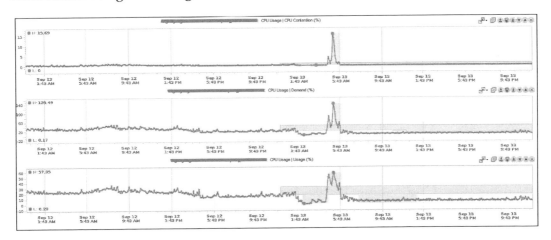

Just like in the case for VMs, vRealize Operations also provides the **Workload** (%) counter for the ESXi host. The next screenshot shows why I prefer **Workload** over **Demand**. The **Workload** chart is easier to read as the value is rounded.

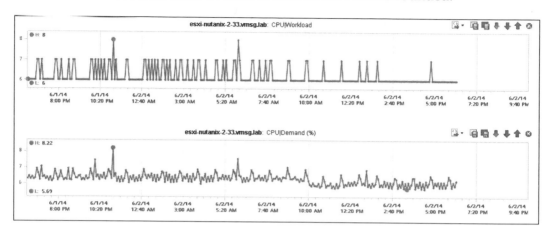

At individual core levels, vRealize Operations retains two metrics to track: **Usage (%)** and **Used (ms)**. The two values are identical as you can see from the following chart. If you take the peak value of **CPU Used** (which is 533.93) and divide it by 20,000, you get the peak value of **Usage** (which is 2.66).

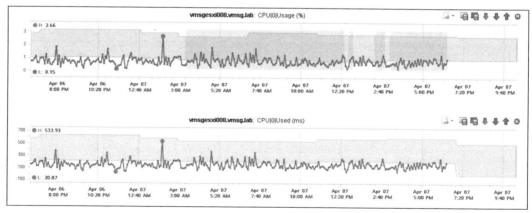

ESXi – CPU core level metrics

I mentioned previously that some counters in ESXi are the sum of the associated counters of all the VMs running in the host. **CPU Wait** is such an example. The next screenshot shows **CPU Wait** hovering around 220,000. The sharp drop to around 170,000 was caused by moving a VM off the host using vMotion. The remaining VMs on the host were then moved using vMotion, causing the counter to drop to zero.

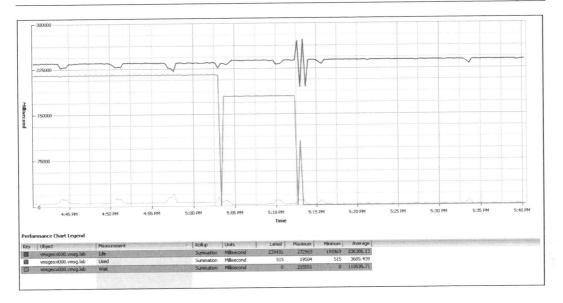

Key	Object	Measurement	Rollup	Units	Latest	Maximum	Minimum	Average
	vmsgesxi008.vmsg.lab	Idle	Summation	Millisecond	239491	272963	193363	236386.13
	vmsgesxi008.vmsg.lab	Used	Summation	Millisecond	515	19504	515	3605.439
	vmsgesxi008.vmsg.lab	Wait	Summation	Millisecond	0	215551	0	110595.71

Now, let's look at **Core Utilization** and **Utilization**. These counters are not available at the VM level. They are also not included in vRealize Operations by default. **Core Utilization** includes hyper-threading, as the value is twice higher. I verified with a few other ESXi (a different model and on a different cluster). The value of **Core Utilization** is higher than the value of **Utilization** and **Usage**, although it is not always double because it takes into account hyper-threading.

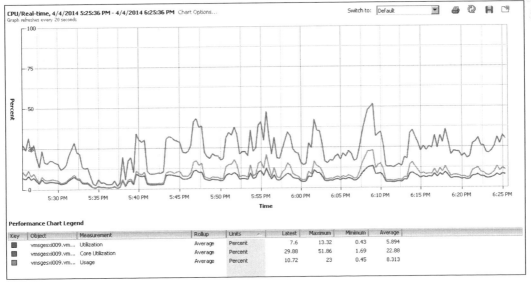

Key	Object	Measurement	Rollup	Units	Latest	Maximum	Minimum	Average
	vmsgesxi009.vm...	Utilization	Average	Percent	7.6	13.32	0.43	5.894
	vmsgesxi009.vm...	Core Utilization	Average	Percent	29.88	51.86	1.69	22.88
	vmsgesxi009.vm...	Usage	Average	Percent	10.72	23	0.45	8.313

ESXi – CPU Utilization and Usage

The preceding screenshot shows **Utilization** at the ESXi host level. Now let's look at a single core. The value of **Core Utilization** is double that of **Utilization**.

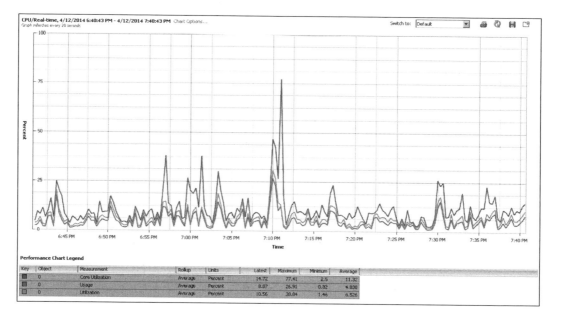

As we already have enough counters for utilization, I do not see a use case to use the **Core Utilization** and **Utilization** counters. Considering they are not included in vRealize Operations, I tend to think that they are considered a corner-case situation. For such troubleshooting, esxtop might be a better tool.

ESXi provides 2 capacity-related counters that are not available at the VM level:

- **Total capacity**: This is the sum of all the physical cores in MHz. It does not take into account hyper-threading. It does take into account CPU power management, as the value is around 11 percent to 18 percent — lower than the stated CPU frequency.

> I verified the value with three ESXi hosts. vRealize Operations provides a much more intuitive tool for capacity management. I also think that capacity management should be done at cluster level, and not at host level. As such, I do not see a use case for this counter. If you do, I'd appreciate your feedback.

- **Reserved capacity**: This counter tracks any reservation made for VM. In the example shown in the following chart, a reservation of 2,000 MHz is set for a VM.

If your cluster uses a lot of VM-level reservations, you can create a super metric that calculates the capacity left from a reservation point of view. You do this by using the following formula:

(Reserved Capacity / Total Capacity) * (100 percent)

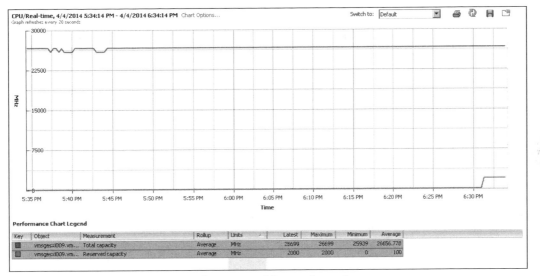

Total capacity and Reserved capacity

CPU Wait, **Swap Wait**, and **Idle** behave the same way in ESXi as they do for VMs. So, you should expect **Swap Wait** to be zero all the time during business as usual, indicating your ESXi is not accessing memory from the disk. None of these three counters are captured in vRealize Operations by default, where there are other counters that can tell us the same information. For example, there are storage and memory counters to indicate issues caused by storage or memory.

ESXi CPU key counters

We talked about **Contention** and **Utilization** being the main metrics to check. The following table summarizes what I recommend you monitor at core level or at an overall object level (host).

The following table shows the ESXi CPU core level counters:

Purpose	vCenter	vRealize Operations
Contention	None	None (as a result)
Utilization	Usage (%)	Usage (%)

The following table shows the ESXi-level CPU counters:

Purpose	vCenter	vRealize Operations
Contention	Ready (ms) Co-stop (ms) Latency (%)	Contention (%)
Utilization	Usage (%)	Workload (%)

CPU counters at the cluster level

vCenter only provides three CPU counters at cluster level (as shown in the next screenshot):

- CPU Usage (**MHz**)
- CPU Usage (**Percent**)
- Total (**MHz**)

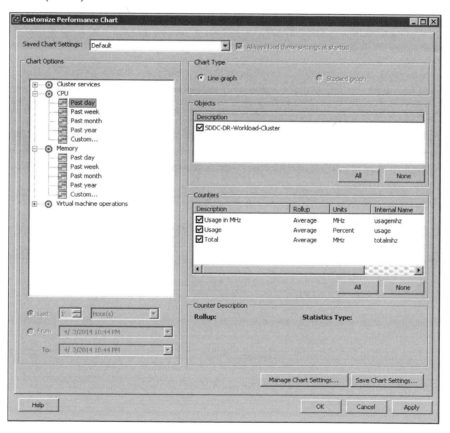

There is no storage or network metric group provided. Also, the data is not available in real time, meaning the data granularity is in intervals of 5 minutes, not 20 seconds.

Let us look at an example of the values of the 2 usage counters. I've excluded the **Total** metric in the next screenshot, as you would not be able to see the fluctuation in the **Usage in MHz** counter if I include it. The **Total** counter is a relatively static counter. It does not take into account **HA**. Changing the cluster setting does not impact this value. However, it does seem to take into account CPU power management. For example, I am getting a total value of 56 GHz whereas the actual total is 63 GHz. I check with a cluster with identical configuration (hardware and CPU power management) and the values differ slightly.

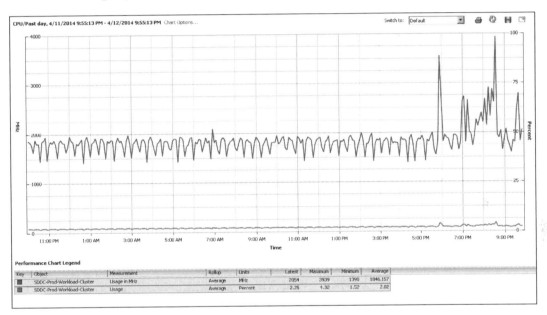

vRealize Operations provides a set of CPU counters at the cluster level. They are useful as performance and capacity management should be done at cluster level. The majority of the counters are an average or a sum of all host members. There are no peak counters. This makes sense, as DRS will balance your cluster. However, in situations where the overall cluster has low utilization, you can have an unbalanced distribution. This also makes sense, as balancing it does not necessarily result in improved performance. Having a peak counter in this case is useful, as the average will not tell the full story. As a result, I recommend that you track both **Average** and **Peak**. You should track both the contention and the utilization. This means that you are tracking four data points. Together, the four points should give you a good insight into CPU utilization for your environment. This table lists the key counters that give you these four data points.

The following table shows the vRealize Operations and cluster counters:

Purpose	Counters	Roll up	Description
Contention	Contention (%)	Average	Use super metric to get the peak.
Utilization	Workload (%)	Average	Use super metric to get the peak. This does not take into account HA. The workload will be higher if HA occurs.

CPU counters at higher levels

Higher level here means data center, vCenter, and World objects. Measuring at this level is useful in a large environment where you have many clusters. In a small environment with fewer than five clusters, it makes more sense to manage at cluster level.

By now, we know that vCenter provides very little information at these levels. It does not provide information about CPU, RAM, disk, or network. vRealize Operations provides a set of key counters, which are useful in overall management. For example, the following 2 counters quickly tell us the state of CPU demand and contention for the entire infrastructure managed by a vCenter:

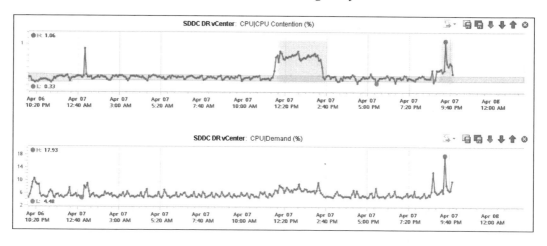

When looking at an object higher than the cluster level, there is no more automatic load balancing. If you have 10 clusters in a single vCenter data center, and the workload is not balanced among the 10 clusters, vSphere will not load balance for you. As a result, it makes more sense to capture peak by taking the highest value from the members of the group. In this example, the cluster with the highest peak will determine the peak value.

We call this *Approach 1* and it was covered in the *When is a peak not a true peak?* section of *Chapter 3, Mastering the Key Counters in SDDC*. Capturing peak by taking the highest value of the data center utilization in a given time period will give a lower value, as the data center utilization is the average of all clusters. We call this *Approach 2* and it was covered earlier. You then complement the peak counter with the average counter. These two counters will serve as your upper and lower threshold in your performance or capacity management. Plot them in a single line chart so you can see the trends. If there is a big gap, that means you have unbalanced deployment. Some clusters are busier than others. You should expect your tier 1 clusters to have lower utilization than your tier 3 clusters.

Because there are three levels above clusters, you need to decide which method of determining the peak makes sense for your environment. How you roll up the peak information will impact the results. You do not have to worry about how you roll up the average information, as vRealize Operations does it for you already. An average of a large group tends to be low, so you need to complement it with the peak.

Let's use an example to make it clearer. Imagine you manage a global environment spread over three continents. You have 10 vCenter Servers managing 6 global data centers and 100 remote branches. There are a total of 100,000 VMs in 5,000 hosts in 500 clusters. If you only use *Approach 1* for all the three levels, you will have a single host giving you the peak of all of your 5,000 hosts. This will be misleading. On the other hand, if you only use *Approach 2* for all the three levels, you will flatten the peak and you will end up with a number that is close to your average (which is already given by vRealize Operations out of the box). So you need to apply some combination. For example, at the World level, the peak could be the peak from a single vCenter (*Approach 1*). At the vCenter level, the peak could be the peak at a certain time (*Approach 2*).

This table lists the key counters you should be using at these levels. Notice how vRealize Operations has provided you with a consistent set of metrics. Nice!

The following table shows the vRealize Operations and cluster counters:

Object	Purpose	Counters	Roll up
Data center	Contention	Contention (%)	Average
Data center	Utilization	Workload (%)	Average
vCenter	Contention	Contention (%)	Average
vCenter	Utilization	Workload (%)	Average
World	Contention	Contention (%)	Average
World	Utilization	Workload (%)	Average

CPU contention guidance

I emphasized throughout this book that the first thing we look at is contention, and not utilization. So I thought I would provide guidance on the value you should set for a contention SLA. This is not an official guidance from VMware, but a recommendation from my own experience. The actual numbers you set may not be the same as mine. You should choose numbers that you are comfortable with, and have been agreed upon by your customers (application team or business units). Not having a defined SLA can result in miscommunication with your customers or management, especially when performance impacts the business. If you do not have a number, the expectation will be by default set to the same as physical.

Once you set your SLA for contention, you should also monitor it. You might need to adjust it based on your specific environment. You should have two numbers. One is the SLA your customers agree on. The other is an internal number for your own proactive monitoring. The second number is naturally lower. For example, you may set 10 percent as the official SLA and 6 percent as the internal threshold for you to start proactive adjustment. The delta is a buffer you have for proactive troubleshooting.

I use three tiers of SLAs as I think the values should differ for a different class of service. Having just a single tier means both mission-critical VM and development VM are getting the same class of service sacrificing either the performance of mission-critical VMs or the cost of the overall solution. On the other hand, having too many tiers adds operational complexity and hence increases cost.

The following table shows my definition of the three tiers—your organization may have different service tiers:

Tier	Purpose	Compute	Storage
1 (highest)	Production	No oversubscription. As a result, there is no need for reservation.	10 VMs per datastore. 10 ms latency.
2	Production Nonproduction	2 times oversubscription for CPU and 1.5 times for RAM. An ESXi host with 24 cores, 48 threads, and 128 GB RAM may run 48 vCPUs and 192 GB vRAM. I use lower oversubscription for RAM as I am assuming the applications use large pages.	20 VMs per datastore. 20 ms latency.

Tier	Purpose	Compute	Storage
3 (lowest)	Nonproduction	3 times oversubscription for CPU and 2 times for RAM. Expect to see contention during peak usage.	30 VMs per datastore. 30 ms latency.

Based on the preceding three tiers, here are the values I would choose for CPU:

Object	Contention	Remarks
VM	Official SLA: • Tier 1: 1 percent • Tier 2: 3 percent • Tier 3: 13 percent Internal threshold: • Tier 1: 1 percent • Tier 2: 2 percent • Tier 3: 10 percent	The number increases drastically from tier 2 to tier 3 as the CPU power management setting is different. I use maximum performance for tier 1 and tier 2, and balance for tier 3. CPU contention cannot be 0 percent as CPU Ready is rarely zero milliseconds. The number is higher for VM compared with cluster as cluster is an average of many VMs. If the cluster in general is performing well, then you would expect the overall contention to be lower at cluster level.

Your customers only care about their own VMs, hence the following numbers are a recommendation for the internal target to complement the agreed SLA. You should have a more stringent threshold internally. This gives you a buffer for troubleshooting.

Object	Contention	Remarks
ESXi	NA	There is no need to track it at ESXi host level due to DRS and vMotion.
Cluster	Internal threshold: • Tier 1: 1 percent • Tier 2: 2 percent • Tier 3: 10 percent	If your cluster contains mixed tiers, you need to take an estimate based on the ratio of tiers in the cluster. Use the total vCPU as a comparison, and not simply based on the number of VMs. This is because large VMs result in higher contention.

Object	Contention	Remarks
Data center	NA	There is no need to track it at this level as data center normally consists of clusters of different service tiers.
		If you have a large environment where there are many clusters, you can create a group that groups each cluster based on their tiers. You can then create a super metric that tracks the average or peak of these clusters. You might need to do both, as average can give a number that is too low (it is an average of a lot of clusters), and peak can be on the high side. It is the number in the middle that you want to track.

Summary

In this chapter, we discussed CPU counters in both vCenter and vRealize Operations. We covered what they mean and what values you should expect for a healthy environment. The relationship between metrics was also explained. We tried to provide screenshots to make the learning easier and add real-world examples.

At the end of the chapter, I provided my personal recommendation on what you should set for each service tier.

Let's now take a journey down memory lane in the next chapter (pun intended).

5
Memory Counters

We have covered CPU in depth in the previous chapter. Let's now take a trip down memory lane. We will take the same approach we did with CPU. The following topics will be covered in the chapter:

- VM memory counters
- ESXi memory counters
- Cluster memory counters
- Memory counters at higher level objects
- Memory contention guidance

Memory – not such a simple matter

Memory differs from CPU as it is a form of storage. Unlike CPU, which executes instructions as they enter the CPU, memory keeps information for a much longer period of time. We are comparing nanoseconds to seconds (or longer, up to months, depending upon the uptime of your VM). Information is stored in memory in standard block sizes, typically 4 KB or 2 MB. Each block is called a **page**. At the lowest level, the memory pages are just a series of zeroes and ones.

Keeping this concept in mind is useful as you review the memory counters. Memory has a very different nature compared to CPU, and the storage nature of memory is the reason why memory monitoring is more challenging than CPU monitoring.

Before you proceed with this section, you need to be familiar with vSphere memory management. The whitepaper at `https://www.vmware.com/resources/techresources/10206` provides a good explanation. It is based on vSphere 5.0, but is still relevant in vSphere 5.5. The only difference is the introduction of reliable memory technology in vSphere 5.5, which does not consume a lot of RAM because it is only for the VMkernel. Many useful things about monitoring are shared in the paper, especially the fact that the hypervisor does not have direct visibility inside the Guest OS. When a Guest OS frees up a memory page, it normally just updates its list of free memory, it does not release it. This list is not exposed to the hypervisor, and so the physical page remains claimed by the VM. This is why the **Consumed** counter in vCenter remains high when the **Active** counter has long dropped. Because the hypervisor has no visibility inside the Guest OS, you may need to deploy an agent to get visibility into your application. You should monitor both at the Guest OS level (for example, Windows and RedHat) and at the application level (for example, MS SQL Server and Oracle). Check if there is excessive paging or the Guest OS experiences a hard page fault. For Windows, you can use tools such as pfmon, a page fault monitor.

Pfmon is not to be confused with perfmon. See the KB article *Excessive Page Faults Generated By Windows Applications May Impact the Performance of Virtual Machines (1687)* at `http://kb.vmware.com/kb/1687`.

It is acceptable for an application to release memory that it does not use, and a well-behaved application will listen to the requests of the Guest OS to release inactive pages. It is advisable to discuss the performance impact of releasing unused memory with the application architect.

Another reason for deploying an agent is the **Active** counter itself. The vSphere manual says that it tracks the amount of memory that is actively used, as estimated by VMkernel based on recently-touched memory pages. In summary, the ESXi host periodically checks a sample of all the consumed pages of the VM and determines the **Active** counter's percentage. ESXi will assume that the sample is representative and derive the **Active** value for the VM as a whole. As a result, using **Active** in isolation can lead to sizing that is too aggressive.

This is covered in more detail by Mark Achtemichuk at `http://blogs.vmware.com/vsphere/2013/10/understanding-vsphere-active-memory.html`.

There are certainly situations where you cannot deploy an agent. For example, in a large environment, it is common that the infrastructure team does not even have read access to the Guest OS, let alone permission to install an agent. You do not know what is running inside the Guest OS, and yet you get a call if there is an issue. In this situation, you can get some visibility if you put the page file into a virtual disk by itself. The entire **vmdk** only contains the swap partition with no temporary directory or other purpose. You can then use the virtual disk I/O counters to track swap activity, as memory read/write becomes disk read/write.

You should also check out the following sections in the VMware vSphere Documentation Center:

- Memory Virtualization Basics
- Administering Memory Resources

I have shown the first one in the following screenshot:

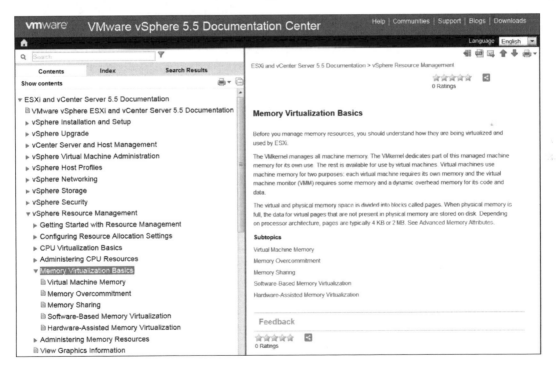

As of late 2014, 256 GB of RAM on a 2-socket ESXi host is becoming more common. Assuming 10 GB is being used by the hypervisor and hypervisor-based services (antivirus, firewall, load balancer, distributed router, and Virtual SAN), that still leaves plenty of RAM for around 20-40 VMs per host (depending upon the size of the VMs). 40 VMs per host is probably the upper limit you want to place for server VMs before concentration risk becomes a real issue that you will need to answer to your customer. In tier 1, the number of VMs per host is likely a lot lower. For VDI, the number can be higher because each desktop VM is likely configured with just 4 GB vRAM and they have many common pages.

Memory counters at the VM level

vCenter 5.5 provides 28 counters for RAM to track the various features of ESXi memory management. Compared with physical servers, where you normally just monitor the memory utilization and swapping, these are a lot counters. I have shown all the counters in the next screenshot. With 28 counters per VM, a vSphere environment with 1,000 VMs will have 28,000 counters just for VM RAM! It is certainly too many to be monitored as part of overall management. I will share, in the later part of this chapter, the three key counters you need to track to manage performance and capacity.

Description	Rollup	Units	Internal Name	Collection Level
☐ Memory saved by zipping	Latest	Kilobytes	zipSaved	2
☐ Decompression rate	Average	KBps	decompressionRate	2
☐ Swapped	Average	Kilobytes	swapped	2
☐ Overhead touched	Average	Kilobytes	overheadTouched	4
☑ Balloon	Average	Kilobytes	vmmemctl	1
☑ Active	Average	Kilobytes	active	2
☐ Shared	Average	Kilobytes	shared	2
☐ Entitlement	Average	Kilobytes	entitlement	2
☐ Host cache used for swapping	Average	Kilobytes	llSwapUsed	4
☐ Active write	Average	Kilobytes	activewrite	2
☐ Reserved overhead	Average	Kilobytes	overheadMax	2
☐ Zipped memory	Latest	Kilobytes	zipped	2
☐ Swap out	Average	Kilobytes	swapout	2
☐ Compressed	Average	Kilobytes	compressed	2
☐ Balloon target	Average	Kilobytes	vmmemctltarget	2
☐ Latency	Average	Percent	latency	2
☐ Swap in rate	Average	KBps	swapinRate	1
☐ Swap in rate from host cache	Average	KBps	llSwapInRate	2
☐ Overhead	Average	Kilobytes	overhead	1
☑ Consumed	Average	Kilobytes	consumed	1
☐ Zero	Average	Kilobytes	zero	2
☐ Swap in	Average	Kilobytes	swapin	2
☐ Compression rate	Average	KBps	compressionRate	2
☐ Swap target	Average	Kilobytes	swaptarget	2
☐ Swap out rate to host cache	Average	KBps	llSwapOutRate	2
☐ Swap out rate	Average	KBps	swapoutRate	1
☑ Granted	Average	Kilobytes	granted	2
☐ Usage	Average	Percent	usage	1

VM – RAM counters

At the ESXi level, vCenter provides 33 counters. As you can expect, some of the counters at the ESXi level are essentially the sum of associated counters of all VMs running in the host, plus VMkernel's own memory counters (since it also consumes memory). This aggregation is useful as VMs do move around within the cluster. Since there are a lot of counters, let's compare the differences first.

The following counters are unique to VM monitoring and they do not exist at the ESXi level:

- **Entitlement**: This makes sense, since entitlement is a property of a VM.

- **Overhead touched**.

- **Reserved overhead**.

- **Zipped memory**.

- **Memory saved by zipping (KB)**: The compression ratio is either 2x or 4x, so this counter tracks the total memory saved. With the availability of other counters, I have yet to find a use case for it. If you find a use case for this counter, let me know.

- **Balloon target**: If you see nonzero value in this counter, it means that the hypervisor has asked this VM to give back memory via the VM balloon driver. This does not necessarily indicate reduction of performance, as it depends upon whether the memory page released by the balloon driver is a free one or not. If it is from the free memory, then the Guest OS does not need to do page out to meet the request of its balloon driver. If it is not, then the Guest OS will page out and this can impact performance. Page out happens when the Guest OS is running high on memory. This means that it is acceptable to see some ballooning so long as both the **Consumed** and **Active** counters are low.

- **Swap target**: This is different from ballooning, as the hypervisor has no knowledge of free memory inside the Guest OS. It is important to note that this is a target, meaning it may not be achieved. The hypervisor is clever enough to do compression instead, if it can compress at least 2x (meaning the 4 KB block becomes less than 2 KB). If it cannot, logically the choice is to swap out. As a result, any value in this counter indicates that the host is unable to satisfy the VM memory requirement. Use vMotion on one or more VMs out of the host until the **Swap target** counter hits zero.

You may notice that there is no **Compression target**. We have **Balloon target** and **Swap target,** so we should expect **Compression target** too. Because both swap and compression work together to meet the **Swap target** counter, I think the counter should be called **Compression or Swap target**.

We looked at counters that do not exist on ESXi. Let's now look at counters that exist so that you can make a comparison. The following counters exist in ESXi but do not exist at the VM level:

- **Used by VMkernel**

  This is obviously not applicable to a VM. With ESXi nowadays sporting more than 128 GB of RAM, the memory consumed by the hypervisor is very small compared to the total RAM.

- **Heap**
- **State**
- **Low free threshold**
- **Reserved capacity**
- **Unreserved**
- **Total capacity**
- **Swap in from host cache**
- **Swap out from host cache**
- **Shared common**

Before we dive into the details of key counters, let's quickly cover what is not available. There is no counter for large pages. This means that you cannot tell whether a VM memory is being backed by large pages or not. At the ESXi level, you cannot tell how many gigabytes of the RAM is made up of large pages. A topic on large pages merits a discussion by itself, as there are many levels to check (ESXi, Guest OS, and application) and factors to consider (performance, cost, and manageability). Personally, I'd enable large page in use cases where performance matters the most (that is, in clusters where there will be no oversubscription) and disable it where cost matters the most (that is, where you want to have heavy oversubscription).

There is also another useful counter that is missing. It exists for CPU but it does not exist in RAM. Go back and look at the list. Can you spot it?

That counter is **Demand**. We will talk about it when we cover **Utilization**. Right now, we need to cover **Contention**. We will use the same approach we used in CPU counter, which is starting with contention, followed by utilization, and ending with other counters.

Contention counters

As expected, vCenter Server does not provide a counter for memory contention. You can certainly check for signs of contention, such as the existence of balloon, swapped, or compressed memory. A nonzero value in any of these counters indicates ESXi had or has memory pressure and it may impact this VM. I use the word *may* because it does not always mean that the VM performance is affected. If the page being swapped out is a free page and the VM does not use it, then there is no performance hit. The performance issue happens when the Guest OS wants to access that page, because the hypervisor has to bring the page back to the physical DIMM first. Certainly the higher the value for balloon, swapped, and compressed, the higher the chance of a performance hit happening in the future if the data is requested later. The severity of the impact depends on the VM memory shares, reservation, and limit. It also depends upon the size of the VM configured RAM. A 10 MB ballooned will have more impact on a 0.5 GB RAM VM than on a 128 GB RAM VM.

It is also possible to have balloon showing zero value while compressed or swapped are showing nonzero values—even though in the order of ESXi memory reclamation techniques, ballooning occurs before compression. This indicates that the VM did have memory pressure in the past that caused ballooning, compression, and swapping then, but it no longer has the memory pressure. Data that was compressed or swapped out is not retrieved unless requested, because doing so takes CPU cycle. The balloon driver, on the other hand, will be proactively deflated when memory pressure is relieved.

Without an SSD as a cache, swapped memory would mean severe memory performance degradation. If your use case requires high ESXi memory utilization and regular swapping is likely, then you should consider implementing SSDs as a cache. For a VM, retrieving swapped pages from a host-side SSD is much faster than from a spinning disk.

 I recommend you check out the write up by Duncan Epping at http://www.yellow-bricks.com/2011/08/18/swap-to-host-cache-aka-swap-to-ssd/.

Once you enable the host cache, you should also track the **Host cache used for swapping**, **Swap out rate to host cache**, and **Swap in rate to host cache** counters.

There is also a counter called **Latency (%)** that tracks the percentage of time for which the VM is waiting as it is accessing swapped memory or compressed memory.

 Latency does not include balloon. The hypervisor is not aware of the Guest OS internal activity.

This is certainly useful. Just because a VM has a portion of its memory compressed does not mean that it is accessing that compressed memory. Therefore, it is acceptable to see **Balloon** or **Compressed** or **Swap** as long as **Latency** is 0.

You should also check **Entitlement** and make sure it is not capping the **Demand** value or the **Consumed** value. It is possible for a VM to not have its memory swapped, compressed, or ballooned, but still not get what it demands. Check if there are reservations on other VMs and limits on this VM. This is why I recommend you do not set these two counters (**Reservation** and **Limit**) and use **Share** instead. With vRealize Operations, you can create a super metric that tracks **Entitlement/Demand** or **Entitlement/Consumed**. You need to use the **This Resource** icon, so the formula is applied to the VM itself. You expect a value of 1 or higher. A value between 0 and 1 means **Demand** is greater than **Entitlement**, which is not what you want. In a healthy environment, all your VMs will give you a value greater than 1. You can create a **Heat Map** that shows all VMs. If you choose a range between 0.8 and 1.0, where 0.8 is red and 1.0 is green, then a small percentage of contention will result in color change, making it visible. For a **Test/Dev** cluster where you deliberately drive for a higher utilization, adjust the range beyond 1.

As you can tell from the preceding part, it is difficult to check contention as there are many counters and factors to consider. This is where the **Contention (%)** metric in vRealize Operations is useful. It is actually derived from the CPU **Swap Wait (ms)** counter, as shown in the next screenshot. The following VM has 4 vCPUs. If you divide 16,539 by 4, you will get 4,134. Then 4,134 ms over 20,000 ms is 20.67 percent.

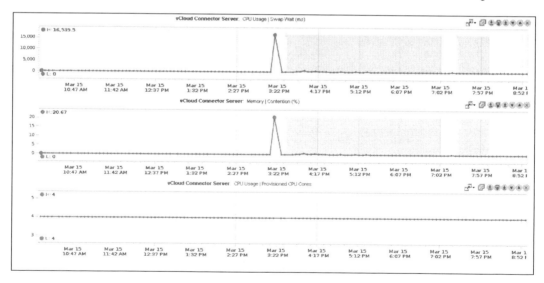

Let's look at another example of **Memory Contention (%)** in action. This time, there are no VMware tools in the VM (the balloon driver relies on VM tools being installed). The VM experienced both **Swapped** and **Compression**. About 33 MB was swapped and 24 MB was zipped, which are low amounts of contention as the VM has 6 GB of RAM. The **Contention (%)** went up to around 0.2 percent, reflecting the low amount of contention. The counter then dropped even though the swapped and zipped counters remained where they were. Can you figure out why **Contention** dropped? The answer is **CPU Swap Wait**. The **CPU Swap Wait** went down, because the VM did not access those pages anymore.

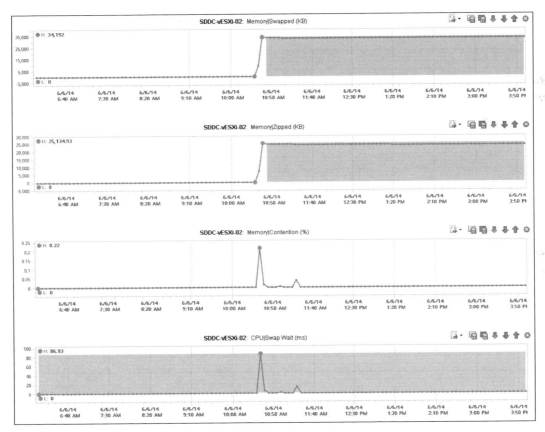

Utilization counters

For utilization, vCenter provides **Active (KB)**, **Active Write (KB)**, **Consumed (KB)**, **Granted (KB)**, and **Usage (%)**. Because you will have VMs with different vRAM sizes, it is easier to use the **Usage (%)** counter.

Pay special attention to the **Usage** counter. It has different formulas depending upon the object. For VM, it is mapped to **Active**. For ESXi, it is mapped to **Consumed**. For cluster, it is mapped to **Consumed** and **Memory overhead**. The effect of this formula is that you will see ESXi **Usage** as much higher than your VM **Usage**. For example, if all the VMs have the same size of RAM and their usage is about the same, you will notice your ESXi **Usage** is higher than the VM. Technically speaking, mapping **Usage** to **Active** for VM and **Consumed** for ESXi makes sense, due to the two-level memory hierarchy in virtualization. Operationally, this can create some confusion, as it is not a consistent mapping. At the VM level we use **Active** as it shows what the VM is actually consuming (related to performance). At host and cluster level, we use **Consumed** because it is related to what the Guest OS has claimed (related to capacity management).

The blog post by Mark Achtemichuk shared earlier explains that using **Active (KB)** alone will normally result in aggressive sizing. For an application that manages its own memory (for example, JVM and database), this can result in poor performance for the application. These applications have their own set of working memory and the Guest OS does not understand it. Doing ballooning in this situation may result in a hard page fault as far as the application is concerned, because the Guest OS does not know how the application uses memory. In some situations, it might be better for the application to be given less memory to begin with. You should use **Consumed (KB)** as a guide for such applications. Because it is application dependent, you should consider deploying vRealize Infrastructure Navigator, which is a component of vRealize Operations, because it can tell you if you have database and Java application servers.

Does this mean we can just give a VM whatever resources the VM owner asks? That is not a wise policy. From experience, we know that applications tend to be oversized if we do not apply a sanity check. This is a common practice for physical servers, as the server comes with a standard RAM configuration. We also know that there are cases where applications simply ask for memory and then never use it again. Oversizing, as you probably have experienced first-hand, can lead to poorer performance. It also takes longer to boot and to use vMotion for a larger VM—more does not always mean better when the underlying platform is virtualized.

There is a need to **right-size**. That requires both the application developer and infrastructure engineer to discuss and agree upon the sizing together. However, this is not always possible: in a global organization with thousands of VMs, it may not be practical. This is why in vRealize Operations, there is a derived counter called **Demand**. It uses **Active** as a starting point. The **Demand** counter takes into account that an OS needs a minimum amount of RAM to function properly. The range is typically 64 MB to 512 MB, depending upon the size of configured RAM and active memory. It also takes into account memory contention.

The worse the contention, the higher the **Demand** counter becomes. This is why it is possible to see **Demand** go up when **Active** does not, signaling memory contention. In an environment where there is no contention, you should see a similar pattern between **Demand** and **Active**, with **Demand** being up to 512 MB higher. The following screenshot shows the two counters have an identical pattern, with **Demand** being approximately 350 MB higher.

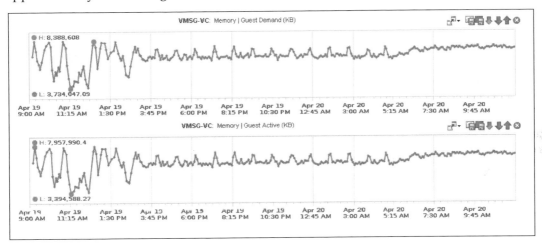

In an environment where there is little memory contention, you will see a pattern like the one shown in the preceding screenshot. Without checking the **Consumed** and **Configured** counters, you cannot tell if **Demand** is high enough. This is because the **Demand** metric is not shown as a percentage. This is where **Workload (%)** comes in. Because it is a percentage, you can also make a relative comparison among VMs.

The **Demand (KB)** counter, because the unit is an absolute amount (instead of a percentage), can be useful when combined with the use of a dynamic group. Let's say your environment has a lot of large VMs mixing with many small VMs in the same cluster. In this situation, you want to know the impact that these large VMs have in your cluster. For that, you need to know if they are using the memory given to them, as large VMs tend to be over-configured. A VM may be configured with 64 GB of RAM, but does it actually use that much RAM? You can create a dynamic group in vRealize Operations whose members are VMs with more than 16 GB of vRAM. Then create a super metric which is applied to that dynamic group and tracks the maximum value of **Demand (KB)** memory. You divide the number by *1,024 * 1,024* to get the value in terms of GB. If the super metric shows a small number most of the time, then you know that these large VMs are over-configured and not really impacting your cluster. If the super metric shows a large number, then you need to check for signs of contention in your cluster, hosts, and VMs.

Other counters

The **Shared memory** counter is not applicable at the VM level, as each VM believes it is alone with the underlying physical resources to match its configured size. The **Shared memory** counter is naturally read only, as a write from any VM will make the page different and therefore no longer shared. If you have a uniform set of VMs yet the **Shared memory** counter is low, it could be that the Guest OS writes a lot to its pages.

The **Overhead touched**, **Reserved overhead**, and **Overhead** counters can generally be ignored as their values are low. The following screenshot shows that their values are barely visible. The following VM has 10 GB RAM. I rebooted the VM towards the middle of the timeline, just to be sure the counters were behaving properly.

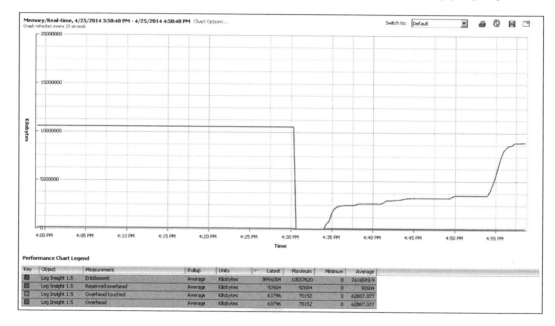

Putting it together

Let us now take an example to see how all the preceding counters relate, using a vCenter 5.5 Appliance. There are differences in memory behavior between the Linux Appliance and vCenter installed on Windows. For this example, the VM is configured with 3 GB vRAM and rebooted to ensure we have a clean start. The following chart shows that it has hit a steady state after the initial boot. The highest line is the **Entitlement** line, as it is **Granted** + **Overhead**. The hypervisor has entitled the VM to the entire 3 GB of RAM as the host has plenty of memory. The **Granted** counter and **Consumed** counter are practically identical. The lines are in fact overlapping, with the **Consumed** line overwriting the **Granted** line. It is a flat line, meaning all the pages the VM asked for are backed by physical DIMM. It is good to see that the **Consumed** value is both high and flat. As we know, **Consumed** goes up when the Guest OS asks for the memory, which means the Guest OS is writing to its physical memory pages (which in turn are backed by hypervisor physical memory). If the VM no longer needs it but ESXi does not use the page, ESXi keeps the pages just in case they are required in the future.

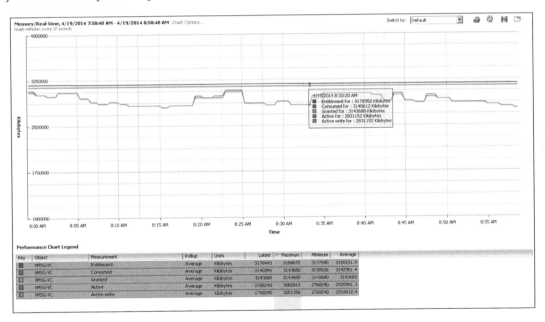

You probably noticed that both the **Active** counter and **Active write** counter are high. These values are close to the **Consumed** value. This indicates the Guest OS is actively using most of its consumed memory. In fact, the value of **Active write** is almost identical to the value of **Active**. The green line is practically covering the gray line. This behavior is specific to vCenter.

If we look at the vCenter Operations 5.8 appliance for example, the pattern is very different. As you can see in the next screenshot, **Active write** is definitely lower than **Active** and both are much lower than **Consumed**.

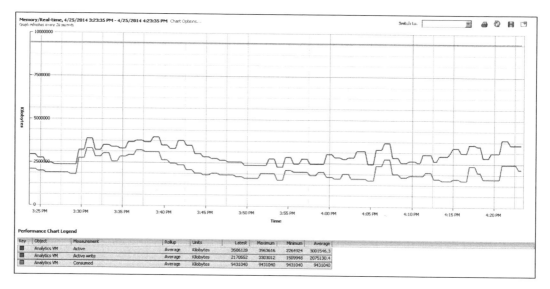

Let's now add the **Usage** counter as follows. I have removed some counters to make the following chart easier to interpret and added the **Balloon** counter. The **Usage** counter tracks the **Active** counter closely. The **Usage** counter shows the VM has very high memory utilization, averaging at 93 percent in the past 1 hour, which triggers a vCenter alert.

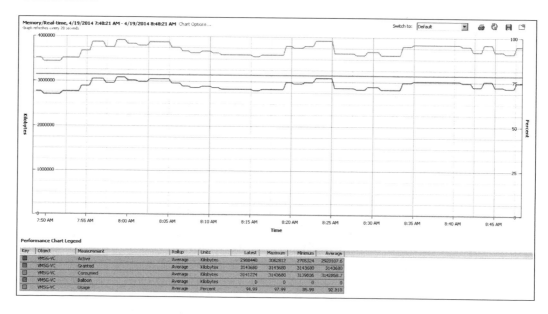

The **Balloon** counter is **0** for the entire duration, indicating there is no memory pressure at all. Let's look at the remaining counters that measure contention. As you can see from the following chart, they are all zeroes. We can deduce that **Latency** should be 0 too.

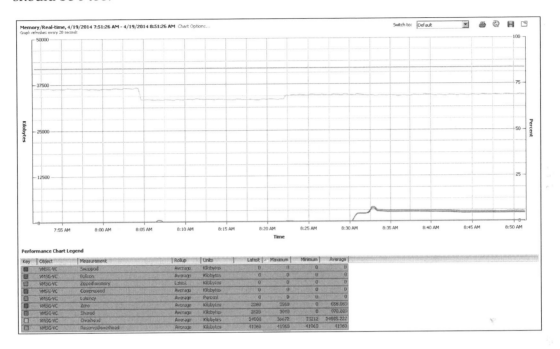

You can also see the **Overhead** and **Reserved overhead** counters. As expected, their value is insignificant as the memory overhead in vSphere 5.5 is low. The **Reserved overhead** is the thin and flat gray line at the top, while the yellow line below it is the **Overhead** counter.

The **Zero** counter tracks all pages with just zeroes on them (unused pages). As expected, the value is low as this is a Linux OS—Linux does not touch any pages until they are actively used. In Windows 2008, you will see a high spike during boot, as Windows initializes all the pages available to it on startup. After a while, it will taper off as this is just part of the initial boot. The next screenshot shows that. The **Active write** counter is identical to the **Active** as this is the period where Windows was writing zeroes.

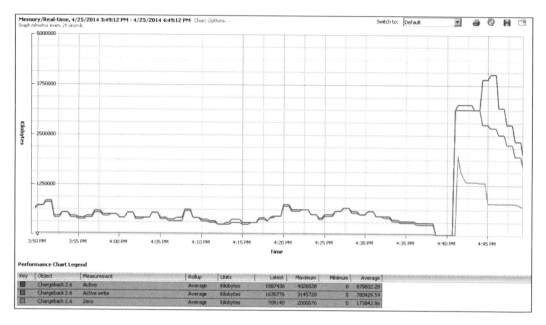

I was curious to see if the high memory utilization experienced in vCenter 5.5 in my earlier example was due to the RAM being undersized. After shutting down the VM, changing the RAM to 8 GB (which is the default setting), and rebooting it, you can see from the following chart that **Usage** drops from around 90 percent to around 70 percent. Soon after that, the alarm in vCenter was cleared.

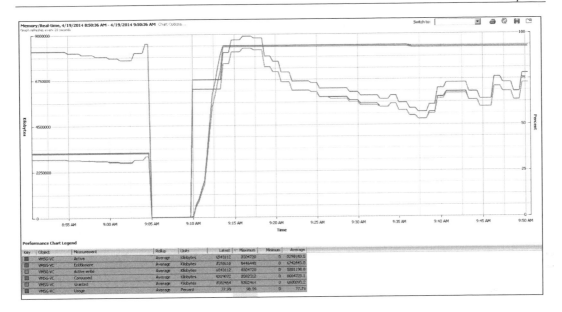

It is interesting to note that **Active** and **Active write** shoots up ahead of **Entitlement** and **Granted** during boot. Testing with another VM (VMware Log Insight 1.5, which is also based on SuSE Linux) led to the same behavior. This is not due to writing to the VM swap file as I set the VM RAM reservation to maximum. This is a normal behavior during VM boot, as the values drop after that to below **Entitlement** and **Granted**.

For Windows, you may see **Consumed** shoots up ahead of **Granted**. As mentioned previously, Microsoft Windows writes zeroes as it initializes the pages and VMkernel is smart enough to do copy-on-write, so all the pages are pointing to the same physical page. This results in the **Consumed** counter being higher than the **Granted** counter, as **Granted** only counts the physical page once. After a while, as the pages are replaced with actual data, the **Granted** counter will go up as each of the new pages is backed by large pages (common in Windows 2008 and Windows 7). The **Granted** counter tends to have a stable value as it only goes down if the host is under memory pressure.

VM memory key counters

We have talked about contention and utilization being the main areas you need to check. The following table summarizes what I recommend you monitor:

Purpose	vCenter	vRealize Operations	Description
Contention	CPU Swap Wait	Contention (%)	Memory Contention is based on CPU Swap Wait.
Utilization	Usage (%)	Workload (%)	For the lower threshold.
Utilization	Consumed (KB)	Consumed (KB)	For the upper threshold. There is no Usage/Usable (%) metric at VM level.

Memory counters at the ESXi level

vCenter provides even more counters at ESXi level: 32 counters for RAM plus 11 for VMkernel RAM. VMkernel has around 50 processes that are tracked. As a result, a cluster of 8 ESXi can have about 800 counters just for ESXi RAM! The counters are shown in the next screenshot. Most of them are not shown as a percentage, making it difficult to compare across ESXi with different memory sizes.

Description	Rollup	Units	Internal Name	Collection Level
☑ Swap used	Average	Kilobytes	swapused	2
☐ Host cache used for swapping	Average	Kilobytes	llSwapUsed	4
☐ Heap	Average	Kilobytes	heap	4
☐ Usage	Average	Percent	usage	1
☐ Swap in	Average	Kilobytes	swapin	2
☐ Swap out rate to host cache	Average	KBps	llSwapOutRate	2
☐ Low free threshold	Average	Kilobytes	lowfreethreshold	2
☐ Swap in rate	Average	KBps	swapinRate	1
☐ Zero	Average	Kilobytes	zero	2
☐ Swap out	Average	Kilobytes	swapout	2
☐ Shared	Average	Kilobytes	shared	2
☑ Granted	Average	Kilobytes	granted	2
☐ Compression rate	Average	KBps	compressionRate	2
☑ Consumed	Average	Kilobytes	consumed	1
☐ Decompression rate	Average	KBps	decompressionRate	2
☐ Used by VMkernel	Average	Kilobytes	sysUsage	2
☑ Active	Average	Kilobytes	active	2
☐ Swap in rate from host cache	Average	KBps	llSwapInRate	2
☐ Compressed	Average	Kilobytes	compressed	2
☑ Balloon	Average	Kilobytes	vmmemctl	1
☐ Reserved capacity	Average	Megabytes	reservedCapacity	2
☐ Overhead	Average	Kilobytes	overhead	1
☐ Latency	Average	Percent	latency	2
☐ Swap in from host cache	Average	Kilobytes	llSwapIn	4
☐ Active write	Average	Kilobytes	activewrite	2
☑ Shared common	Average	Kilobytes	sharedcommon	2
☐ Unreserved	Average	Kilobytes	unreserved	2
☐ Total capacity	Average	Megabytes	totalCapacity	2
☐ Swap out rate	Average	KBps	swapoutRate	1
☐ State	Latest	Number	state	2
☐ Swap out to host cache	Average	Kilobytes	llSwapOut	4
☐ Heap free	Average	Kilobytes	heapfree	4

ESXi: RAM counters

As for the VMkernel processes, they are not shown under the **Memory** group, but under the **System** group. In most cases, you do not need to track the CPU or RAM consumed by the kernel processes. If you are curious, you can see the individual process (for example, vMotion, storage vMotion, hostd, vpxa, and dcui) consumption of CPU or RAM, as shown in the following chart. While Virtual SAN is a kernel module, the vSphere 5.5 Update 2 performance counter does not track it. You will need a separate tool for now to track Virtual SAN.

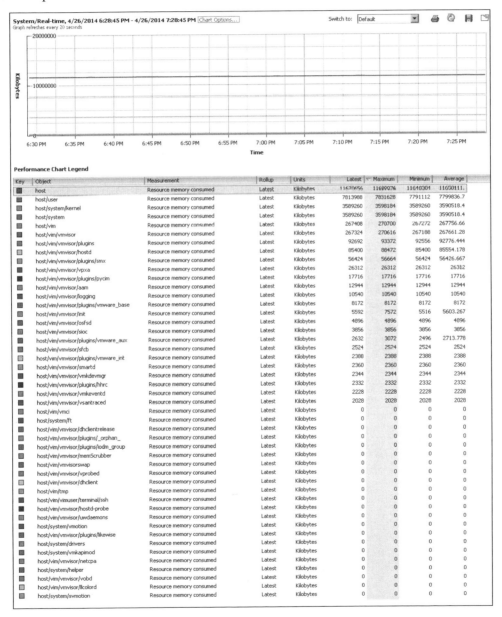

System/Real-time, 4/26/2014 6:28:45 PM - 4/26/2014 7:28:45 PM | Chart Options... | Switch to: Default

Performance Chart Legend

Key	Object	Measurement	Rollup	Units	Latest	Maximum	Minimum	Average
■	host	Resource memory consumed	Latest	Kilobytes	11670656	11680076	11640301	11660111.
■	host/user	Resource memory consumed	Latest	Kilobytes	7813988	7831628	7791112	7799836.7
■	host/system/kernel	Resource memory consumed	Latest	Kilobytes	3589260	3598184	3589260	3590518.4
■	host/system	Resource memory consumed	Latest	Kilobytes	3589260	3598184	3589260	3590518.4
■	host/vim	Resource memory consumed	Latest	Kilobytes	267408	270700	267272	267756.66
■	host/vim/vmvisor	Resource memory consumed	Latest	Kilobytes	267324	270616	267188	267661.28
■	host/vim/vmvisor/plugins	Resource memory consumed	Latest	Kilobytes	92692	93372	92556	92776.444
■	host/vim/vmvisor/hostd	Resource memory consumed	Latest	Kilobytes	85400	88472	85400	85554.178
■	host/vim/vmvisor/plugins/smx	Resource memory consumed	Latest	Kilobytes	56424	56664	56424	56426.667
■	host/vim/vmvisor/vpxa	Resource memory consumed	Latest	Kilobytes	26312	26312	26312	26312
■	host/vim/vmvisor/plugins/pycim	Resource memory consumed	Latest	Kilobytes	17716	17716	17716	17716
■	host/vim/vmvisor/aam	Resource memory consumed	Latest	Kilobytes	12944	12944	12944	12944
■	host/vim/vmvisor/logging	Resource memory consumed	Latest	Kilobytes	10540	10540	10540	10540
■	host/vim/vmvisor/plugins/vmware_base	Resource memory consumed	Latest	Kilobytes	8172	8172	8172	8172
■	host/vim/vmvisor/init	Resource memory consumed	Latest	Kilobytes	5592	7572	5516	5603.267
■	host/vim/vmvisor/osfsd	Resource memory consumed	Latest	Kilobytes	4896	4896	4896	4896
■	host/vim/vmvisor/sioc	Resource memory consumed	Latest	Kilobytes	3856	3856	3856	3856
■	host/vim/vmvisor/plugins/vmware_aux	Resource memory consumed	Latest	Kilobytes	2632	3072	2496	2713.778
■	host/vim/vmvisor/sfcb	Resource memory consumed	Latest	Kilobytes	2524	2524	2524	2524
■	host/vim/vmvisor/plugins/vmware_int	Resource memory consumed	Latest	Kilobytes	2388	2388	2388	2388
■	host/vim/vmvisor/smartd	Resource memory consumed	Latest	Kilobytes	2360	2360	2360	2360
■	host/vim/vmvisor/vmkdevmgr	Resource memory consumed	Latest	Kilobytes	2344	2344	2344	2344
■	host/vim/vmvisor/plugins/hhrc	Resource memory consumed	Latest	Kilobytes	2332	2332	2332	2332
■	host/vim/vmvisor/vmkeventd	Resource memory consumed	Latest	Kilobytes	2228	2228	2228	2228
■	host/vim/vmvisor/vsantraced	Resource memory consumed	Latest	Kilobytes	2028	2028	2028	2028
■	host/vim/vmci	Resource memory consumed	Latest	Kilobytes	0	0	0	0
■	host/system/ft	Resource memory consumed	Latest	Kilobytes	0	0	0	0
■	host/vim/vmvisor/dhclientrelease	Resource memory consumed	Latest	Kilobytes	0	0	0	0
■	host/vim/vmvisor/plugins/_orphan_	Resource memory consumed	Latest	Kilobytes	0	0	0	0
■	host/vim/vmvisor/plugins/iodm_group	Resource memory consumed	Latest	Kilobytes	0	0	0	0
■	host/vim/vmvisor/memScrubber	Resource memory consumed	Latest	Kilobytes	0	0	0	0
■	host/vim/vmvisorswap	Resource memory consumed	Latest	Kilobytes	0	0	0	0
■	host/vim/vmvisor/vprobed	Resource memory consumed	Latest	Kilobytes	0	0	0	0
□	host/vim/vmvisor/dhclient	Resource memory consumed	Latest	Kilobytes	0	0	0	0
■	host/vim/tmp	Resource memory consumed	Latest	Kilobytes	0	0	0	0
■	host/vim/vimuser/terminal/ssh	Resource memory consumed	Latest	Kilobytes	0	0	0	0
■	host/vim/vmvisor/hostd-probe	Resource memory consumed	Latest	Kilobytes	0	0	0	0
■	host/vim/vmvisor/uwdaemons	Resource memory consumed	Latest	Kilobytes	0	0	0	0
■	host/system/vmotion	Resource memory consumed	Latest	Kilobytes	0	0	0	0
■	host/vim/vmvisor/plugins/likewise	Resource memory consumed	Latest	Kilobytes	0	0	0	0
■	host/system/drivers	Resource memory consumed	Latest	Kilobytes	0	0	0	0
■	host/system/vmkapimod	Resource memory consumed	Latest	Kilobytes	0	0	0	0
■	host/vim/vmvisor/netcpa	Resource memory consumed	Latest	Kilobytes	0	0	0	0
■	host/system/helper	Resource memory consumed	Latest	Kilobytes	0	0	0	0
■	host/vim/vmvisor/vobd	Resource memory consumed	Latest	Kilobytes	0	0	0	0
□	host/vim/vmvisor/llcolord	Resource memory consumed	Latest	Kilobytes	0	0	0	0
■	host/system/svmotion	Resource memory consumed	Latest	Kilobytes	0	0	0	0

Contention counters

Just like in the case of VM, vCenter Server does not provide a counter for **Contention** for ESXi. You check the same set of counters for a sign of contention, which are **Balloon, Swapped, Compression**, and **Latency**. You should also check for **CPU Swap Wait**, as that counter tracks when the CPU is waiting for memory.

We know that contention happens at hypervisor level, not at VM level. The VM is feeling the side effects of the contention, and the degree of contention depends on each VM's shares and reservation. ESXi begins taking action if it is running low on free memory. This is tracked by a counter called **State**. The **State** counter has four states:

- **high**
- **soft**
- **hard**
- **low**

ESXi uses this to trigger when it reclaims memory from VM. Unless you are deliberately aiming for high utilization, all the ESXi should be in the high state. The *spare host* you add to cater for HA or maintenance mode will help in lowering the overall ESXi utilization. The value of high state is 0, so you can create a super metric that tracks the maximum value of all the hosts across your entire data center. Having said that, just because the host is low on free physical RAM does not mean that the VMs are performing poorly. I have mentioned earlier that even the presence of swapping out does not mean VMs are performing poorly when the swapped memory is not being accessed by the OS. Poor VM performance only happens on **Swap in** or **Decompression**. The **State** counter indicates that free memory is running low on the host, and the host is proactively making freer physical RAM to reallocate as requested by VMs.

The **Low free threshold (KB)** counter provides information on the actual level below which ESXi will begin reclaiming memory from VM. This value varies in hosts with different RAM configurations. Check this value only if you suspect ESXi triggers ballooning too early. You should not be seeing this behavior with the changes in ESXi 5.0. It uses an algorithm that results in a lower threshold on ESXi hosts with large RAM configuration. Without this, an ESXi with 256 GB of RAM would see the occurrence of ballooning when 15.3 GB (6 percent) of RAM is still available. With this sliding scale, the threshold would be around 3.3 GB, a more reasonable number. In the next screenshot, the threshold is sitting at around 1 GB for an ESXi with 48 GB of RAM.

 For more information, check out the blog post by Frank Denneman at `http://blogs.vmware.com/vsphere/2012/05/` `memminfreepct-sliding-scale-function.html`.

The following screenshot also shows **0** ballooning, which is a sign that the ESXi host has no memory pressure. **Latency** is also **0**, which means it has not accessed memory that is swapped or compressed.

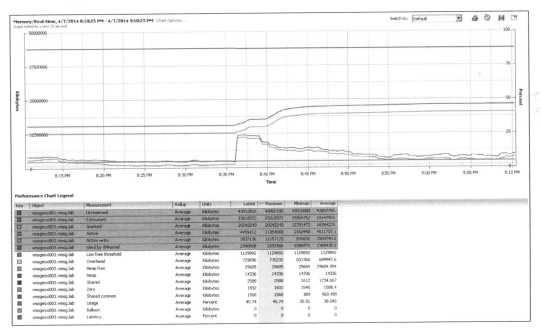

At the ESXi level, **Contention (%)** is the aggregate of all its VM **Contention (%)** counters. The next screenshot shows that relationship. In this ESXi host, the only VM experiencing contention is the **SDDC-vESXi-02** VM. All other VMs are not experiencing contention. So at the ESXi level the pattern reflects this, with a much lower value at the ESXi level. To complete the picture, the contention happened because ESXi had high memory utilization. The usage suddenly went up from a stable 88 percent to 92.52 percent, triggering ESXi to free up memory.

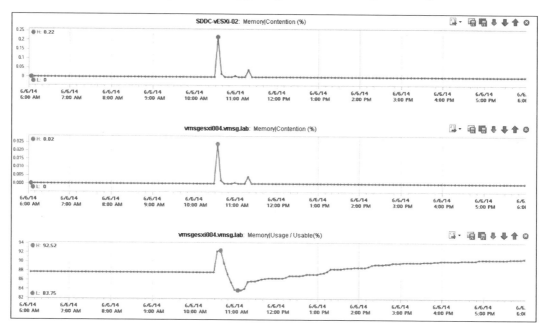

Utilization counters

vCenter provides **Active (KB)**, **Active write (KB)**, **Consumed (KB)**, **Granted (KB)**, and **Usage (%)** for utilization. **Granted** at the host is the total of the granted counters of VMs running on the host. It includes the shared memory. **Consumed** is the amount of memory used on the host. It includes both VM memory and hypervisor memory, so it is slightly higher than **Granted**. In other words, *Consumed = Total host memory - Free host memory*.

You should check both **Active (KB)** and **Usage (%)** to give you the average and peak utilization. **Active** would give you the *average* while **Usage (%)** indicates the *peak*. If you have a lot of applications that need to manage their own memory (for example, JVM and database), then you would gravitate toward **Usage (%)**. If not, you would gravitate towards the **Active** counter. Just like the situation with VMs where vRealize Operations provides a new counter called **Demand**, vRealize Operations also has the **Demand** counter at ESXi level. It is called **Machine Demand (KB)**.

The **Workload** counter translates **Machine Demand** into percentage, making it possible to compare it with **Usage (%)**. As you can see in the following chart, plotting them on the same chart gives you the range of memory utilization:

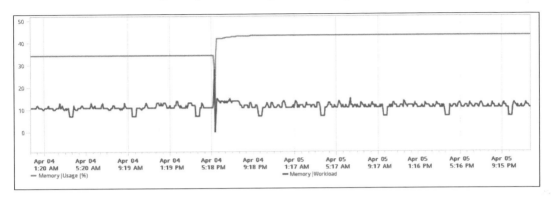

Memory shared is the sum of all the VM memory pages that are pointing to a shared page. **Memory shared common** is the sum of all the shared pages. As a result, **Memory shared common** is at most half the value of **Memory shared**, as sharing means at least two blocks are pointing to the shared page. If the value is a lot less than half, then you are saving a lot. A majority of today's ESXi hosts should be sporting the hardware-assisted memory virtualization from Intel or AMD. With this technology, VMkernel uses large pages to back the VM memory. As a result, the possibility of shared memory is low, unless the host memory is highly utilized. In this state, the large pages are broken down into small, shareable pages. So you can also use the **Memory shared common** counter to track for signs of host memory under pressure.

The **Heap** counter shows the memory used by VMkernel heap and other data. This is normally a constant and small value. In some hosts with 48 to 64 GB RAM, I see the heap size has a constant value of 14 MB, which is negligible.

The **Total capacity** counter is not the same as the total RAM in the host. Generally speaking, I find it to be around 98 percent of the host physical RAM. For example, on a host with 64 GB physical RAM, the **Total capacity** counter will report around 62.6 GB. vRealize Operations provides a metric called **Provisioned Memory (KB)**, which will show you the actual configured RAM (64 GB in this example).

Reserved Capacity (MB) only counts reservation. Therefore the value will be a lot lower than **Total capacity,** as most customers do not use reservation. It also includes memory reserved by VMkernel, which should be less than 0.5 GB and hence negligible.

ESXi memory key counters

We talked about contention and utilization being the main areas you should check. The following table summarizes what I recommend you monitor at the host level for RAM:

Purpose	vCenter	vRealize Operations	Description
Contention	CPU Swap Wait	Contention (%)	Memory contention is based on CPU Swap Wait
Utilization	Active (KB)	Workload (%)	For the lower threshold
Utilization	Usage (%)	Usage/Usable (%)	For the upper threshold

Memory counters at the cluster level

vCenter does not provide a lot of memory counters at the cluster level. From the following performance chart dialog box, you can see that the number of counters drop to just five. Counters related to contention such as **Compression, Swap**, and **Latency** are no longer available. The **Latency** counter would be especially useful to track at cluster level if you have a large environment.

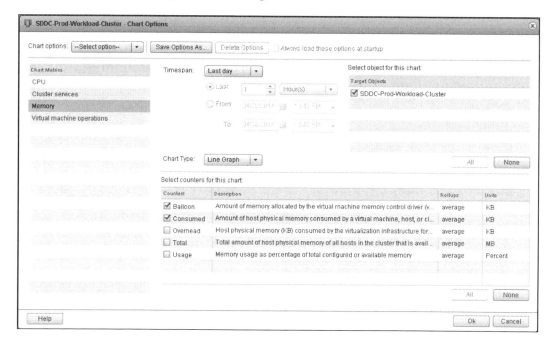

The data is not available in real time. This means the data granularity is at 5-minute intervals, not 20 seconds. As the rollup is an average, it means any spike within a 5-minute period may not be visible. In practice however, most performance problems would still likely be detectable with 5-minute data points.

The counters do not take HA into account. For example, the **Total** counter sums all the host physical memory.

The **Consumed** memory does not take into account the host memory. So the memory used by VMkernel is not included. This is practically negligible as most ESXi hosts sport more than 128 GB of RAM.

Unlike the other counters, which just sum up each host in the cluster, the **Usage** counter is an average of all hosts. So if a large cluster (more than 8 nodes) has an unbalanced RAM utilization, you may not see a high value. I recommend you to create a super metric that tracks the maximum RAM among all the hosts in the cluster. You can then plot this chart together with the Cluster average chart. This will give you both the average and the peak.

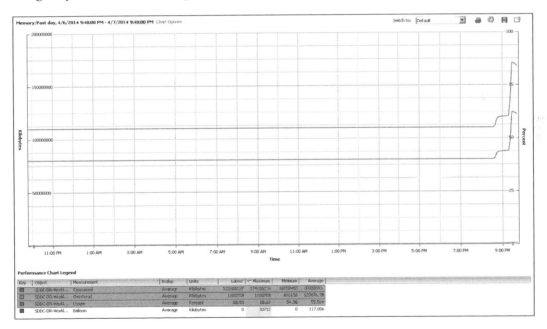

The **Usage (%)** and **Usage/Usable (%)** counters provide the same data. The following screenshot shows that they are identical over a period of one week:

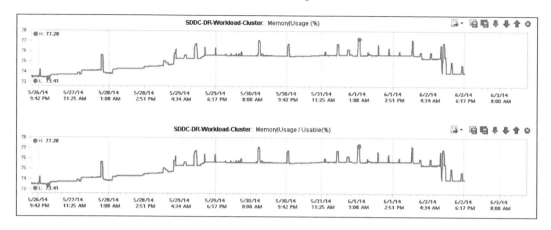

vRealize Operations provides a set of counters at the cluster level. Please refer to the *CPU counters at cluster level* section from *Chapter 4, CPU Counters*, as the approach is similar for memory. The following table lists the key counters. The **Workload** counter uses the active memory, while the **Usage** counter uses the consumed memory. Therefore, I consider them to be the lower and upper limits, respectively.

Purpose	Counters	Roll up	Description
Contention	Contention (%)	Average	As it is an average, you should complement it with a super metric that is based on peak contention of a member host
Utilization	Workload (%)	Average	For the lower threshold
Utilization	Usage/Usable (%)	Average	For the upper threshold

Memory counters at higher levels

As covered earlier in the book, vCenter does not provide information at this level. vRealize Operations provides a set of counters at the vCenter level. There are, naturally, fewer counters for these higher-level objects, as we just need a summary.

Object	Purpose	Counters	Roll up	Description
Data center	Contention	Contention (%)	Average	As it is an average, you should complement it with a super metric that is based on peak contention of a member cluster
Data center	Utilization	Workload (%)	Average	For the lower threshold
Data center	Utilization	Usage/Usable (%)	Average	For the upper threshold
vCenter	Contention	Contention (%)	Average	As it is an average, you should complement it with a super metric that is based on peak contention of a member data center
vCenter	Utilization	Workload (%)	Average	For the lower threshold
vCenter	Utilization	Usage/Usable (%)	Average	For the upper threshold
World	Contention	Contention (%)	Average	As it is an average, you should complement it with a super metric that is based on peak contention of a member host
World	Utilization	Workload (%)	Average	For the lower threshold
World	Utilization	Usage/Usable (%)	Average	For the upper threshold

Memory contention guidance

The following table provides a general guidance on memory contention. It must be read in conjunction with the *CPU contention guidance* section from the previous chapter. I must emphasize that this is just a guideline, which needs to be adjusted to meet the needs of your environment.

Object	Contention	Remarks
VM	• Tier 1: 0 percent • Tier 2: 5 percent • Tier 3: 10 percent	Because every single VM has its memory backed by the hypervisor, there will be no ballooning, swap, or compression. As a result, the value for Contention in tier 1 will be 0 percent.

Your customers only care about their own VMs, so the numbers in the following table are for your internal targets only. You should certainly have a more stringent threshold internally. This gives you a buffer for troubleshooting.

Object	Contention	Remarks
ESXi	NA	Please see the *CPU contention guidance* section from the previous chapter as the same logic applies here.
Cluster	Internal threshold: • Tier 1: 0 percent • Tier 2: 4 percent • Tier 3: 8 percent	Just like CPU, there is no need to track at individual ESXi host level. I'm using a lower number for clusters, as it is an average of all hosts in the cluster, which in turn is an average of all VMs in the respective hosts. As a result, the number will be lower than individual VMs.
Data center	NA	Please see the *CPU contention guidance* section in the previous chapter as the same logic applies here.

Summary

I hope you enjoyed this short travel down memory lane. In this chapter, we discussed memory counters in both vCenter and vRealize Operations. We covered what they mean and what values you should expect for a healthy environment. The relationship between metrics were also explained. We provided screenshots to make the learning easier and added real-world examples.

I'd like to emphasize again that hypervisor does not have visibility inside the Guest OS memory. Be careful when performing right sizing based solely on the data from the hypervisor. For an application that manages its own memory, this can result in poor performance due to excessive paging.

I also shared a tip that by separating the page file into its own vmdk file, you get some level of visibility on whether the Guest OS is reading or writing into the file, as it gets translated into disk activity.

We have now covered both CPU and memory, which means we are done with compute. Let's now go through the **Network** counters in the next chapter.

6
Network Counters

We will continue our exploration of counters by covering Network counters in this chapter. We will take the same approach as we did with CPU and RAM. We will cover the following topics:

- VM Network counters
- ESXi Network counters
- Cluster Network counters
- Distributed Virtual Switch Network counters
- Network counters at higher levels

Network monitoring and management

For complete network monitoring, you need to complement vSphere with another tool. vSphere does not provide protocol analysis functionality, which is instead available through a packet analyzer or sniffer program, such as **Wireshark** and **Netflow Logic**. With vSphere alone, you will not know, for example, which VMs are talking to which VMs, what kind of latency they experience, and what protocols are traveling in your network. At the time of writing, there is also no management pack for vRealize Operations that provides network protocol analysis. This means you need to have two consoles for complete network monitoring. NetFlow Logic is developing a new management pack, which you can follow up at `https://www.netflowlogic.com/products/for-vmware/`.

vSphere 5.5 provides an enhancement for capturing network packets. The previous tool, tcpdump-uw, did not let you capture packets at points such as virtual port and switch. The new tool, pktcap-uw, can capture at any points within the vSphere stack. I recommend you read the blog at `http://blogs.vmware.com/vsphere/networking`, as it provides examples that the KB article at `http://kb.vmware.com/kb/2051814` does not.

Good network management is about understanding the application. In a way, we should treat vCloud Suite as an application. There are now two layers of applications in a **Software-Defined Data Center (SDDC)**: infrastructure applications and applications that serve a business function. This is consistent with the fact that you will have two layers of network when the network is virtualized. When you virtualize your network with NSX, vRealize Operations provides visibility via its management pack for NSX. You can download it at VMware Solution Exchange by visiting `https://solutionexchange.vmware.com`.

Network counters at the VM level

The following screenshot shows the counters vCenter provides for the Network at a VM layer. The counters are available at each individual vNIC level and at the VM level. Most VMs will only have one vNIC so the data at VM level and vNIC level will be identical. The vNICs are named using the convention "400x". That means the first vNIC is 4000, the second vNIC is 4001, and so on.

Description	Rollup	Units	Internal Name	Collection Level
Data receive rate	Average	KBps	bytesRx	2
Broadcast receives	Summation	Number	broadcastRx	2
Data transmit rate	Average	KBps	transmitted	2
Multicast transmits	Summation	Number	multicastTx	2
Packets transmitted	Summation	Number	packetsTx	2
Data receive rate	Average	KBps	received	2
Transmit packets dropped	Summation	Number	droppedTx	2
Data transmit rate	Average	KBps	bytesTx	2
Packets received	Summation	Number	packetsRx	2
Multicast receives	Summation	Number	multicastRx	2
Usage	Average	KBps	usage	1
Broadcast transmits	Summation	Number	broadcastTx	2
Receive packets dropped	Summation	Number	droppedRx	2

VM Network counters

As usual, let's approach the counters starting with **Contention**. There is no **Latency** counter, so you cannot track how long it takes for a packet to reach its destination. There are, however, counters that track dropped packets. A dropped packet needs to be retransmitted and therefore increases network latency from the application's point of view. vRealize Operations provides a Latency counter, which uses packet drops as an indicator. Using a percentage is certainly easier than dealing with the raw counters in vCenter. The packet drop percentage is based on the packets transmitted and packet received in that collection period. These two counters are not collected by default.

You certainly want to avoid having packet drop in your network. To monitor if any VM is experiencing packet drop, you can build a super metric and develop a dashboard with a line chart and Top-N widgets. The super metric tracks the maximum packet drop of all VMs.

You apply it at the appropriate level (for example, cluster, data center, vCenter) and plot a line chart. You should expect a flat line at 0 when the Network is performing well. The line chart, however, does not tell you which VM experiences packet drop if you have any. This is where the Top-N chart comes in. You can set it at, say Top-25 VM, and make the time range long (for example, 1 month). This is available in an existing dashboard.

For *Utilization*, vCenter provides the data both in terms of the number of TCP/IP packets and network throughput. There is also a **Usage** counter, which is the sum of **Data Transmit Rate (TX)** and **Data Receive Rate (RX)**. The **Usage** counter cannot exceed the physical wire speed, even with full duplex. So if the VM is sending 800 Mbps to another VM in another ESXi host, it can only receive 224 Mbps as the total (TX + RX) cannot exceed 1 Gbps (1024 Mbps). The limit can certainly be exceeded if the communication is between two VMs in the ESXi hosts, as the packets move at memory speed.

The following chart shows that **Usage** is the sum of RX and TX. In vRealize Operations, use the **Usage Rate** counter. The counter **4000 | Usage Rate** will only give the data for the first vNIC; hence, it will be incomplete if you have a VM with two vNICs (for example, those with a LAN-based backup, or have access to multiple networks).

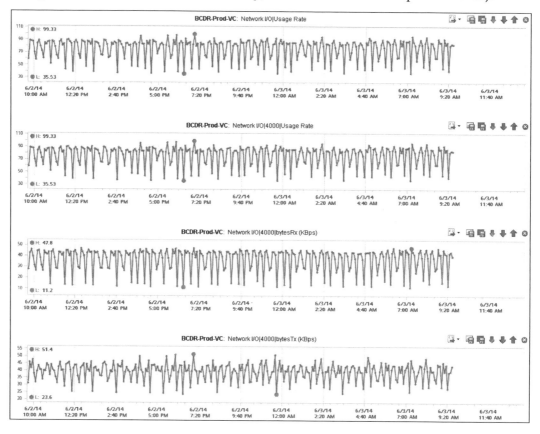

You will notice that the numbers provided by vCenter and vRealize Operations are given in KBps, whereas your vmnic is in Gbps. 1 Gbps equals to 131,072 KBps, so this is the theoretical maximum for a 1 GE physical card. Because vCenter takes a 20 second average, you will not see this number most of the time as that means the throughput is sustained for the full 20-seconds. vRealize Operations will provide an even lower figure as the number is averaged over 5 minutes.

There are duplicate counters as shown in the next screenshot. There are two data transmit rates and two data receive rates. The following data is from vCenter 5.5 Update 1 Appliance. As you can tell, there is a regular spike every few minutes or so. The load is primarily due to two vRealize Operations (5.8.1 and 6.0) accessing the vCenter.

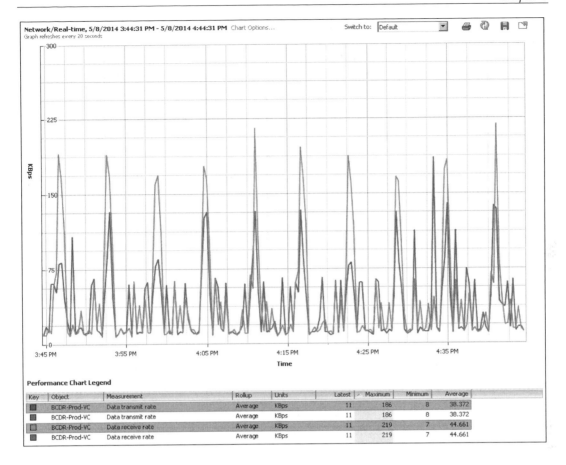

You may want to know if any given VM hits the network limit. Assuming you are on a 1 GE network, you can do this by creating a super metric that tracks the maximum **Usage** (KBps) of all VMs, multiplying it by 8, and then dividing it by *1024 * 1024* to convert to Gbps. If you see a number nearing 1, it means you have a VM hitting 1 GE (which is the limit that the VM sees; the actual limit is likely to be lower since many VMs will be sharing the 1 GE vmnic).

Besides unicast traffic, which should form the bulk of your network, vSphere also provides information about broadcast traffic and multicast traffic. If you are not expecting any of these two variety of traffic from certain VMs (or clusters) and want to be alerted if it does occur, you can create a group for the objects and then apply a super metric. The super metric would add the four counters that capture broadcast and multicast. You should expect a flat line as the total should be 0.

We have talked about contention and utilization being the main areas you should check. The following table summarizes what I recommend you monitor for the Network. Notice that vCenter does not provide the total packet drops. Also, the unit is in the number of packet drops, not in percent. For utilization, vCenter does not have the equivalent of workload. I have left the table cell blank for ease of comparison.

VM - Network counters:

Purpose	vCenter	vRealize Operations
Contention	Transmit packets dropped (number)	Packet dropped (%)
	Received packets dropped (number)	
Utilization	Usage (KBps)	Usage rate (KBps)
Utilization		Workload (%)

Network counters at the ESXi level

vCenter provides three additional counters at the host level. It can track **Packet receive errors**, **Packet transmit errors**, and **Unknown protocol frames**. The counters are provided at either the host level or vmnic level. They are not provided at the switch or port group level. This means you cannot gauge the performance at the port group level or switch level easily using vCenter.

Description	Rollup	Units	Internal Name	Collection Level
Multicast receives	Summation	Number	multicastRx	2
Usage	Average	KBps	usage	1
Data receive rate	Average	KBps	bytesRx	2
Multicast transmits	Summation	Number	multicastTx	2
Unknown protocol frames	Summation	Number	unknownProtos	2
Data transmit rate	Average	KBps	transmitted	2
Packet receive errors	Summation	Number	errorsRx	2
Packet transmit errors	Summation	Number	errorsTx	2
Packets transmitted	Summation	Number	packetsTx	2
Data receive rate	Average	KBps	received	2
Transmit packets dropped	Summation	Number	droppedTx	2
Receive packets dropped	Summation	Number	droppedRx	2
Packets received	Summation	Number	packetsRx	2
Broadcast receives	Summation	Number	broadcastRx	2
Data transmit rate	Average	KBps	bytesTx	2
Broadcast transmits	Summation	Number	broadcastTx	2

ESXi Network counters

Just like vCenter, vRealize Operations also does not provide the counters at the standard switch or port group level. This means you cannot aggregate or analyze the data from these network objects' point of view. This is one reason why I prefer to use Distributed Switch. It simply has a much richer monitoring capability.

Usage, Data Received Rate, and **Data Transmit Rate** are all available at the host level and at the individual NIC level. I'm showing just **vmnic3** and the host in this screenshot:

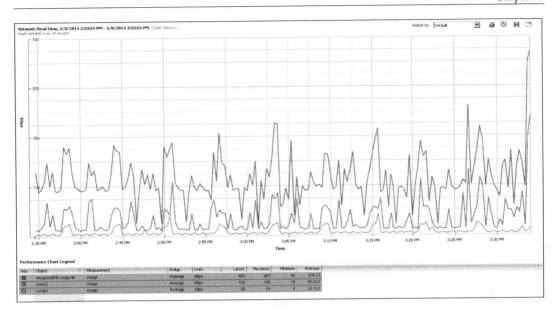

You should expect the value for packets dropped and unknown packet frames to be 0. A packet is considered unknown if ESXi is unable to decode it and hence does not know what type of packet it is. Discuss with your network admin if you are seeing either a dropped packet or an unknown packet.

Packets dropped and unknown packet frames counters are available at the host level and individual NIC level. I'm showing just **vmnic1** and the host in this screenshot:

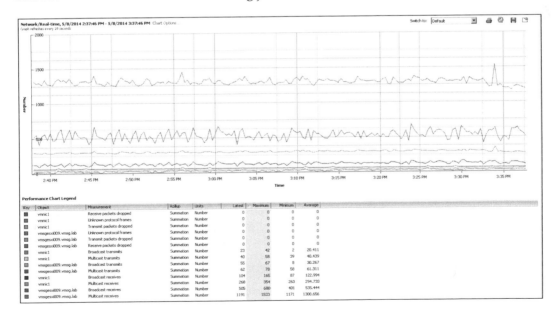

The key counters to track for ESXi are consistent with the key counters for a VM. Again, vCenter does not provide the total packets dropped and the equivalent of the Workload counter. I have left the table cell blank for ease of comparison. The table for ESXi Network counters is as follows:

Purpose	vCenter	vRealize Operations
Contention	Transmit Packets dropped (number) Received Packets dropped (number)	Packet Dropped (%)
Utilization	Usage (KBps)	Usage Rate (KBps)
Utilization		Workload (%)

Network counters at the cluster level

vRealize Operations provides a set of counters at the cluster level. Please refer to the *CPU counters at the cluster level* section of *Chapter 4, CPU Counters*, as the approach is similar for Network. Ensure you create the super metrics so that you complement the average with peak. The following table lists the key cluster counters of vRealize Operations:

Purpose	Counters	Roll up
Contention	Packet Dropped (%)	Average
Utilization	Usage Rate (KBps)	Summation
Utilization	Workload (%)	Average

Network counters at the Distributed Switch level

As discussed earlier, vCenter does not provide information at this level. This makes monitoring difficult, as you cannot slice the data from the switch point of view. This is one major enhancement in vRealize Operations. It provides a set of counters at the Distributed Switch level and for its port groups. Putting network as a first-class object is one of the major enhancements in Versions 6.0 and 5.8.2. If you are using VMware **NSX**, you will see that the management pack for NSX provides even deeper visibility into the virtual network.

For Contention, vRealize Operations provides the Packet Dropped (%) metric. You will not find the Contention (%) metric. For Utilization, you use both the metric Usage Rate (KBps) and Workload (%). You need to use both due to the dynamic nature of the upper limit.

The following screenshot shows an example of visibility at the Distributed Switch level:

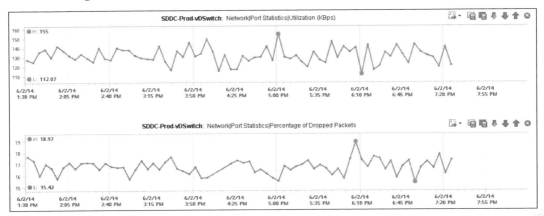

In addition to the preceding, vRealize Operations provides some configuration-related metrics that can be useful in monitoring your environment. The next screenshot shows the metrics. For example, you can create a super metric that tracks the maximum of **MTU Mismatch**, **Unsupported MTU**, **Teaming Mismatch**, and so on. You should expect a flat line with 0 as the value. You can then create an alert if the value goes beyond 0.

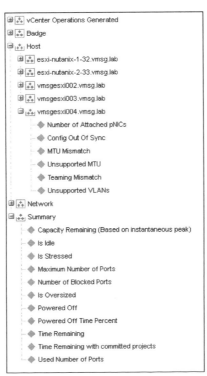

Network counters at higher levels

As covered earlier, vCenter does not provide information for the network at these levels (data center, vCenter, and World). vRealize Operations provides a set of counters for the network at these levels, which are useful for overall visibility. This table lists the key counters. The only exception is that the packet dropped information is not available at the World level. I have left the table cell blank for ease of comparison. The table for vRealize Operations cluster counters is given as follows:

Object	Purpose	Counters	Roll up
Data center	Contention	Packet Dropped (%)	Average
Data center	Utilization	Usage Rate (KBps)	Summation
Data center	Utilization	Workload (%)	Average
vCenter	Contention	Packet Dropped (%)	Average
vCenter	Utilization	Usage Rate (KBps)	Summation
vCenter	Utilization	Workload (%)	Average
World	Contention		
World	Utilization	Usage Rate (KBps)	Summation
World	Utilization	Workload (%)	Average

Summary

In this chapter, we covered network counters. The set of counters is relatively short compared to CPU, RAM, and storage, because vCenter 5.5 does not provide protocol analysis capability. In terms of network monitoring, it is also clear that distributed switch has far superior management. This visibility provides another reason for choosing it over the standard switch.

In the next chapter, we will cover the last of our infrastructure group. We will dive into the storage counters.

7
Storage Counters

We will complete our exploration of counters by covering the storage counters in this chapter. We will take the same approach we did with CPU, RAM, and network. We will cover the following topics in this chapter:

- The layers in the storage subsystem
- VM storage counters
- ESXi storage counters
- Cluster storage counters
- Datastore storage counters
- Storage counters at high-level objects, such as data center, vCenter, and World

The multilayer storage

Virtualization increases the complexity in troubleshooting storage performance. Just like memory, where we have more than one level, we have three levels for storage. At the highest level we have VMs. A VM typically has two to three virtual disks (or RDMs), such as OS drive, paging file drive, and data drive. A large database VM will have even more. We are interested in data both at the VM level and individual virtual disk level. If you are running a VM with a large data drive (for example, a Oracle database), the performance of the data drive is what the VM owner cares about the most. At the VM level, you get the average of all drives, so the performance issue can be masked. Below the VM level we have the datastore. Multiple VMs share a datastore, so it is common to have an **I/O blender** effect, where sequential writes on individual vmdk files become random writes at the datastore level. This can occur in either VMFS or NFS. The datastore is normally backed one to one by a LUN, so what we see at the datastore level should match what we see at the LUN level. Multiple LUNs reside on a single array, which represents the third and lowest level.

I did not include ESXi as a level in our discussion of storage counters, as in general it is not a cause of storage bottlenecks. Yes, the VMkernel prioritizes and queues every I/O, but all these should be less than 1 millisecond. If the I/O is held at the kernel, there is a good chance that the physical device latency is more than 10 milliseconds.

The following table shows the level of visibility available at each level. I added VMs as you need to look at this level before diving into a specific vDisk of the VM. I am assuming that the array level provides the necessary information and this can be presented to vRealize Operations via a management pack (for example, NetApp, HDS, and EMC)

Level	Latency	IOPS	Throughput
vDisk	Yes.	Yes.	Yes.
VM	Yes. Tracks the highest latency at datastore or disk metric group. Tracks latency at the datastore counter.	Yes. Uses the datastore or disk metric group.	Yes.
Datastore	Yes.	Yes.	Yes.
Array	Yes.	Yes.	Yes.

The preceding table is for a *typical* VM. A typical VM has multiple virtual disks but they are all in the *same* datastore. It does not use RDMs. If your VM has an RDM, you will notice in the Disk metric group that vSphere can only track the highest latency. This is actually not the highest latency. It is the latency at the point of collection. It cannot track the average latency on a 20,000 millisecond-collection period. This means that there is no read latency or write latency per disk either. If your VM's its vmdk files reside in multiple datastores, then you can only track the highest latency among all datastores (for VMFS or NFS) or LUNs (for VMFS or RDM) – there is no breakdown. For each datastore, vShpere can track read or write latency, but cannot track the overall latency.

The same limitation for the preceding latency applies for IOPS and throughput. This is another reason to minimize the usage of RDMs or spread the vmdk files of a single VM across multiple datastores.

All the above apply to a classic physical array. A distributed storage such as Virtual SAN needs a thorough discussion, which is outside the scope of this book.

We covered what you can see at various levels of storage. Let's now move on to the actual counters. We will use the same approach we used for CPU and other counters: starting with contention, followed by utilization, and ending with other counters as required.

For storage, the counter for contention is clear. First, ensure that you do not have dropped packets for your IP storage or SCSI commands aborted for your block storage. They are a sign of contention as the datastore (VMFS or NFS) is shared. The SCSI lock was more common in the earlier versions of vSphere, before a more granular locking was introduced. The **Bus Resets** and **Commands Aborted** counters should be zero all the time. As a result, it should be fine to track them at high-level objects. Create a super metric that tracks the maximum or summation of both, and you should expect a flat line.

Once you have ensured that you do not have dropped packets on the IP storage or aborted commands on the block storage, you can use the latency counter to define and measure your **Service Level Agreement (SLA)**. In most cases, it is sufficient to measure the average latency, without the need to comply at both read latency and write latency. The total latency is not *read latency* + *write latency* because it is not a simple summation. In a given second, a VM issues many IOPS. For example, a VM issues 100 reads and 10 writes in a second. Each of these 110 commands will have their own latency. The "total" latency is the average of these 110 commands. In this example, the total latency will be more influenced by the read latency, as the workload is read dominated. For those of you using the IP storage, take note that read latency and write latency do not map 1:1 to **Transmit (Tx)** and **Receive (Rx)** in networking counters. Read latency and write latency are both mapped to the Transmit counter as the ESXi host issues commands, hence transmitting the packets.

vCenter also provides information about the number of I/Os that have been issued but not yet completed. The number of outstanding I/O counters tracks these, and it provides a separate counter for read latency and write latency. Certainly, the greater the number of outstanding I/Os, the higher the latency becomes.

The following chart shows that 148 outstanding write requests resulted in a write latency spike of 505 milliseconds that was sustained for 20 seconds. The level to which the latency will increase for each outstanding I/O depends upon many factors, such as the drive specification and the overall storage throughput.

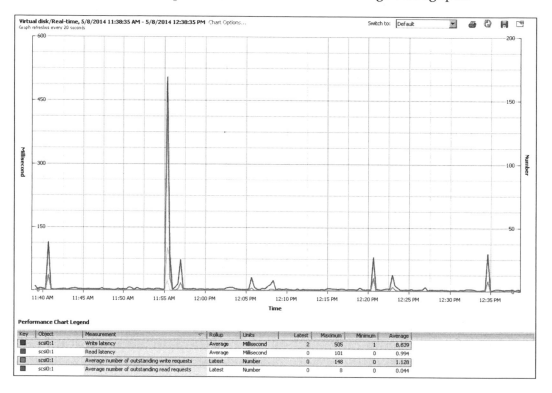

For Utilization, we need to look at both IOPS and throughput. You will find a number of counters that provide these data points, depending on the objects you analyze.

Ideally, we should be able to figure out the root cause behind the poor storage performance. These are some possibilities to keep in mind while performing the analysis:

- **Array**: Look into the array if the physical device latency counter is high. There are many possible causes, as an array has many layers and components. As most arrays now have a few SSDs or are purely SSD based, the array causing an issue related to IOPS has become less likely.

- **Network**: Look into the network if the fabric is saturated or if you are using IP storage. Even if you are on a 10-gigabit network, it is possible to have contention if you do not turn on network I/O control.

- **ESXi host**: Look into this to determine whether the poor storage performance is caused by bad configuration, such as the wrong multipath policy chosen or insufficient HBA queue depth. You should also look at non-VM workloads such as vSphere Replication and host-based security services.

- **VM**: Look into the VM if the workload is high. The most common VM-related storage performance issues are the snapshot that was not removed, an anti-virus update or scan, Windows patches, and backup. Backup jobs are a common performance hit, especially if they hit several related VMs at once—either on the same host or the same datastore. Another cause could be a developer running IOmeter (http://www.iometer.org/) or a database test. If the VM workload is low and yet it has a storage issue, check whether the disk length is full inside the Guest OS.

Storage counters at the VM level

vCenter 5.5 provides 17 counters for storage at the VM level. 7 are new counters compared to vCenter 5.0. The new additions are number of seeks (small, medium, large), latency in microseconds, and size of requests (read latency and write latency). At the VM level, you can look at counters at the individual virtual disk level, datastore level, and disk level:

- If you look at the virtual disk counters, you can see VMFS vmdk files, NFS vmdk files, and RDMs. However, you don't get data below the virtual disk layer. For example, if the VM has a snapshot, the data at virtual disk level will know show it. Also, a VM typically has multiple virtual disks (OS drive, swap drive, data drive), so you need to add them manually if you use vCenter. In vRealize Operations, you use the aggregate of all instances.

- If you look at the datastore counters, you can see VMFS and NFS, but not RDM. Because snapshots happen at the datastore level, the counter will include it. Datastore figures will be higher if your VM has a snapshot. You don't have to add the data from each virtual disk together as the data presented is already at the VM level. It also has the **Highest latency** counter, which is useful for tracking the peak latency.

- If you look at the disk counters, you can see VMFS and RDM, but not NFS. The data at this level should be the same as at the datastore level because your blocks should be aligned. You should have a 1:1 mapping between the datastore and LUN without extents. It also has the **Highest latency** counter, which is useful for tracking the peak latency.

The following three screenshots show the counters available in the virtual disk group, datastore group, and disk group respectively. For a typical VM, these counters will be the same as all the vmdk files are on the same datastore, which in turn is mapped 1:1 with the underlying disk.

Description	Rollup	Units	Internal Name	Collection Level
Write rate	Average	KBps	write	2
Average number of outstanding write requests	Latest	Number	writeOIO	2
Number of small seeks	Latest	Number	smallSeeks	4
Number of large seeks	Latest	Number	largeSeeks	4
Write Latency (us)	Latest	Microsecond	writeLatencyUS	4
Read workload metric	Latest	Number	readLoadMetric	2
Read Latency (us)	Latest	Microsecond	readLatencyUS	4
Write latency	Average	Millisecond	totalWriteLatency	1
Read request size	Latest	Number	readIOSize	4
Average read requests per second	Average	Number	numberReadAveraged	1
Average number of outstanding read requests	Latest	Number	readOIO	2
Read latency	Average	Millisecond	totalReadLatency	1
Write request size	Latest	Number	writeIOSize	4
Number of medium seeks	Latest	Number	mediumSeeks	4
Read rate	Average	KBps	read	2
Write workload metric	Latest	Number	writeLoadMetric	2
Average write requests per second	Average	Number	numberWriteAveraged	1

VM Virtual Disk counters

The datastore metric group shows the metrics for this VM only, and not for every VM in that datastore. To see the data at the datastore level, look at the datastore object.

Description	Rollup	Units	Internal Name	Collection Level
Read rate	Average	KBps	read	2
Highest latency	Latest	Millisecond	maxTotalLatency	3
Average write requests per ...	Average	Number	numberWriteAvera...	1
Write rate	Average	KBps	write	2
Average read requests per ...	Average	Number	numberReadAvera...	1
☑ Read latency	Average	Millisecond	totalReadLatency	1
☑ Write latency	Average	Millisecond	totalWriteLatency	1

VM datastore counters

The disk is the physical LUN backing up the datastore. If the datastore does not span multiple LUNs, then Disk counters will be very similar to the datastore counters.

Description	Rollup	Units	Internal Name	Collection Level
☐ Average write requests per second	Average	Number	numberWriteAveraged	1
☐ Highest latency	Latest	Millisecond	maxTotalLatency	1
☐ Commands issued	Summation	Number	commands	2
☐ Average read requests per second	Average	Number	numberReadAveraged	1
☐ Read requests	Summation	Number	numberRead	3
☐ Average commands issued per second	Average	Number	commandsAveraged	2
☐ Write requests	Summation	Number	numberWrite	3
☐ Write rate	Average	KBps	write	2
☐ Commands aborted	Summation	Number	commandsAborted	2
☐ Usage	Average	KBps	usage	1
☐ Read rate	Average	KBps	read	2
☐ Bus resets	Summation	Number	busResets	2

VM Disk counter

For latency, vCenter provides the **Write latency** and **Read latency** counters. There is no counter for the total average latency, but there is a counter called **Highest latency**. If you have an RDM, use the counter at the Disk metric group. If you have NFS, use the counter at the datastore metric group. If you have vmdk, you can use either. vCenter provides the data in both milliseconds and microseconds. As you can see in the next chart, microseconds just provide a more granular view than milliseconds, which can be useful in latency-sensitive applications:

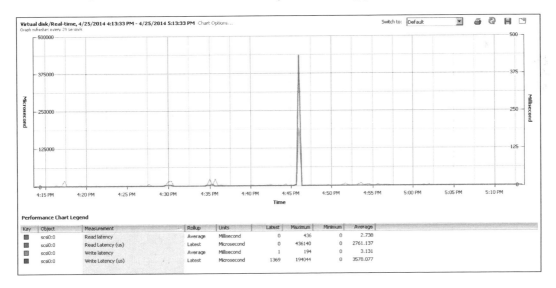

At the datastore and Disk levels, vCenter also provides the **Highest latency** counter. This tracks the highest latency among all datastores and disks. It is based on the latest data, and not on the average or peak of the sample period. You can see in vCenter that the rollup technique used is **Latest**. This is why it can be lower than the individual disk or datastore metric. This metric is useful when the VM has multiple datastores or disks. It is also useful if the VM resides on a single datastore or disk. Note that this is *not* the total latency. **Highest latency** is the peak of either write latency or read latency, not the aggregate of both. This can be used to track the peak as vRealize Operations takes an average of 5 minutes, which may hide any spike within the 5-minute period.

For Utilization, vRealize Operations provides the Workload (percent) counter. Since the Workload counter is in percentage, it becomes easier to understand and manage. I will cover this counter in the datastore section.

Putting it all together

Let's now take a look at an example to see how these three metric groups (virtual disk, datastore, and disk) work together. We will use a vCenter 5.5 appliance in this example. The event that caused the spike shown in the following screenshot was the vCenter web client server restarting. The administrator will see the message that the web client server was restarted when attempting to log in to vCenter.

At the virtual disk level, the total IOPS went up till 3,000, as shown in the following screenshot. The VM has two virtual disks: **scsi0:0** and **scsi0:1**.

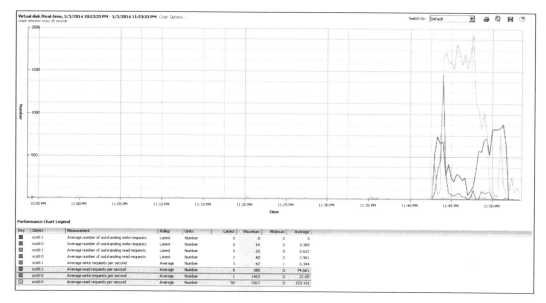

At the datastore level, the pattern is consistent. While there are other VMs in the datastore, the counters only show the IOPS from this VM. Notice how we lose the detail: there is no data at the virtual disk level. On the other hand, if we have a snapshot, the result will be visible at this level:

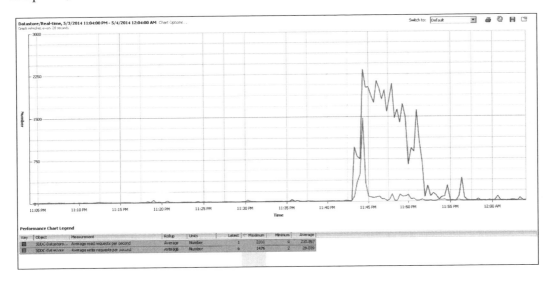

The pattern is again consistent at the disk level. The next screenshot shows the total I/O issued. If you divide the number by 20 (as the timeline is 20 seconds), you get a similar result with the IOPS you see at the datastore level.

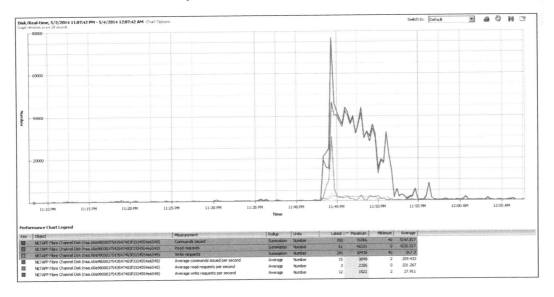

All the previously shown charts are for IOPS. Let's now check the throughput. From the following screenshot, the workload is small as the total value is below 400 megabits per second, which is much lower than the physical limit. To get the total value, carry out the following steps:

1. Add **Read rate** and **Write rate** to get the total throughput.
2. Then, multiply the throughput value by 8 to convert it from byte to bit.
3. Finally, divide it by 1,024 to convert from kilo to mega.

Please note that this is an average of 20 seconds. It is possible that there is a spike within the 20 seconds.

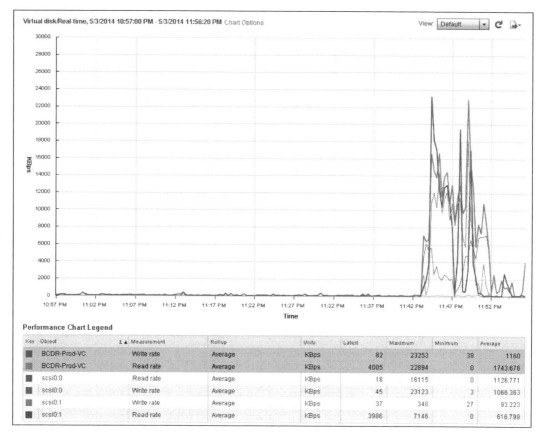

Key	Object	Measurement	Rollup	Units	Latest	Maximum	Minimum	Average
■	BCDR-Prod-VC	Write rate	Average	KBps	82	23253	38	1160
■	BCDR-Prod-VC	Read rate	Average	KBps	4005	22894	0	1743.676
■	scsi0:0	Read rate	Average	KBps	18	18115	0	1126.771
■	scsi0:0	Write rate	Average	KBps	45	23123	3	1066.363
■	scsi0:1	Write rate	Average	KBps	37	346	27	93.223
■	scsi0:1	Read rate	Average	KBps	3986	7146	0	616.799

Even though the throughput is low, it does not mean the latency is low. In our example, the latency went up to 25 milliseconds at the datastore level. Please note that the **Highest latency** counter can be a little lower than the **Write latency** or **Read latency** counter. Can you figure out why? It's because of the difference in the roll-up technique. The **Highest latency** takes the last data in that 20-second sampling interval, and not the average of the entire 20 seconds.

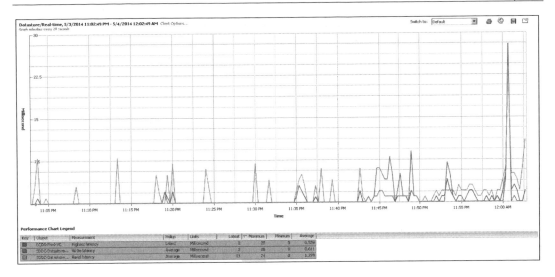

As shown in the next chart, the latency also went up to 25 milliseconds at Disk level. This is expected as we have a 1:1 mapping.

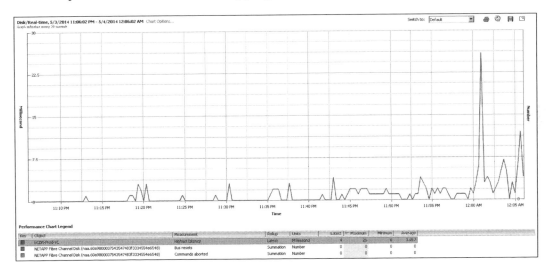

VM storage key counters

We talked about contention and utilization as the main areas you should check. The following table summarizes what I recommend you monitor at the virtual disk level or VM level (which will be an average of all its virtual disks). For the virtual disk, vCenter does not provide a total value, which means you need to add them together manually (read latency and write latency). vRealize Operations provides both the summary and breakdown (read latency and write latency).

vCenter also does not provide utilization in a percentage. It only provides the raw data. I have left the table cell blank for ease of comparison.

The following table shows the virtual disk counters of the VM storage:

Purpose	vCenter	vRealize Operations
Contention	Read latency Write latency	Total latency
Utilization	Average read requests per second Average write requests per second	Commands per second
Utilization	Write rate (KBps) Read rate (KBps)	Usage

The following table shows the VM counters of the VM storage:

Purpose	vCenter	vRealize Operations
Contention	Highest latency (milliseconds)	Disk command latency (milliseconds)
Utilization	Commands issued (number)	Commands per second
Utilization	Usage (KBps)	Usage average (KBps)
Utilization		Workload (%)

Storage counters at the ESXi level

The storage counters at ESXi level are similar to those at the VM level. They provide the same set of information (latency, throughput, and IOPS). Each of the metric groups gives insight from the vantage point of the object. For example, the ESXi adapter metric group provides the data from each adapter (vmhba).

The following two tables show the set of counters available for each ESXi adapter and its associated storage paths.

 Notice that in the screenshot there is no total throughput counter, so you need to add write latency and read latency manually. vRealize Operations provides the total throughput counter via the **Total Usage** counter.

As shared earlier, you normally set four paths between an ESXi host and its target LUN. You set two HBAs (in case either one of them fails), and each HBA sees a port on each SP in the array (in case either SP fails).

Description	Rollup	Units	Internal Name	Collection Level
☐ Read latency	Average	Millisecond	totalReadLatency	2
☐ Average write requests per second	Average	Number	numberWriteAveraged	2
☐ Average commands issued per second	Average	Number	commandsAveraged	2
☐ Highest latency	Latest	Millisecond	maxTotalLatency	3
☐ Read rate	Average	KBps	read	2
☐ Average read requests per second	Average	Number	numberReadAveraged	2
☐ Write rate	Average	KBps	write	2
☐ Write latency	Average	Millisecond	totalWriteLatency	2

ESXi adapter counters

This means that in the following storage path counters, you will have four sets of values. You can use vRealize Operations to get their total, average, or peak.

Description	Rollup	Units	Internal Name	Collection Level
☐ Read rate	Average	KBps	read	3
☐ Read latency	Average	Millisecond	totalReadLatency	3
☐ Write latency	Average	Millisecond	totalWriteLatency	3
☐ Write rate	Average	KBps	write	3
☐ Average read requests per second	Average	Number	numberReadAveraged	3
☐ Average write requests per second	Average	Number	numberWriteAveraged	3
☐ Average commands issued per second	Average	Number	commandsAveraged	3
☐ Highest latency	Latest	Millisecond	maxTotalLatency	3

ESXi storage path counters

At the datastore level, ESXi provides visibility of the operation of Storage DRS and Storage I/O Control. The **Highest latency** counter is useful, as most of the time an ESXi host will have multiple datastores. This tracks the highest among all the datastores.

Description	Rollup	Units	Internal Name	Collection Level
☐ Storage I/O Control normalized latency	Average	Microsecond	sizeNormalizedDatastoreLatency	1
☐ Storage DRS datastore outstanding write requests	Latest	Number	datastoreWriteOIO	1
☐ Storage DRS datastore normalized read latency	Latest	Number	datastoreNormalReadLatency	2
☐ Storage I/O Control datastore maximum queue depth	Latest	Number	datastoreMaxQueueDepth	1
☐ Write rate	Average	KBps	write	2
☐ Datastore latency observed by VMs	Latest	Number	datastoreVMObservedLatency	1
☐ Storage DRS datastore read I/O rate	Latest	Number	datastoreReadIops	1
☐ Average write requests per second	Average	Number	numberWriteAveraged	1
☐ Write latency	Average	Millisecond	totalWriteLatency	1
☐ Storage DRS datastore bytes read	Latest	Number	datastoreReadBytes	2
☐ Storage DRS datastore read workload metric	Latest	Number	datastoreReadLoadMetric	4
☐ Storage DRS datastore write workload metric	Latest	Number	datastoreWriteLoadMetric	4
☐ Storage I/O Control aggregated IOPS	Average	Number	datastoreIops	1
☐ Read latency	Average	Millisecond	totalReadLatency	1
☐ Storage DRS datastore bytes written	Latest	Number	datastoreWriteBytes	2
☐ Storage DRS datastore write I/O rate	Latest	Number	datastoreWriteIops	1
☐ Read rate	Average	KBps	read	2
☐ Storage DRS datastore outstanding read requests	Latest	Number	datastoreReadOIO	1
☐ Storage DRS datastore normalized write latency	Latest	Number	datastoreNormalWriteLatency	2
☐ Average read requests per second	Average	Number	numberReadAveraged	1
☐ Storage I/O Control active time percentage	Average	Percent	siocActiveTimePercentage	1
☐ Highest latency	Latest	Millisecond	maxTotalLatency	3

ESXi datastore counters

You can tell how much action has been taken by **Storage I/O Control (SIOC)** by following the **Storage I/O Control active time percentage** counter. The next screenshot shows a datastore cluster with two members. The first chart shows that SIOC was quite active because the datastore latency exceeded 30 milliseconds several times. The second chart shows the aggregate latency. The third and fourth charts show the latency of individual datastores, which are members of the group. As you can see, the aggregate is the average of both. Note that the aggregate is the average per I/O, it is not just a simple average of the values of the different datastores, because the datastores had different amounts of I/O.

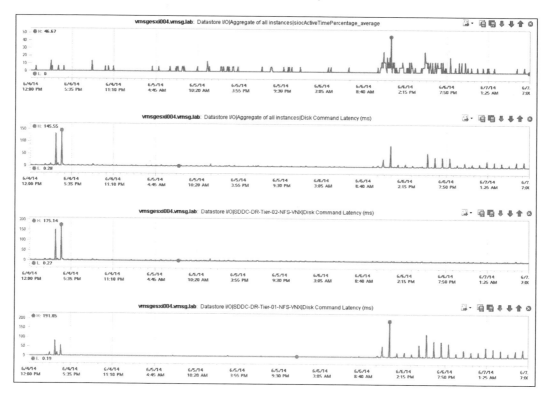

The ESXi Disk metric group, shown in the next screenshot, provides visibility into the VMkernel storage stack. For example, there are counters that track the amount of time a command spends sitting in the kernel queue. As shared earlier, the VMkernel latency should be less than 1 millisecond most of the time, as the main bottleneck should be at the physical device layer. You can create a super metric that tracks the maximum value of the Queue command latency and Kernel command latency for all ESXi hosts in your data centers. You should expect a value of 0 or 1 for the super metric, indicating a healthy situation.

Description	Rollup	Units	Internal Name	Collection Level
☐ Queue command latency	Average	Millisecond	queueLatency	2
☑ Write rate	Average	KBps	write	2
☐ Bus resets	Summation	Number	busResets	2
☐ Write latency	Average	Millisecond	totalWriteLatency	2
☐ Average commands issued per second	Average	Number	commandsAveraged	2
☐ Kernel read latency	Average	Millisecond	kernelReadLatency	2
☐ Queue write latency	Average	Millisecond	queueWriteLatency	2
☐ Read requests	Summation	Number	numberRead	3
☐ Average write requests per second	Average	Number	numberWriteAveraged	1
☐ Physical device command latency	Average	Millisecond	deviceLatency	1
☐ Write requests	Summation	Number	numberWrite	3
☐ Maximum queue depth	Average	Number	maxQueueDepth	1
☐ Commands aborted	Summation	Number	commandsAborted	2
☐ Kernel command latency	Average	Millisecond	kernelLatency	2
☑ Read rate	Average	KBps	read	2
☐ Physical device write latency	Average	Millisecond	deviceWriteLatency	2
☐ Read latency	Average	Millisecond	totalReadLatency	2
☐ Average read requests per second	Average	Number	numberReadAveraged	1
☑ Highest latency	Latest	Millisecond	maxTotalLatency	1
☐ Commands issued	Summation	Number	commands	2
☐ Physical device read latency	Average	Millisecond	deviceReadLatency	2
☐ Queue read latency	Average	Millisecond	queueReadLatency	2
☐ Kernel write latency	Average	Millisecond	kernelWriteLatency	2
☐ Command latency	Average	Millisecond	totalLatency	3
☑ Usage	Average	KBps	usage	1

The storage array provides access to many datastores, which are mounted by multiple ESXi hosts, sometimes in multiple clusters. Seeing the datastore counters at the ESXi level or cluster level means that we do not get the full picture. To see the full picture, we need to look at the datastore level or the array level. Keep in mind that most ESXi hosts have a local datastore that gets included in the ESXi level storage information. You need to manually exclude the local datastore information if you only need the data for a shared datastore.

For these reasons, I normally do not track storage performance at ESXi or cluster level.

Storage counters at the cluster level

vCenter does not provide information for storage at cluster level but vRealize Operations does, including counters such as IOPS, throughput, and latency. The main reason why I do not look at storage at the cluster level when working with traditional arrays is that the cluster is a *compute* cluster, not a storage cluster, so the boundary a cluster provides for compute may not apply to storage. The other reason is that the data at this level, as for the ESXi host level, includes all the *local datastores*. They can impact the overall result, especially those that give an average of all the datastores. If you have a cluster with 10 nodes that share 5 datastores, you will have 15 datastores in the clusters. The 10 local datastores will skew the total result, masking important data such as the average latency.

For a view beyond disk and datastore, the datastore cluster is a much more useful object to look into.

Storage counters at the datastore level

vCenter only provides the following screen for datastores. It is a fixed set of charts with a fixed configuration.

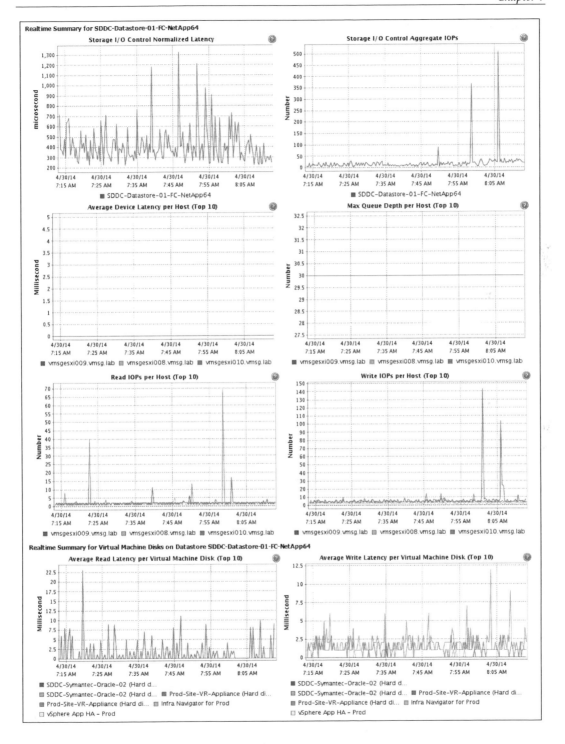

The complete list of charts available in vCenter is listed as follows:

- **Storage I/O Control Normalized Latency**
- **Storage I/O Control Normalized Aggregate IOPS**
- **Average Device Latency per host (Top 10 only)**
- **Maximum Queue Depth per host (Top 10 only)**
- **Read IOPS per host (Top 10 only)**
- **Write IOPS per host (Top 10 only)**
- **Average Read Latency per VM vDisk (Top 10 only)**
- **Average Write Latency per VM vDisk (Top 10 only)**
- **Read IOPS per VM vDisk (Top 10 only)**
- **Write IOPS per VM vDisk (Top 10 only)**

As you can see, this list is rather limited. For example, there are no counters for throughput, be it read, write, or total. Most charts only show the top 10 data points.

vRealize Operations provides a richer set of data for storage at the datastore level, including IOPS, throughput, latency, and outstanding I/O. For most of them, you get the data for Read, Write, and Total. In addition to these basic counters, vRealize Operations provides a **Workload** (%) counter, which provides good comparable information on storage utilization. In reality, different datastores will experience different IOPS and throughput. Even in the same datastore, different VMs will have different demands. For example, when someone says, "the datastore has high storage workload", what does that person normally mean? Usually, they mean high IOPS, high throughput, or high outstanding requests. All these factors are considered by the **Workload** (%) counter, as you can see in the following chart. It does not consider the latency, as high latency does not necessarily mean that the VMs in the datastore generate a lot of workload.

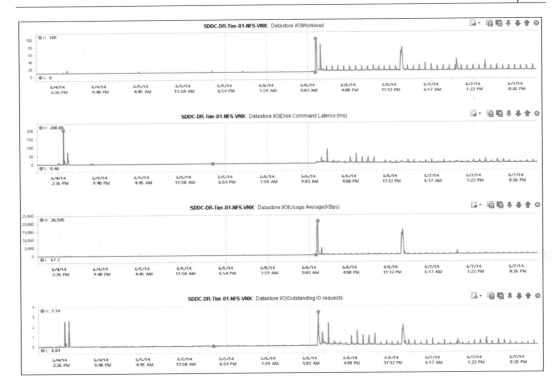

I find the **Workload** counter useful to compare across datastores. Unfortunately, there is no **Workload** counter at the datastore cluster level. This means you need to compare it at the datastore level, or create a super metric. The following table shows the counters I recommend you check at the datastore level:

Purpose	vCenter	vRealize Operations
Contention	Not available at datastore level	Disk command latency (milliseconds)
Utilization	Not available at datastore level	Commands per second
Utilization	Not available at datastore level	Usage Average (KBps)
Utilization	Not available at datastore level	Workload (%)

Storage counters at the datastore cluster level

vCenter only provides the following screen for Storage at the datastore cluster level. Just like with datastores, the screen is a fixed set of charts, the details of which cannot be modified.

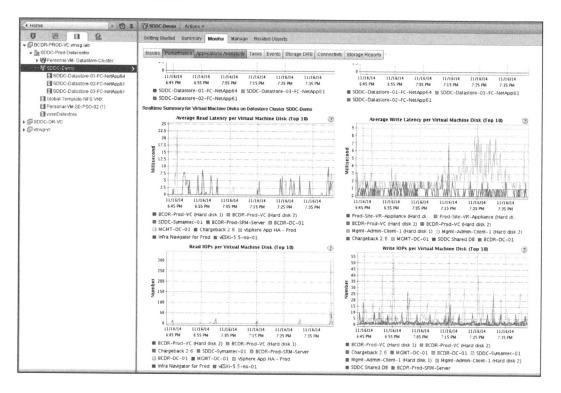

The complete list of charts provided by vCenter is mentioned as follows:

- **Normalized Latency per datastore (Top 10)**
- **Aggregate IOPS per datastore (Top 10)**
- **SIOC Activity report per datastore (Top 10)**
- **Storage I/O Control Normalized Latency**
- **Storage I/O Control Normalized Aggregate IOPS**
- **Average Device Latency per host (Top 10 only)**
- **Maximum Queue Depth per host (Top 10 only)**
- **Read IOPS per host (Top 10 only)**

- Write IOPS per host (Top 10 only)
- Average Read Latency per VM vDisk (Top 10 only)
- Average Write Latency per VM vDisk (Top 10 only)
- Read IOPS per VM vDisk (Top 10 only)
- Write IOPS per VM vDisk (Top 10 only)

As you can see from this list, it's rather limited. Just like with datastores, there are no counters for throughput and most charts only show the top 10 data points.

vRealize Operations provides a rich set of data. You get the IOPS, throughput, latency, and outstanding I/O. For most of them, you get the data for read, write, and total. The following table summarizes what I recommend you monitor. vCenter does not provide a counter for throughput. I have left the table cell blank for ease of comparison.

The following table shows the counters at the datastore cluster level:

Purpose	vCenter	vRealize Operations
Contention	Normalized latency per datastore	Disk command latency (milliseconds)
Utilization	Aggregate IOPS per datastore	Commands per second
Utilization		Usage average (KBps)

Storage counters at the higher level

As you can expect by now, vCenter does not provide information for storage at this level, but vRealize Operations does. The following table lists the key counters. Except for the World object, the rest of the objects provide all the counters. Take note that their values include local datastores. If you want to exclude the local datastores, create a group.

I included the **Workload (%)** counter as it may be easier for the operations team to deal with a percentage rather than raw data. For example, if you have 20 vCenter Servers and they show different KBps numbers, it is difficult to understand the significance of that value at a glance—is it higher or lower than, or the same as, last time? If you use the 0-100 range as a percentage, you can color code the range to help the operations team.

The following table shows the cluster counters of vRealize Operations:

Object	Purpose	Counters	Roll up
Data center	Contention	Disk Command Latency (millisecond)	Average
Data center	Utilization	Usage Rate (KBps)	Average
Data center	Utilization	Commands per second (number)	Average
Data center	Utilization	Workload (%)	Average
vCenter	Contention	Disk Command Latency (milliseconds)	Average
vCenter	Utilization	Usage Rate (KBps)	Average
vCenter	Utilization	Commands per seconds (number)	Average
vCenter	Utilization	Workload (%)	Average
World	Contention		
World	Utilization	Usage Rate (KBps)	Average
World	Utilization	Commands per second (number)	Average
World	Utilization	Workload (%)	Average

Storage contention guidance

The following table provides *general* guidance on storage contention. It *must* be read in conjunction with the *CPU Contention Guidance* section in *Chapter 4, CPU Counters*. I must emphasize that these are just guidelines—you should set the values according to the unique needs of your environment.

Object	Contention	Remarks
VM	Official SLA: • Tier 1: 10 milliseconds • Tier 2: 20 milliseconds • Tier 3: 30 milliseconds Internal threshold: • Tier 1: 5 milliseconds • Tier 2: 15 milliseconds • Tier 3: 20 milliseconds	The internal threshold is lower as it serves as a buffer.

Your customers only care about their own VMs, so the following numbers are for your internal targets. You should have a more stringent internal threshold. This gives you a buffer to troubleshoot.

Object	Contention	Remarks
ESXi	NA	There is no need to track at this level because of the following reasons: • You already track contention at the VM level, datastore level, and array level. • VMs get vMotion-ed in the cluster. Due to DRS and vMotion, a cluster is the smallest logical building block from a performance viewpoint. • You need to exclude local datastores.
Cluster	NA	There is no need to track at this level because of the following reasons: • You already track at the VM level, datastore level, and array level • You may have datastores that are mounted by multiple clusters • You need to exclude local datastores.
Datastore	Internal threshold: Tier 1: 5 milliseconds Tier 2: 10 milliseconds Tier 3: 15 milliseconds	The data at this level is an average of all VMs in that datastore. Hence, you should set a more aggressive target as the average latency will certainly be lower than the highest latency (which is experienced by one VM in that datastore).
Array	Internal threshold: Tier 1: 5 milliseconds Tier 2: 10 milliseconds Tier 3: 15 milliseconds	I recommend you use the respective vRealize Operations storage management pack. Discuss this with the storage architect.

Summary

In the previous four chapters, we covered many counters and objects. We covered CPU, RAM, network, and storage respectively. We covered each of them from both the contention and utilization point of view.

Now that we have mastered all the counters, we are in a position to apply them. The next chapter shows some real-life use cases, where we will put all these counters into a set of dashboards that will give us an insight into the environment.

8
Dashboard Examples and Ideas

This chapter provides real-life examples of dashboards that my customers have found to be useful. It is broken into a set of use cases. Here are the use cases we are going to cover in this chapter:

- Use case—is virtualization causing a problem?
- Use case—managing the overall SDDC performance
- Use case—dashboards for the big screen
- Use case—storage performance management
- Use case—storage capacity management
- Use case—network performance management
- Use case—right-sizing large VMs
- Use case—capacity planning

For each use case, I will provide the rationale behind it. This will enable you to review the context and requirements behind the dashboard, so you can then tailor the dashboard to your own needs. Each use case may need more than one dashboard, as a big dashboard takes longer to load and increases complexity. Having said that, I strongly recommend you use full HD resolution so the widgets are not too small.

Planning for your dashboards

During my interaction with customers, I learned that there are two types of dashboards:

- The first kind is for management purposes, be it to manage performance, capacity, availability, health, configuration, or compliance

- The second kind is for troubleshooting purposes, the use of which is normally triggered by performance issues

In a virtual environment, performance management and performance troubleshooting are relatively more distinct from each other than they are in a traditional physical environment. As resources are shared, performance management becomes more important to reduce the need to troubleshoot often. Here is a breakdown of the differences between performance management and performance troubleshooting:

- Troubleshooting means you currently have or you had a problem. Even if the problem is no longer active, you normally need to know what caused it. Management, on the other hand, is about preventing the problem in the first place. Troubleshooting is about correcting the problem. Management is about optimizing and planning.

- Troubleshooting tends to start from a specific problem (for example, a VM running slow, the network has dropped packets, the storage array has high latency). Management tends to start from the big picture. You need to ensure the overall situation is good before diving into a particular trouble spot.

- When you are troubleshooting, you are focused on the present, as you have a live fire to put out. When you are managing, you are focused on the future, anticipating problems, and taking action before they occur. In some sense, performance management is related to capacity management. This relationship is reflected in the vRealize Operations dashboard, where the capacity management major badge is **risk**—indicating the risk of future health and performance problems.

- In troubleshooting, the utilization of the resource is secondary. A VM can generate 10,000 IOPS, or it might be using 128 GB vRAM, and so on. So long as its high demands are being met, there is no performance problem. In troubleshooting, we are concerned with demands not being met. The utilization of the VM and the infrastructure are technically irrelevant. In management, you care about utilization and track it so that it does not grow beyond your physical resources and become a problem in the future.

The preceding differences directly impact how we use the vRealize Operations dashboards. From my experience, performance troubleshooting requires on-demand dashboards, on top of the dashboards used for performance management. Depending on the symptoms, I would either clone existing dashboards or create a brand new one. The dashboard may require new super metrics, groups, or tags. Depending on the complexity of the problem, we may need to create multiple widgets or dashboards. This is why I spent a lot of time in the previous chapters covering all the counters as you need to know exactly what they mean. Even if you choose the right counters, the wrong interpretation will still lead to the wrong conclusion.

Because of this wide variation, this chapter only focuses on management. Creating troubleshooting dashboards on the fly is a skill best picked up with experience. I will share some dashboards that demonstrate how vRealize Operations helps in performance and capacity management. There are many possibilities for these dashboards. For example, you can enhance them to include availability-related information as even a single fault can certainly impact performance. You may also decide to combine performance, capacity, and configuration into a series of dashboards that you check as one set.

Using the right counters

In *Chapter 4*, *CPU Counters*, to *Chapter 7*, *Storage Counters*, we've spent a considerable amount of time covering all the counters. It is important that you pick the right counters. The following table provides a summary for the two most fundamental counters:

- Contention
- Workload (representing utilization)

I've listed all the vSphere objects in the following table. For each object, a "No" under the **Contention** counter column means you will not find a counter called **Contention** for that object. The same goes for the **Workload** counter column. This is because the **Contention** counter and the **Workload** counter do not exist for all objects. For example, **Distributed switch** does not have a **Contention** counter, but it does have a **Workload** counter.

When there is no actual counter called **Contention** or **Workload**, you can use other counters as a workaround. For example, you can use **Latency (millisecond)** as a replacement for **Contention (%)**.

Object	Contention counter	Workload counter	Remarks
VM	• Overall: no • CPU: yes • RAM: yes • Storage: no • Network: no	• Overall: yes • CPU: yes • RAM: yes • Storage: yes • Network: yes	For storage, use the **Latency** counter. It is available for datastore only and not for RDM.
ESXi	• Overall: no • CPU: yes • RAM: yes • Storage: no • Network: no	• Overall: yes • CPU: yes • RAM: yes • Storage: yes • Network: yes	Same as VM.
Cluster	• Overall: no • CPU: yes • RAM: yes • Storage: no • Network: no	• Overall: yes • CPU: yes • RAM: yes • Storage: yes • Network: yes	Same as VM.
Data center	• Overall: no • CPU: yes • RAM: yes • Storage: no • Network: no	• Overall: yes • CPU: yes • RAM: yes • Storage: yes • Network: yes	Same as VM.
vCenter	• Overall: no • CPU: yes • RAM: yes • Storage: no • Network: no	• Overall: yes • CPU: yes • RAM: yes • Storage: yes • Network: yes	Same as VM.
World	• Overall: no • CPU: no • RAM: yes • Storage: no • Network: no	• Overall: yes • CPU: yes • RAM: yes • Storage: yes • Network: yes	Same as VM.

Object	Contention counter	Workload counter	Remarks
Distributed switch	• Network: no	• Network: yes	CPU, RAM, and disk are not relevant for this object, hence they are not shown. Use the **Dropped Packet** counter to measure contention.
Distributed port group	• Network: no	• Network: yes	Same as distributed switch.
Datastore	• Storage: no	• Storage: yes	CPU, RAM, and network are not relevant for this object. Use the **Latency** counter to measure contention.
Datastore cluster	• Storage: no	• Storage: no	Same as datastore.

Figuring out who will use which dashboard

As you create many dashboards for different roles in your organization, you will find that some of the information or widgets apply to more than one user or role. For example, the VMware administrator may need a dashboard that shows information about VMs, ESXi, network, and storage on a single screen. The network widget in that dashboard is also useful for the network administrator. So don't worry if you find yourself duplicating information as you build your dashboards. What start as very similar dashboards may evolve over time with user requirements.

In general, there are some differences between dashboards for senior management (for example, CIO) and dashboards for the ground-level technical team (for example, VMware administrator). This table lists the main differences:

Senior management	Ground-level team
A simple dashboard with minimal interaction and widgets. The dashboard fits into a notebook's display.	A rich dashboard, which may have complex interaction and many widgets. Ideally, the dashboard occupies a full HD screen.
It shows the big picture. It also tends to be application focused.	It shows the big picture but complemented with detailed information. It focuses on the infrastructure or application, depending on the role.

Senior management	Ground-level team
The number presented is relative, normalized to 0-100 for ease of comparison and understanding.	The data presented shows both the absolute data (raw figure) and the normalized data. It requires technical knowledge on counters.
It focuses on the long term timeline (normally 1-3 months). The data is averaged out. A 30-minute spike will not show up.	Some dashboards will focus on the long term timeline, whereas others will focus on the short term. For the short term timeline, it tends to show both peak and average values. A 5-minute spike will be visible in the chart.
Normally, it is updated daily. Users are not expected to log in multiple times a day.	The short-term dashboard will be updated every 5 minutes. Users may have the dashboard open all the time.

You will also tailor the built-in dashboards to fit your needs. Do not be afraid to change them in any way, as they do not impact the way vRealize Operations works. The dashboards that you create should complement the built-in dashboards, as there is no point in duplicating them.

How many dashboards do I need to have?

The number of dashboards you will have depends on the size of the environment and the number of people managing it. An environment with 100 VMs in just 5 hosts and 1 cluster will need far fewer dashboards than an environment with 100,000 VMs spread over 5,000 ESXi, 500 clusters, 20 data centers, and 15 vCenter Servers.

In a large environment, where you have many physical data centers and even more vSphere clusters, you will likely need to display the information per physical data center. There are several reasons for this:

- Aggregating data at a global level, which spans many physical data centers, will hide too much information. Presenting data at such a level means you are getting an average of thousands of objects. If your environment is generally healthy (and it should be), the average will logically fall within a healthy range.

- In most cases, the performance in a given physical data center is independent from that of other data centers. For example, your Singapore data center typically does not impact the performance of your London data center. An exception to this case is when you link your data center at the network (stretched L2) and storage layers (synchronous replication). From my experience in troubleshooting such a scenario, I recommend you keep the physical layer independent from each other. Assuming your data centers are independent, it makes more sense to display the chart on a per data center basis.

- VMs typically do not move from one physical data center to another (unless they are paired with storage replication and your network is stretched), so an imbalance among multiple data centers does not translate into a realistic rebalancing action.

The following picture should help you visualize the situation. Imagine you have two vCenter Servers. They manage five large data centers, located in different cities or countries. Each data center has multiple clusters. From here, you can plan what data you want to see at what level. Think of both techniques of rolling up (across time and across member), which we covered earlier.

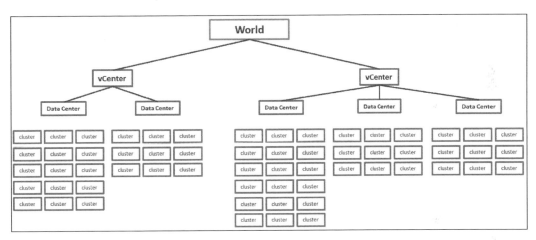

The use cases given in this chapter are only a small subset of the possible use cases for vRealize Operations dashboards. For more real-world cases of how to implement vRealize Operations, I recommend you check out the blogs of Lior Kamrat at `http://imallvirtual.com/` and Sunny Dua at `http://vxpresss.blogspot.sg/`. They have individual blogs and are also contributing authors to the official VMware Cloud Management blogs at `http://blogs.vmware.com/management/`. I have not duplicated use cases that Lior and Sunny have already covered in their blogs.

Providing a step-by-step guide on how to build the vRealize Operations dashboards in the use cases is out of the scope of this book, as materials on how to build vRealize Operations dashboards is freely available online. I am assuming that you know or can access information on how to build the dashboard—the purpose of this section is to help you work out what to build. I aim to give you some examples from which you can start creating your own dashboard ideas.

Use case – is virtualization causing a problem?

The target user for this use case is the VM Owner (via the operations team).

It is common for the application team (or the VM Owner) to suspect that virtualization is behind any performance degradation. After all, resources are shared and there are many IaaS workloads.

The workflow here is that the operations team gets a call from a VM Owner asking for proof on whether or not the VM is being held back by the infrastructure. In other words, does the infrastructure give whatever resources the VM is asking for? To prove this, we need to show the following information about the VM:

- CPU contention
- Memory contention
- Disk latency
- Network dropped packets (as covered at the beginning of *Chapter 6*, *Network Counters*, vCenter does not provide network latency information)

All the preceding information has to be provided in a line chart format, so that any peak in the past can be shown. The line chart will also enable the operations team to look back to see whether the problem has occurred previously or not.

This dashboard is meant to be simple and quick for level 1 or level 2 support in a large organization with thousands of VMs. If you want to enhance it, here are some ideas you can use:

- Provide Guest-OS-level information. The following counters will provide visibility into the OS:
    - CPU run queue
    - Memory paging activity
    - Outstanding disk I/O at the Guest filesystem level
- Provide network latency information.
- Provide individual vCPU utilization. This provides visibility into whether any cores are saturated. This covers the situation of a VM with multiple vCPUs, where the VM does not use all its given cores.

- Provide individual vmdk latency. The information at the VM level is an average of all its vmdk files.

The preceding enhancements will likely require an agent to be installed on the Guest OS. This is where **Hyperic**, a part of vRealize Operations, comes in. For Windows, you can also use **Windows Management Instrumentation (WMI)**.

If your environment has a standard where the page.file is always on a separate vmdk (for example, scsi1:0), you can use vRealize Operations to display its read/write information without the need of an agent.

What the dashboard looks like

The resultant dashboard looks like the following screenshot. It is split into three columns. Ideally, your screen resolution is full HD, so the line charts can display sufficient information:

- The first column is for the VM
- The second column is for the ESXi host where the VM runs
- The third column is for the datastore where the VM resides

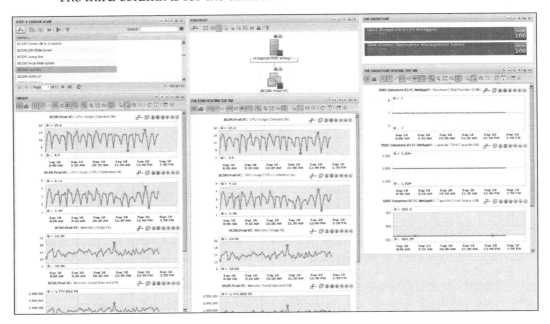

As the preceding screenshot may not be clear, I've zoomed in to the key parts of the dashboard in the following screenshot:

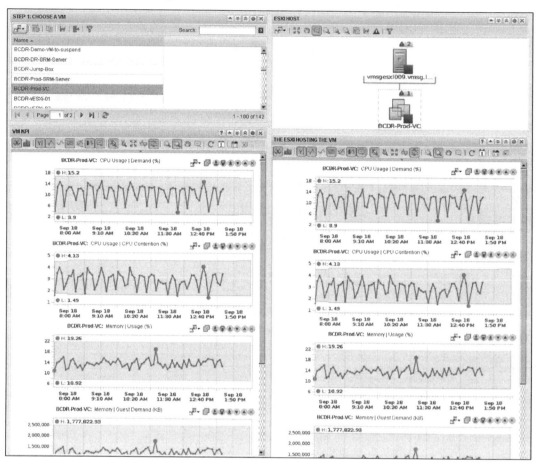

The dashboard contains several widgets with interactions among them. The first widget is **Resource List**, which lists all the VMs in the environment. This is ideally a World level object, so you get all the VMs from all vCenter Servers. You need to navigate to **Resource Kind | VM** so that it only shows the VM and not all the other objects. In the **Resource List** widget, you can display an additional column from the VM resource kind.

The widget below the first widget is named **VM KPI**. It shows the contention information. This is specific to the chosen VM, so it is driven by the first widget. You need to specify this in the **Widget Interaction** step. You can set the default information to display data at any length of time. I chose 1 day as it is a good balance between the details and the big picture.

The widget displays the following metrics:

- CPU contention
- CPU demand
- Memory contention
- Memory demand
- Disk latency
- Network drop packet

CPU demand and memory demand are included to verify whether the slowness is because of high utilization.

Views are a new feature in Version 6.0. In Version 5.x, you needed to create a custom XML file if you wanted to display specific metrics. In Version 6, you just need to create a view for a specific metric. There is no need to manually edit and upload an XML file anymore. The catch is that you get one chart per view, which cannot be split. If you want multiple charts, you need to have multiple views, and hence multiple widgets.

Moving on to the second column, the ESXi host is automatically shown. The line chart widget below the ESXi host provides the same information as the second widget, but only for the ESXi host where the VM in question is running. Although technically it is not relevant, the information provides assurance to the VM owner that the underlying ESXi host is coping well. This covers the scenario that ESXi is busy doing non-VM work, such as vMotion or other VMkernel-level workload.

The last column shows the datastore automatically. The line chart widget below it provides the storage latency information at the datastore where the VM resides. Although technically it is not relevant, it provides assurance if the underlying datastore is coping well.

Use case – managing the overall SDDC performance

The target user for this use case is an SDDC overall architect.

This use case presents dashboards for someone who is keen on the overall infrastructure performance. This is typically the starting point of any performance troubleshooting, as one needs to know the overall situation before diving into a particular problem. This dashboard is not for the overall health. Health is more than performance. It takes into account anomalies and faults. Health is also affected when the capacity is near full, and it takes into account the vSphere HA setting.

The dashboard is suited for the overall SDDC architect, the person who will perform troubleshooting. However, the dashboard can be modified to suit other roles, such as the head of infrastructure.

As this is an overall dashboard, it needs to be complemented with a set of more detailed dashboards. The detailed dashboards will cover storage, network, and compute, separately. This dashboard just shows the big picture. It does not show capacity information, as this is a performance dashboard.

The overall performance can be broken down into two levels: VM and infrastructure.

For each level, we need to cover the four main components, which are as follows:

- CPU
- RAM
- Disk
- Network

VM level

At the VM level, we need to ensure not a single VM experiences a contention that exceeds the agreed SLA. If you have multiple tiers, you naturally have a different SLA per tier. This means you need to plot one chart for each service tier.

In a smaller environment, where you mix multiple service tiers in a cluster, you need to manually create groups. Create one group for each tier, and place the VMs into their respective tier.

In a larger environment, where you have dedicated clusters for each service tier, you can simply use the cluster. If you have many clusters, you need to create a group for each tier. Add the clusters to their groups manually. This is a one-time setup that you need to do for each cluster. In an environment where you have many physical data centers, these groups can contain clusters from different vCenter Servers and different physical data centers. A tier 1 VM is a tier 1 VM, regardless of where it physically resides. You should have consistent SLAs throughout your organization.

When you create the group, the group will naturally be an object that is one level higher, as it has to encompass all the members of the group. The following screenshot shows a group named **Tier 1 Clusters**. It has two clusters as its members.

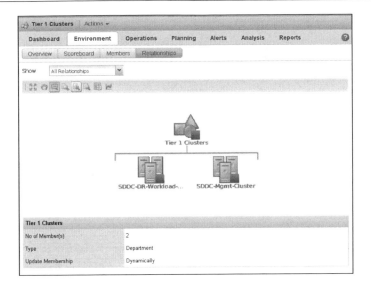

When I clicked on one of the member clusters, I got the following screenshot. It drills down into the cluster, showing all the ESXi hosts belonging to that cluster.

This understanding is important because it impacts the way you create the super metric. You cannot create a super metric on top of another super metric. So the way you get the summary at the group level is by specifying **depth=3**, instead of **depth=2** in the super metric formula.

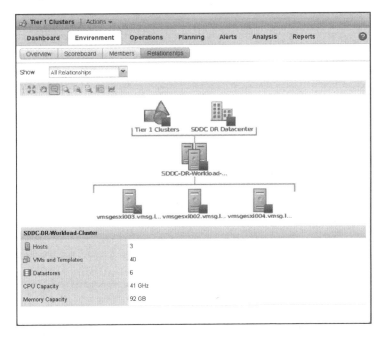

You need to look at both the maximum and average lines. The maximum line will give the peak result. For the maximum line, you should get a value that is below your SLA for that specific tier. This means that you meet your SLA, as not a single VM goes above the threshold. For the average line, you would like to see a line that is much lower than the maximum line. This means that you have room as most VMs get a good service from the hypervisor.

If the maximum is above the SLA, but the average is far lower than the maximum, it means that only a small percentage of VMs are breaching the SLA. If the average is near the maximum, and the maximum is higher than the SLA, you have a widespread problem.

The line charts will look like the next screenshot. The top chart shows the average, and the bottom one shows the maximum. In this example, the problem is not widespread as the maximum is around 10 times higher than the average.

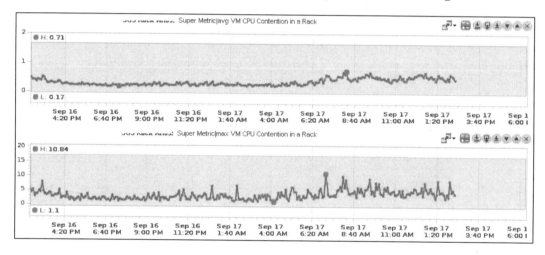

You need to create three charts for each tier. Each chart will have two lines. The charts are as follows:

- Maximum CPU contention and average CPU contention for all VMs in that tier

- Maximum RAM contention and average RAM contention for all VMs in that tier

- Maximum storage latency and average storage latency for all VMs in that tier

All the previously shown charts rely on the super metric. An example of the super metric is shown in the next screenshot. This shows the maximum CPU contention for all VMs in a cluster. Notice **depth=2** in the formula. If you are using a group, you have to use **depth=3** and apply the formula at the group level instead.

In the next screenshot, I also previewed the result using a cluster called **SDDC-Mgmt-Cluster**. I find the preview feature very useful in validating that the super metric is configured correctly.

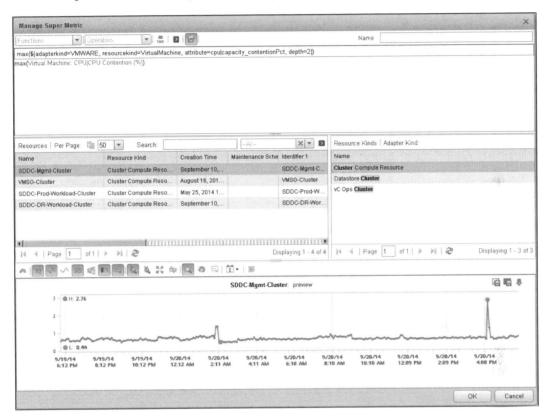

For tier 1, where you should not oversubscribe, you can skip the average and just show the maximum. You should expect a flat line for memory. It should look like the example in the next screenshot, where there is no memory contention for a long period of time:

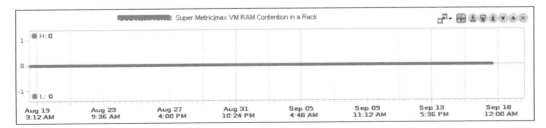

The vRealize Operations line chart does not tell you which VM hits the maximum latency at any given moment. Hovering a mouse over a particular point does not show the object providing the value. You need to complement it with a top-N chart. This lets you see which VMs are experiencing contention in that specific time range. You need to modify the time line of the top-N widget manually to match the line chart because the line chart does not drive the top-N widget.

There is no need to add the network as the default dashboard provides it already. You should expect no drop packet or error. The chart will look like the following one. This one shows that there is no dropped packet for the entire week.

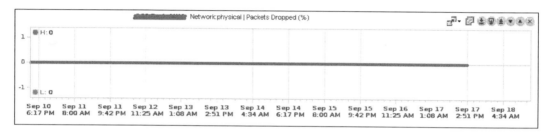

The overall dashboard looks like the following screenshot. This is only for one service tier. As you can see, it is more practical to create one dashboard per tier, especially if you do not mix tiers in a cluster.

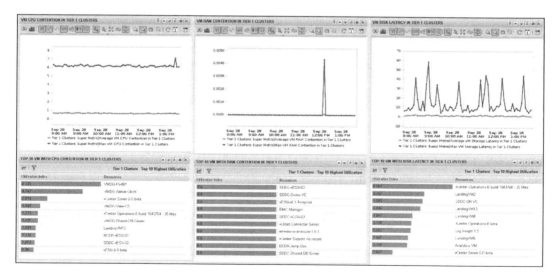

As the preceding screenshot may not be clear, I've zoomed in to a part of the dashboard in the following screenshot:

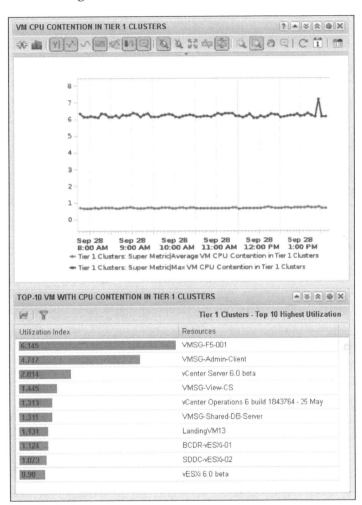

Infrastructure level

At the infrastructure level, you will focus on utilization, not contention. As discussed in our exploration of the metrics, contention is covered at the VM level. Although looking at the same information from the infrastructure level is useful, it is not necessary for this big picture, and the leaner the big picture dashboard is while still providing the necessary information, the more useful it is. The detailed dashboards can deliver the additional information.

The dashboard is split into two parts:

- Compute
- Storage

There is no need to add a network as you should have it already in the default dashboard. You should expect no dropped packet or error.

For the compute part, you need to show the following:

- A line chart showing the maximum CPU demand and average CPU demand for all hosts per service tier:
  - Notice I use host, not cluster. It is more granular this way.
  - If you need to show the data in one screen, you can combine the tiers. If you do this, bear in mind that tier 3 hosts will dominate the result as it should have higher utilization due to higher oversubscription.

- A line chart showing the maximum RAM consumed and the maximum RAM demand for all hosts per tier:
  - I have to use both consumed and demand due to the two-level memory hierarchy.
  - I am using maximum for both as I am tracking peak utilization here.

- A heat map showing the CPU demand distribution:
  - Color by CPU demand. You can set your threshold at 80 percent to provide some buffer as you need to cater for HA. It also takes time to procure new hardware, so setting the threshold at 100 percent is risky. Setting it at 80 percent means a host with a CPU demand of 80 percent will be shown in full red.
  - Size by the number of physical cores. This is assuming that the greater the number of cores, the more powerful the host is, which is generally the case. Using the CPU frequency is not a good indicator as the frequency no longer equates to the performance.

- A heat map showing the RAM demand distribution:

  ○ Color by RAM demand. As with the CPU, you can set the threshold at 80 percent.

  ○ Size by RAM size. This means the more RAM the host has, the bigger the box. You should expect a uniform size if you have standardized your ESXi host. You should standardize as it lowers complexity.

An example of the line chart is shown in the next screenshot. This shows the charts for **Tier 1 Clusters**.

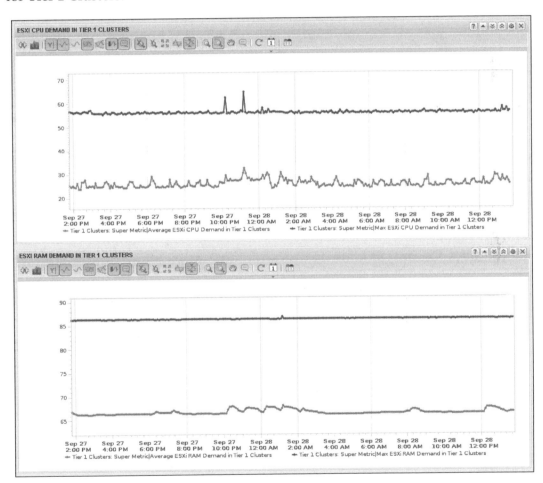

For a heat map, you need to set the interaction and drive the heat map from another widget if you need to filter it. In our case, we only want to show the ESXi hosts from a specific service tier (for example, **Tier 1 Clusters**). The problem is that the host object is not a member of the group; the cluster object is. So we cannot filter it from within the widget. We can, however, filter it from outside the widget. The following screenshot shows how we can select a particular tier, and it shows only the hosts on that tier.

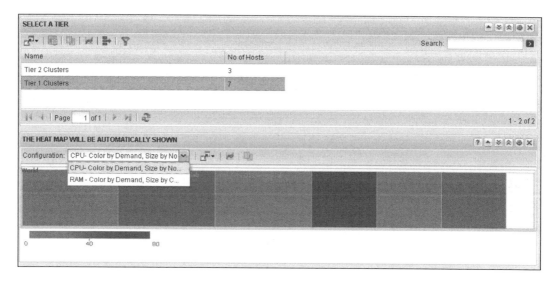

As you can see in the preceding screenshot, I put two configurations for the heat maps to save space: one for the RAM and one for the CPU.

For storage, there is no need to display the information per tier if all the tiers reside on the same physical array. Since many components of the array are shared, it is better to do the dashboard at the physical array level. An exception to this is if your physical array is capable of providing different tiers. If you have many physical arrays, it is best to display the chart per array.

Because you are showing data at the array level, you will be deriving the overall trends. You should see a gradual increase over time. You may have a daily, weekly, and monthly spike if you have many scheduled jobs.

You need to have two line charts per array. You cannot put them in the same chart as their values are vastly different in terms of scale. The charts are as follows:

- Total IOPS for all nonlocal datastores. If you have RDM, use disk (LUN) instead of datastore. This is assuming that your ESXi is not configured with SAN boot (most customers do not boot from SAN).

- Total throughput (gigabits/second) for all nonlocal datastores. This should be lower than the physical connection that your storage has, preferably with 30 percent headroom. You need to use a super metric to convert the number from kilobytes/second to gigabits/second.

vRealize Operations does not distinguish between local and shared datastores. To exclude the local datastores, you need to create a group or tag in vRealize Operations. If your shared datastore has a different naming pattern than your local datastore, you can create a dynamic group based on the name. If not, then you can use **Tag**, and manually drag all the shared datastores into that **Tag**. An example of how to use **Tag** is shown in this screenshot:

Once the preceding tag is created, I simply select all my shared datastores and drag-and-drop them from the UI to the tag. The tag is like a container, so it is an object one level higher than the datastore. This means that the super metric must be applied one level below; for example, to get the total throughput from all the datastores, I used the following formula:

To convert from KBps to Gbps, you have to multiply by 8, divide it by 1,024, and divide by 1,024.

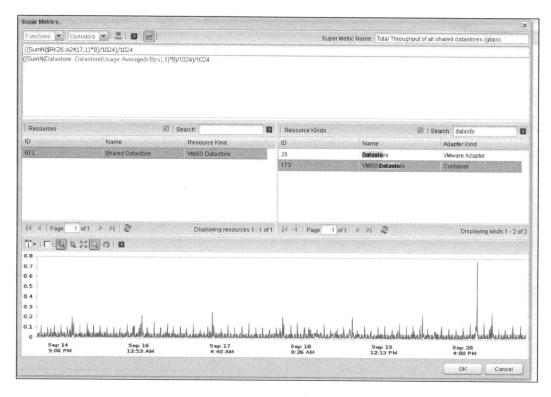

You need to complement the preceding line chart with a heat map. The heat map shows latency and IOPS for all datastores, so you know the relative distribution among all your datastores:

- Color by latency so all the high-latency datastores will be highly visible. Because this is for all tiers, you need to group the information per tier in the heat map to differentiate the tiers. If you have a lot of datastores, you can create a separate heat map for each tier in the same widget.

- Size by IOPS so you can quickly see if there is an IOPS unbalanced among the datastores. If you have RDMs, choose **Disk** instead of **Datastore**.

The following screenshot shows the configuration of the heat map. In this example, my physical array does not support multiple tiers, so I only have 1 tier. I have a tag called **Shared Datastores** and I used it to filter the result. I set the latency value to 30 milliseconds. I size it by IOPS. Notice that the counter is parked under the **Devices** category, and not under **Datastore**.

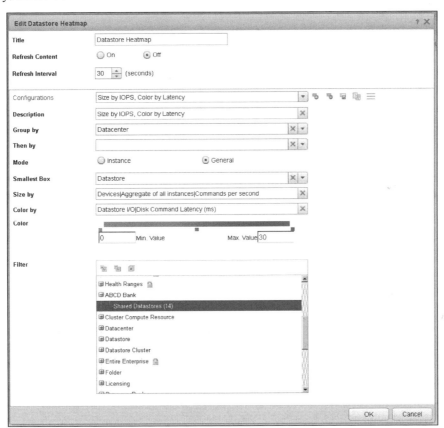

The preceding information is not sufficient to conclude that you need to invest in more hardware. There are factors such as read/write ratio, block size distribution, nature of the I/O (random, sequential), and cache. However, this is a mandatory input to discuss with the storage teams as to how demand hits the physical array. They would appreciate the feedback as they cannot see the VMs hitting the array in vSphere 5.5.

Use case – dashboards for the big screen

The target user for this use case is the operations team.

This set of dashboards serves a similar purpose with the previous use case (managing the overall SDDC) because typically you would show the key indicators for both. There are, however, differences in the implementation. For the operations team control center, where key operations information is displayed on a large screen dashboard, the following key characteristics apply:

- There is no interaction, as there is no user clicking on any part of the dashboard.

- The dashboards will automatically cycle every 1 minute. You can modify this time period, add more dashboards, and change the order.

- The dashboards show minimal information, typically with large numbers. They do not show detailed charts as that is hard to read from afar. Ideally, all the numbers are in percentage, with 0 being bad and 100 being perfect.

- The dashboards typically use color to classify information. Color is much easier to digest from afar and at a glance. A good approach is to use the vRealize Operations key colors (green, yellow, amber, and red).

- The screen is simplified and the browser is set to full screen. To minimize the vRealize Operations functionality, create an ID with the least amount of access. This will hide some of the menu and buttons, resulting in a neater screen.

- The content is chosen so that it drives the viewer into action. If you display something that is red most of the time, after a while the viewer will ignore it, hence defeating the very purpose of displaying on the big screen. When something on the big screen is red, you want action to be taken. Thus, the color changes in vRealize Operations should be chosen such that if everything is functioning normally, everything is green.

The following screenshot provides an example of this type of control center operations dashboard. This is the first dashboard in a series of four dashboards. This first dashboard focuses on availability, and the remaining three dashboards focus on performance and capacity. This dashboard looks at Business VM, Management VM, ESXi host, and physical arrays. We are using a heat map for this dashboard as availability, unlike performance, is binary in nature. We set the size to fixed so it is easier to compare. If the size is not fixed, it will change every minute, making it difficult to read. There are 12 physical NetApp devices distributed throughout Asia. The first four show white boxes instead of green as NetApp DFM integration has not been completed. The arrays were detected by the plugins, but no data was received.

Use case – storage performance management

The target user for this use case is a storage administrator or storage architect.

This is the use case for the storage administrator or VMware administrator who wants to know how the overall storage is performing. As a result, this is a storage-centric view, not a VMware-centric view. In this dashboard, we will not focus on non-storage items.

Following the IaaS business model, you need to match the supply and demand. The supply comes from the physical infrastructure, and the demand comes from VM and ESXi (the workload is not generated by VMs, such as vSphere Replication). When you purchase an array, you are given certain specifications in terms of IOPS, throughput, and capacity. You will have to assume a certain read/write ratio or block size as it's impossible to predict the demand in advance. The specifications have to deliver more than the total demand hitting the array; otherwise, the storage latency will go up. In addition, having a good latency today does not mean you will have a good latency in three months. So knowing how close the demand is to the supply is important.

The example dashboards here focus on performance. For the capacity, refer to the next example.

You need to show several line charts:

- Maximum read latency and maximum write latency from all datastores mounted on the array in the past one month:
    - Exclude the local datastores, as discussed previously.
    - Separate the read and write latencies, as you want to know how the ESXi host and storage cache cushion the I/O.
    - Use datastores and not VMs as there are many workloads that are not generated by VMs. We covered this previously and called them **IaaS** workloads. Examples of IaaS storage workloads are vSphere replication, VM cloning, and storage vMotion.
    - Expect the latency number to be below 30 milliseconds because the data is a 5-minute average. This means not a single datastore experienced a sustained 30 milliseconds of latency for 5 minutes. 5 minutes is 300 seconds or 300,000 milliseconds. That is a long time in milliseconds, so an average of 30 milliseconds means the peak within those 5 minutes could be much higher than 30 milliseconds. I have seen a peak hit several hundred milliseconds when the 5-minute average was only 11 milliseconds.
    - Use monthly data so we can see if there is a month-end effect.

- The average (latency) from all datastores mounted on the array in the past 1 month:

  ○ This chart complements the first chart as the peak tends to hide the big picture. You should expect your average to be well below the peak. If it is near the peak, you have a widespread problem. If it is well below the peak, and the peak value is not good, then the problem only impacts a few datastores. Check the spindles where the affected datastores reside.

  ○ Expect the number to be below 10 milliseconds, indicating a healthy overall array. This number should certainly be tied to your business SLA. If your array is predominantly serving non-production workloads, and you have agreed on a less stringent SLA, you may tolerate a higher average latency as you want to maximize your investment.

- Maximum read latency and maximum write latency from all VMs:

  ○ This is the same as for chart 1, but zoomed in on the VM's point of view. You want to know how your customer (the VM) is being served.

  ○ If you want, you can complement this chart with the average version. However, I do not see a real need as you already have chart 2.

- Maximum (IOPs) from all VMs mounted on the array in the past 1 month:

  ○ The value should be mostly below 2,000, or a number that you think is the highest generator of IOPS (not throughput) for the VM. As a storage administrator, you need to be aware of the highly demanding VMs and understand their pattern. For example, do they spike together at the start of the day or the end of the month?

- Average (IOPS) from all VMs mounted on the array in the past one month:

  ○ The value should be mostly below 200, especially if you have a large VM population. You should also be able to see a daily pattern if many VMs are inactive after office hours.

As usual, you should complement the line charts with a heat map and a top-N widget, providing more detailed information on the present situation. For example, you can add the following:

- A heat map showing how your infrastructure is coping with the demand:
    - ° The heat map shows the latency and IOPS for all VMs, so you know how demands are met.

- Color by latency so all the high-latency VMs will be easily visible. Because this is for all tiers, you want to group the information per tier in the heat map. If you have many VMs, you can create separate heat maps for each tier in the same widget. Using separate heat maps allows you to set a different threshold. Showing a different threshold is useful as you have a different SLA.

- Size by IOPS so you can see if you have highly demanding VMs dominating your array. This lets you quickly find those VMs that generate the bulk of the IOPS.

- A top-N listing of the top 20 VMs in terms of IOPS:
    - ° This complements the heat map as now the VM names are listed along with their actual IOPS.
    - ° A useful feature in top-N is that you can go back in time. For example, you can know exactly which VM generated the most IOPS when you had a huge spike in your array eight days ago from 9 a.m. to 10 a.m.

- A top-N listing the top 20 datastores in terms of IOPS:
    - ° This is similar to the top-N for VMs, except you show datastores instead.
    - ° If a datastore is heavily hit, you can then drill into the datastore to see if this is a consistent workload.

Use case – storage capacity management

The target user for this use case is the storage administrator or storage architect.

I like this particular dashboard as it demonstrates how you can be creative with super metrics. This dashboard is courtesy of my colleague Yuval Tenenbaum, a lead SE for Cloud Management based in the UK.

As a storage administrator, you may have a policy of not placing more than 15 VMs per datastore. You also want to keep 20 percent free space to cater for snapshots and growth. In a large environment, this can be difficult to enforce and track. If you have hundreds of datastores, it can be cumbersome to show the degree of compliance on a single screen. Ideally, you would like to see a heat map showing all datastores; the higher the number of VMs, or the lesser the capacity left in percentage, the more the datastore should be highlighted (in red). So the heat map would show the information at a glance, if the boxes in the heat map are closer to green, that all of your datastores have good buffer in terms of both the number of VMs and the capacity remaining. Achieving this requires a super metric that tracks the maximum of both the high number of VMs and the capacity remaining.

Let me explain the preceding section with an example.

The first table below addresses the capacity portion. In this example, the size of the datastore is 2 TB, and you have set 80 percent as the threshold. If the consumed space is 800 GB, the ratio is 800/1600 or 50 percent. As the consumed space grows, so does the ratio. At 1.7 TB, which is still below the 2 TB configured space, the ratio is already above 1. If you set 1 as red and 0 as green in the heat map, you will get a full red box as 1.07 is above 1, even though you still have some room to react (in this example, 300 GB remains).

Consumed	Provisioned	Threshold	Ratio
800	2000	1600	0.50
1600	2000	1600	1.00
1700	2000	1600	1.07
1800	2000	1600	1.13

The second table addresses the number of VMs portion. In this example, the policy is to not have more than 20 VMs per datastore. You decide to set the threshold at 75 percent, which equals to 15. If a datastore has 15 VMs, the ratio will be 15/15 or 1.0. If you set 1 as red and 0 as green in the heat map, you will get a full red box even though you have a buffer of 5 more VMs.

Number of VMs deployed	Threshold	Ratio
5	15	0.33
10	15	0.67
15	15	1.00
20	15	1.33

We now need to combine the two portions into a single super metric. We will take the maximum of their values, so we get a full red box when either threshold is reached. The super metric needs to use the `This Resource` function as you need to point to the resource itself. The actual formula is shown in this screenshot:

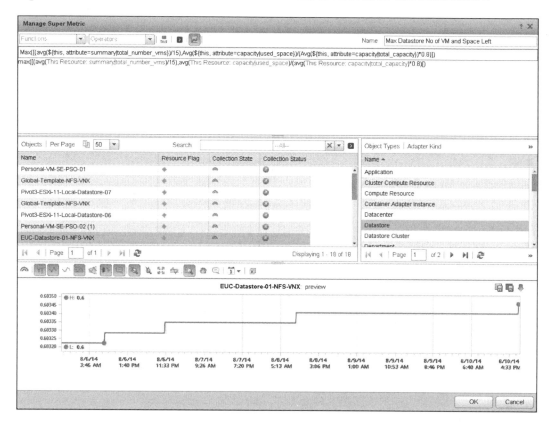

The following is the formula that is mentioned in the screenshot:

Max([(avg(${this, attribute=summary | total_number_vms})/15), Avg(${this, attribute=capacity | used_space})/(Avg(${this, attribute=capacity | total_capacity})*0.8)])

Use case – network performance management

The target user for this use case is the network administrator.

Networking in the SDDC can be divided into three layers:

- The first layer is the VM, which typically has only one vNIC. From a performance management point of view, this is relatively the simplest layer.

- The second layer is the hypervisor, which has multiple components. The hypervisor has virtual switches, typically distributed across many hosts. The switches are connected to the physical NICs, which serve as uplinks. There are many settings and policies that can be applied to the switch and its port groups. With NSX, the hypervisor has a distributed router, a distributed firewall, and a load balancer. This layer can be quite complex to monitor.

- The third layer is made up of the physical switches and routers in the data center. This also includes the WAN link and Internet connectivity. This layer is typically monitored by the network team. If the physical layer has a firewall and a load balancer, that might be monitored by a different team.

The VMware or SDDC architect needs to cover the first two layers at least. Work together with the network team so you can achieve end-to-end monitoring. You will likely need to use a management pack, such as NetFlow Logic, so that the data can appear in vRealize Operations and be analyzed.

To prove that the network is performing well, you need to do a few things:

- Show that there is no error:
    - This can be done with a line chart, which shows that not a single ESXi or VM has experienced dropped packets or error packets. For the ESXi host, you need to get the data from all vmnics.

- Show that the network latency is low:
    - As shared, this is not provided by vCenter and you need to deploy additional tools.

- Show that utilization is below capacity:
    - This can be done with a line chart showing that utilization is below the physical capacity. The physical capacity is either 1 gigabit or 10 gigabits, and you want a number below that.
    - You need to show that not a single ESXi or VM is hitting its limit.

- Special packets:
    - You should expect that the broadcast and multicast packets are kept to a minimum.

Let's discuss how we can deliver the preceding points.

To show that there is no error, you need to check if any VM or ESXi has error packets or dropped packets. Let's show them in two separate charts so it's easier to see if the problem is at the VM level or ESXi level. This means that we need to create two super metrics that track the maximum of dropped packets or error packets. The first one will track all VMs in the data center; the second one will track all ESXi hosts.

If your network is healthy, the charts will be a flat line at 0. This means not a single ESXi host or VM in the entire data center is experiencing packet drops in any of its NICs.

In the event that you have a dropped packet or error packet, you can show it with a top-N widget. I prefer top-N to heat map as top-N allows you to go back in time. The line chart will show the time when the problem occurred, and the top-N time line can be changed to match it. You need to have four top-N widgets. Assuming you just need to show the top 20, you will have:

- The top 20 VM with dropped packets
- The top 20 VM with error packets
- The top 20 ESXi with dropped packets
- The top 20 ESXi with error packets

It is easier to show four widgets than combining the counters as this means that you do not have to create a super metric. It also means that you get to see more detail, which is the objective here.

To show utilization, you apply the same concept, which is using a super metric that tracks the maximum value of network utilization. For a VM, you should expect the value to be below 1 Gbps. If your ESXi uses 10 gigabits, and your VM sees this, it is possible that a network-intensive VM will sustain 1 Gbps for 5 minutes. You need to know about such a VM as it can impact the performance of other VMs or the host. For ESXi, you should expect the value to be below 1 Gbps or 10 Gbps per vmnic, depending upon whether you are using a 1 gigabit or 10 gigabit ethernet.

If the value is too close to the physical wire speed, you need to dig deeper to see whether it is caused by a VM or non-VM workload. For a VM, you can complement the preceding line chart with a top-N widget. For example, show the top 30 VMs in terms of network utilization. A small percentage of your VMs will have their backup via the LAN. You can track them separately (another super metric) if you standardize them to use the second vNIC. You are probably using a second vNIC as your backup network should be a different network.

For ESXi, this is harder, as an ESXi host, typically, has multiple vmnics, and features such as load-based teaming can move workloads from one vmnic to another.

The distributed switch can tell the utilization of the port group. However, it does not tell which port belongs to which ESXi host. You do not know how much network utilization is generated by each member host in the distributed port group.

For the special packets (broadcast and multicast), we do expect them to exist, so the value will not be 0. We do, however, expect them to be minimal and remain low. They should not be trending upwards. We can track them by plotting a line chart that shows the sums of broadcast traffic from all ESXi hosts in the entire data center, expressed in the number of packets. It is enough to just plot TX as we are concerned if an ESXi host generates broadcast traffic.

We do not expect a VM to send regular broadcast and multicast packets, so their value should be 0 most of the time. It is sufficient to use top-N, as we can go back to any moment in time. The value should be minimal as a VM should not be sending broadcast and multicast packets for 5 minutes.

Use case – right-sizing large VMs

The target user for this use case is the VM owner.

This is the most popular request from my clients. It is common for VMs to be sized conservatively by the application team. The result is that many VMs have too many vCPUs and vRAM. A larger VM does not necessarily mean a better-performing one. Once VMs are in production, it can be difficult to right-size them as it requires downtime and testing.

Besides wasting company resources, there are several disadvantages of having an oversized VM:

- It takes longer to boot. If a VM does not have a reservation, vSphere will create a swap file the size of the configured RAM.
- It takes longer to vMotion.
- The RAM or CPU may be spread over a single socket. Due to the NUMA architecture, the performance will be inferior.
- It will experience higher CPU co-stop and CPU ready time. Even if not all vCPUs are used by the application, the Guest OS will still demand all the vCPUs be provided by the hypervisor.

- It takes longer to snapshot, especially if the memory snapshot is included.

- The processes inside the Guest OS may experience ping-pong. Depending on your configuration, the Guest OS may not be aware of the NUMA nature of the physical motherboard, and may think it has a uniform structure. It may move processes within its own CPUs, as it assumes it has no performance impact. If the vCPUs are spread into different NUMA nodes, for example, a 20 vCPU VM on an ESXi host with two sockets and 20 cores, it can experience a ping-pong effect. For more details, I recommend an article by Mark Achtemichuk available at `http://blogs.vmware.com/vsphere/2013/10/does-corespersocket-affect-performance.html`.

- Lack of performance visibility at the individual vCPU or virtual core level. As covered earlier in this book, the majority of the counters are at the VM level, which is an aggregate of all of its vCPUs. It does not matter whether you use virtual sockets or virtual cores.

Reducing the number of vCPUs means that you need to show proof that they are indeed not being used. To do this, you need to show the utilization of every single vCPU, and you need to show it over a long period. I find that 3 months is considered acceptable.

What the dashboard looks like

This is what the dashboard will look like:

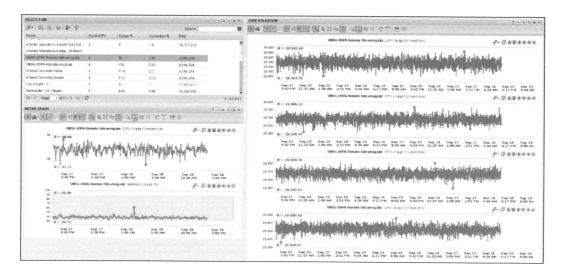

As the preceding screenshot may not be clear, I've zoomed in to the key parts of the dashboard in the following screenshot:

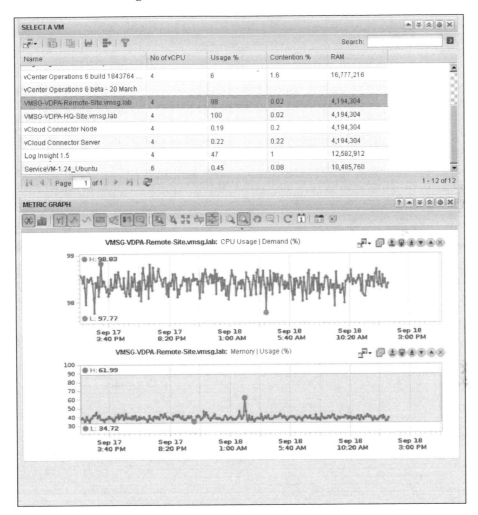

The first step is to create a group that contains all the large VMs. This should be a dynamic group, so VMs are added or removed as they change their configuration. You can start with VMs that have 8 or more vCPUs, because those with just four vCPUs have less room to be adjusted.

The dashboard contains several interactive widgets. The first widget is a **Resource List** widget that lists all the large VMs in the environment. So you choose the group instead of the entire VM population. You can enhance this widget by displaying the vCPU and vRAM configuration. If you have space, you should also display the **CPU Demand** and **Memory demand** counters. In the screenshot, I've added the additional information.

The previously shown widget displays the other two widgets, which are line charts. Each of these line charts shows the utilization of CPU and RAM, respectively, in the past 3 months. The first line chart shows the utilization of each vCPU. Hence, if you have eight vCPUs, there will be eight lines. If the number shows a low utilization for some of the vCPUs, it means that you should reduce the vCPU count.

The line chart can be difficult to read if the VM has highly fluctuating CPU utilization. It also does not answer quickly where the utilization is based on a certain percentile. You can complement it with a distribution chart, which can show you the value for the 75th, 90th, and 95th percentile.

The next screenshot shows two examples. In the first example, the VM has a very high CPU demand. It has an average of more than 98 percent in the past 30 days, as you can see the curve peaks above the 98 percent point. In the second example, the VM has low CPU demand. It has an average of about 12 to 13 percent in the past 30 days. If you take the top 5 percent utilization (that is the 95th percentile), it is still below 15 percent. This means 95 percent of the time, the CPU demand is below 15 percent. It is relatively safe to reduce the vCPU by four times, as the VM never demands beyond 25 percent.

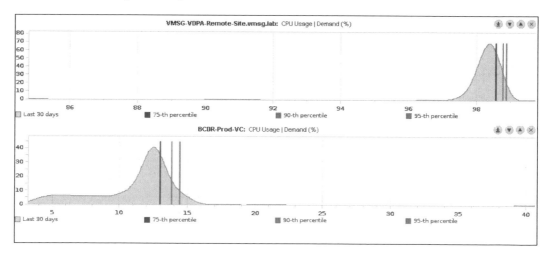

The main limitation of the distribution chart is that it can only go back to the past 30 days.

I understand that this is a manual check, and you need to check the VMs one by one and discuss them with the VM owner. On the other hand, a VM owner will certainly want a detailed discussion and proof before agreeing to reduce the size of a VM. You can avoid this problem in the first place by educating the application team on the importance of right-sizing, providing a wide range of vCPU choices (a banking customer told me it does not complicate their environment), and implementing a chargeback model that encourages the right behavior (for example, non-linear costing, where an 8 vCPU VM is charged more than 8 times that of a 1 vCPU VM).

Use case – capacity planning

The target user for this use case is the capacity manager and the VMware administrator.

This use case is written by Lior Kamrat.

Iwan Rahabok requested me to contribute a use case, as his customers find my blog informative. We discussed various use cases, even trying to come up with a new one, but both of us strongly feel that there are more customers who can benefit from my capacity-planning dashboard. Since it's already documented extensively on my blog, I am only providing the summary here. I am also adding additional information that is not on my blog.

vRealize Operations comes with a capacity-management engine. It performs the calculation and projection automatically. There are customers who like this intelligence. On the other hand, both Iwan and I have met many customers who want to do this task semi-manually, and want the tool to provide the right information. They will do the analysis. They want the tool to be simple to use and tailored to their environment.

In a small environment, performing that calculation for one cluster is not hard to do. In a large environment, where there are many clusters, each with its own set of metrics, characteristics, and availability requirements (that is, vSphere HA), the task can be time consuming and error prone. This is why I created the *1-Click Capacity Planning* custom dashboard. Ever since I shared it on my blog, `http://imallvirtual.com/` and VMware blog `https://blogs.vmware.com`, I have received lots of good feedback from customers and colleagues all over the world. They like the simplicity, and they like that they can customize it to their own needs.

Using some vRealize Operations interaction XML magic, **Resources Widget** and **Metric Graph Widget**, you can extract all the information you need. The following diagram shows the high-level design of the dashboard:

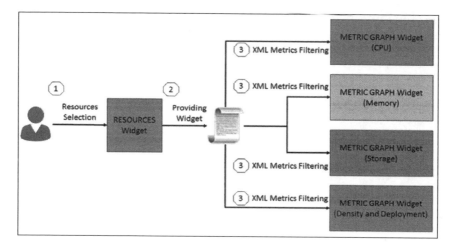

From the preceding diagram, the user interacts with **Resources Widget**, which lists all the clusters in the environment. You can customize this widget to just list a subset of your environment, and add additional information for each cluster if you want.

Once the user selects a cluster, the key information about that cluster will automatically be shown. The information is grouped into four parts:

- **CPU**
- **Memory**
- **Storage**
- **Density and Deployment**

The information is presented in line charts and the user can interact with the chart.

The metrics shown in each group are controlled by an XML file, one for each group. A sample of a generic XML file is shown in the next screenshot. The XML file specifies exactly the metrics to be shown, hence locking the display. You do not actually need to use an XML editor. I simply use Windows Notepad when I do not have access to an editor.

```
1    <?xml version="1.0" encoding="UTF-8" standalone="yes"?>
2    <AdapterKinds>
3      <AdapterKind adapterKindKey="VMWARE">
4        <ResourceKind resourceKindKey="HostSystem">
5          <Metric attrkey="badge|workload" label="Workload" unit="%" yellow="50" orange="60" red="80" />
6          <Metric attrkey="mem|host_usage" label="Host Usage" unit="%" yellow="50" orange="60" red="80" />
7          <Metric attrkey="cpu|usage_average" label="Usage Avg" unit="%" yellow="50" orange="60" red="80" />
8        </ResourceKind>
9        <ResourceKind resourceKindKey="VirtualMachine">
10         <Metric attrkey="badge|workload" label="Workload" unit="%" yellow="50" orange="60" red="80" />
11         <Metric attrkey="disk|usage_average" label="Usage Avg" unit="%" yellow="50" orange="60" red="80" />
12         <Metric attrkey="mem|host_usage" label="Host Usage" unit="%" yellow="50" orange="60" red="80" />
13       </ResourceKind>
14     </AdapterKind>
15     <AdapterKind adapterKindKey="bbb">
16     </AdapterKind>
17   </AdapterKinds>
```

What does the end result look like? The following screenshot shows this. I've added the arrows manually to show that the selected row in the list of clusters will drive the other four widgets. This is specified in the widget interaction screen.

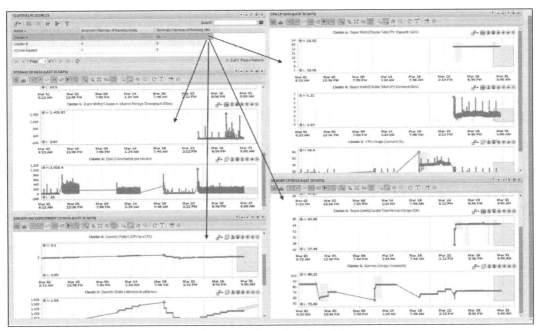

Key information about the selected cluster

As the preceding screenshot may not be clear, I've zoomed in to the key parts of the dashboard in the following screenshot:

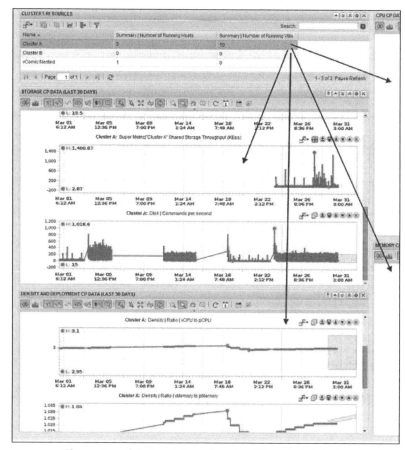

Closer view of the key information about the selected cluster

This dashboard is pretty straightforward and can be developed quickly. For details on how to build it, visit my blog at `http://imallvirtual.com/`.

Summary

Thank you for reading this all the way through. I hope you enjoyed reading it as much as I enjoyed writing it. One thing I particularly liked about writing this book is it's basically about documenting the collective experience I gained from dealing with customers. As someone working on the vendor side, I only know the theory. It is the customers who live with the implementation once the consultants leave, facing the production environment and end users directly.

I'd like to recap the key messages that you read. I hope they resonate and you see the practicality in your environment.

In the first chapter, I set out to explain why virtualization is a much larger change in the evolution of IT. I highlighted the common misconceptions about virtualization, with the goal of setting a strong foundation for the rest of the book. This chapter provided an extensive comparison between the physical server and the virtual machine, and between the physical data center and a virtual data center. The second chapter took one topic, capacity management, deeper, as it is an area that becomes much more complex with virtualization.

Once the foundation was set, *Chapter 3*, *Mastering the Key Counters in SDDC*, to *Chapter 7*, *Storage Counters*, went deep into the world of counters. I covered the four main elements of infrastructure: CPU, RAM, disk, and network. I also covered them from every vSphere object's point of view, so we can see the relationship among counters as they are rolled up to the high-level object. It is clear that vCenter does not provide you with the visibility you need when you look at your environment at the high-level object. This is where vRealize Operations complements it very well.

The last chapter provides real-life examples of the dashboard. Most of them were developed by collaborating with customers. I hope it gives you a good idea about what's possible with vRealize Operations.

We covered a lot of ground, and yet there is so much more to cover. I covered the areas that have been excluded in *Preface*. These are just some of the areas we can cover as we embark on this once-in-a-lifetime journey to the weird and wonderful world of virtualization

In the meantime, let's continue learning from one another. There are many places online to network and socialize with your peers in the industry. A place that I check in regularly is a Facebook group that I set up more than three years ago. It started as a Singapore-based group, but then expanded to Asia Pacific with more users joining in. By now, it has become one of the largest VMware groups globally on Facebook. There are many active users and good discussions. Join us at `https://www.facebook.com/groups/vmware.users` and network with your peers.

References

- VMware, Inc. *The CPU Scheduler in VMware vSphere® 5.1: Performance Study* is available at `http://www.vmware.com/resources/techresources/10345`

- VMware, Inc. *vSphere Monitoring and Performance, vSphere 5.5.* EN-001121-00

Index

Thank you for buying
VMware vRealize Operations Performance and Capacity Management

About Packt Publishing

Packt, pronounced 'packed', published its first book, *Mastering phpMyAdmin for Effective MySQL Management*, in April 2004, and subsequently continued to specialize in publishing highly focused books on specific technologies and solutions.

Our books and publications share the experiences of your fellow IT professionals in adapting and customizing today's systems, applications, and frameworks. Our solution-based books give you the knowledge and power to customize the software and technologies you're using to get the job done. Packt books are more specific and less general than the IT books you have seen in the past. Our unique business model allows us to bring you more focused information, giving you more of what you need to know, and less of what you don't.

Packt is a modern yet unique publishing company that focuses on producing quality, cutting-edge books for communities of developers, administrators, and newbies alike. For more information, please visit our website at www.packtpub.com.

About Packt Enterprise

In 2010, Packt launched two new brands, Packt Enterprise and Packt Open Source, in order to continue its focus on specialization. This book is part of the Packt Enterprise brand, home to books published on enterprise software – software created by major vendors, including (but not limited to) IBM, Microsoft, and Oracle, often for use in other corporations. Its titles will offer information relevant to a range of users of this software, including administrators, developers, architects, and end users.

Writing for Packt

We welcome all inquiries from people who are interested in authoring. Book proposals should be sent to author@packtpub.com. If your book idea is still at an early stage and you would like to discuss it first before writing a formal book proposal, then please contact us; one of our commissioning editors will get in touch with you.

We're not just looking for published authors; if you have strong technical skills but no writing experience, our experienced editors can help you develop a writing career, or simply get some additional reward for your expertise.

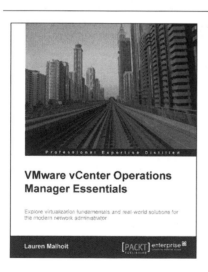

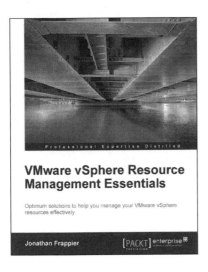

VMware vSphere Resource Management Essentials

ISBN: 978-1-78217-046-4   Paperback: 112 pages

Optimum solutions to help you manage your VMware vSphere resources effectively

1. Understand the requirements to build a strong virtual foundation and the features that can support your VMware environment.

2. Monitor and automate the tools available to make your VMware vSphere environment more efficient.

3. Packed with practical methods and techniques that will enhance your resource management in VMware.

VMware vSphere 5.x Datacenter Design Cookbook

ISBN: 978-1-78217-700-5   Paperback: 260 pages

Over 70 recipes to design a virtual datacenter for performance, availability, manageability, and recoverability with VMware vSphere 5.x

1. Innovative recipes, offering numerous practical solutions when designing virtualized data centers.

2. Identify the design factors—requirements, assumptions, constraints, and risks—by conducting stakeholder interviews and performing technical assessments.

3. Increase and guarantee performance, availability, and workload efficiency with practical steps and design considerations.

Please check **www.PacktPub.com** for information on our titles